THE
COLD
START
PROBLEM

THE
COLD
START
PROBLEM

HOW TO START
AND SCALE
NETWORK EFFECTS

ANDREW CHEN

**HARPER
BUSINESS**

An Imprint of HarperCollins*Publishers*

HarperCollins books may be purchased for educational, business, or sales promotional use. For information, please email the Special Markets Department at SPsales@harpercollins.com.

Illustrations by Andrew Chen

Graphs by Greg Truesdell

Author photograph on page 387 by Ethan Pines

FIRST EDITION

Designed by Kyle O'Brien

Library of Congress Cataloging-in-Publication Data has been applied for.

ISBN 978-0-06-296974-3

21 22 23 24 25   FB   10 9 8 7 6 5 4 3 2 1

CONTENTS

INTRODUCTION

I t was a Friday evening in December 2015, and the office was buzzing. Amid the vast, monochromatic corridors of Uber's San Francisco headquarters at 1455 Market Street—two football fields' worth of gleaming LED lights, light woods, concrete, and steel—the office was still mostly occupied at 8 p.m. Some sat at their desks quietly typing emails while others debated energetically with colleagues over videoconference. Others were drawing on whiteboards, hosting impromptu jam sessions to tackle the tricky operational problems facing who-knows-what. And a few pairs of employees were walking up and down the main flow in one-on-one meetings, some in intense discussion and others just catching up.

Everywhere you looked, there were reminders of the global scale of Uber's business as well as the international heritage of the team driving it. Colorful flags from every country hung from the ceiling. Conference room screens hosted videoconferences with colleagues from faraway offices in Jakarta, São Paulo, and Dubai—sometimes simultaneously! Flat-screen TVs were scattered throughout the floor showing metrics, broken down by mega-region, country, and city, so that teams could monitor progress. The global culture seeped into the naming conventions for conference rooms: near the entrance, the names started with Abu Dhabi and Amsterdam, and at the far other end of the floor, they ended with Vienna, Washington, and Zurich.

At first glance Uber might just look like a simple app—after all, the premise was always to hit a button and get a ride. But underneath its deceptively basic user interface was a complex, global operation required to sustain the business. The app sat on a vast worldwide network of smaller networks, each one representing cities and countries. Each of these networks had to be started, scaled, and defended against competitors, at all hours of the day.

It was in my role at Uber that I really came to viscerally understand networks, supply and demand, network effects, and their immense power to shape the industry. As you might imagine, the Uber experience had its ups and downs—it was a rocketship and a roller coaster, rolled into one. I've come to call it a "rocketcoaster" experience, which is an appropriate description for a company that had gone from an idea to a tiny startup to a massive global company with more than 20,000 employees in less than a decade.

The worldwide operations of the company were complex and intense, and much of the command and control radiated from the center of Uber's San Francisco headquarters. In the middle of the main floor, built from gleaming surfaces of glass and metal, stood the War Room.

To many, it was a big mystery—the War Room didn't share the normal naming convention of city names where Uber operated. It couldn't be booked for meetings as the others could, and was sometimes attended to by security guards. That's because it wasn't a normal meeting room. Many companies (inside and outside tech) have the notion of "war rooms." But, they are typically conference rooms converted temporarily to dedicated use by a product team, working intensely to tackle an emergency product. After the situation is resolved, the room is quickly converted back to normal use. For Uber, perhaps appropriate to its unique needs, this War Room was not temporary at all—it was built to operate twenty-four hours, around the clock. It was built as a huge, permanent room with dark wood walls, multiple flat-screen TVs, a large conference table that could fit a dozen people, and additional sofa seating. Red digital clocks gave the current times in Singapore, Dubai, London, New York, and San Francisco. Given the company's global footprint, there was almost always some kind of emergency situation somewhere in the world that needed attention, and this was often the room where it was dealt with.

That December, the emergency was in San Francisco, the company's hometown.

Scheduled to start at 7 p.m. and run into the night, the urgent meeting was booked on everyone's calendar as "NACS," which stood for the North American Championship Series, an oblique reference to its agenda focusing on operations, product road map, and competitive strategy in the top markets in the United States and Canada. This meeting was a key mechanism for the CEO of Uber, Travis Kalanick—called "TK" within the company—to review the entire business, city by city.

A small group of about a dozen executives and leaders attended the meeting, including myself and the heads of finance, product, and critically, the RGMs—short for "Regional General Managers." The RGMs ran the largest teams at Uber, constituting the on-the-ground Operations city teams that engaged with drivers and riders. The RGMs were thought of as the CEOs of their markets, holding responsibility for revenues and losses, the efforts of thousands of Ops folks, and were always closest to the trickiest problems in the business. I was there to represent the Driver Growth Team—a critical team responsible for recruiting the scarcest asset in the entire business, Uber drivers. It was a big effort for Uber—we spent hundreds of millions just on driver referrals programs, and nearly a billion in paid marketing. Adding more drivers to the Uber network was one of the most important levers we had to grow the business.

The weekly NACS meeting opened with a familiar slide: a grid of cities and their key metrics—tracking the top two dozen markets. Each row represented a different city, with columns for revenue, total trips, and their week-over-week change. It also included operational ratios like the percentage of trips that hit "surge pricing," where riders had to pay extra because there weren't enough drivers. Too much surge, and riders would switch to competitors. Uber's largest markets, New York, Los Angeles, and San Francisco, were always near the top of the list, representing billions of annual gross revenue each, with smaller cities like San Diego and Phoenix near the bottom.

TK sat closest to the screen, dressed casually in a gray T-shirt, jeans, and red sneakers. At the sight of the numbers, he sprung up from his chair and walked up close to the screen. He squinted, staring intensely at the numbers. "Okay, okay . . ." he said, pausing. "So why did surge increase in San Francisco so much? And why is it up even more in LA?" He began to pace up and down the side of the War Room, the intensity of the questions increasing. "Have we seen referral sign-ups dip in the last week? How's the conversion rate in the funnel going? Were there big events this week? Concerts?" Folks in the room began to chime in, answering questions and raising their own.

A Network of Networks

It was my first year at the company, and although many companies have weekly reviews, Uber's were different. First, in the discussion about each city, the level of detail surprised me. For San Francisco, the group began to discuss the surge percentages in the city's seven-mile by seven-mile center, versus East Bay, versus the Peninsula. This was a senior group of executives, but the granularity and level of detail was incredible. But this was a requirement to run a complex, hyperlocal network like Uber where supply and demand depended on the dynamics of popular neighborhoods and frequent "lanes"—like Marina and the Financial District—that tended to be poorly served by other transportation options.

In the weekly dashboard, each row represented a city—yes—but more important, each city was an individual network in Uber's global network of networks that needed to be nurtured, protected, and grown. It was deeply and uniquely ingrained in Uber's DNA to talk about metrics at the hyperlocal network level. In my several years there, it was un-usual to ever hear about an aggregate number—like total trips or total active riders—except as a big vanity milestone at a company all-hands. Those aggregate metrics were regarded as mostly meaningless. Instead, the discussion was always centered on the dynamics of each individual network, which could be nudged up or down independently of each other, with increased marketing budget, incentive spend for either drivers or riders, product improvements, or on-the-ground operational efforts.

The NACS meetings were used to evaluate the health of each of the networks and the global network as a whole—a central means of ac-counting for the twenty or so cities that represented the majority of rev-enue to the company. Furthermore, it was important to go even further in granularity and break the network into the two sides, both the rider side (demand) and the driver side (supply), to make sure each side was healthy but also that they were in balance with each other. Too much surge, and riders stop taking trips. Too little surge, and drivers start to go offline and head home after a long night.

The slides continued. Several of us on the NACS team, including myself, had been working on a hypothesis over the past few days. Ops teams had reported seeing large increases in driver referrals by our primary US competitor, Lyft, over the past few weeks, which was caus-ing drivers to switch over in droves. Driver referrals were typically structured as a give/get incentive—give $250 and get $250 when your friend signs up to drive. A dramatic rise in demand during the holiday season was causing a big undersupply of drivers in the key competitive markets on the West Coast, primarily San Francisco, Los Angeles, and San Diego. For riders, this resulted in a terrible experience—if you request a ride, it would take far longer than usual, sometimes twenty minutes, which meant more riders were canceling their requests. They might even decide to check our competitor's pricing and service level, and book there instead. These cancels were frustrating for Uber's driv-ers, who might have already driven for a few minutes. Piss them off too many times, and it might cause a chain reaction as they'd have even more incentive to stop for the night, and switch off to a competitor's network.

TK grew more intense and agitated as the hypothesis was presented. "This is not good, guys. Not good." He exhaled deeply. What was the right solution? With the years of experience from operating these networks, it was likely that one solution would quickly rebalance the sides of the market. The right solution would need to start on the supply side, to grow our base of drivers quickly and lower ETAs and the cancel rate, and that meant a driver incentive. "What if . . . we did a $750/$750 referral bonus here in SF, LA, and San Diego?"

This would be a big move, a far bigger number than had ever been thrown out. But San Francisco, Los Angeles, and San Diego needed the help. These were some of the most competitive markets that would need to be quickly rebalanced with more supply. TK looked around the room, pausing, and then answered his own question. "Yeah. That would get their attention. That'll wake them up!" he said, smiling and nodding.

Others were not so quick to jump to incentives as the solution. The past year had been good for Uber in the United States, turning it into a cash-flow positive area as the competition in the new China business simultaneously generated both incredible trips growth and severe losses. Uber was in a vicious fight with Didi—its Chinese rideshare competitor—burning on the order of a billion dollars a year primarily because of incentive spending. We started to bat around other ideas, including improving how to display ETA estimates as well as ways to discourage riders from canceling. There were other ways to rebalance the various networks without using incentives, which is a powerful tool but not the only one. The conversation went in circles, and TK grew visibly frustrated.

TK paced around the room again. "No, no! Look, guys. Our network is collapsing. We need to stop the bleeding . . . now!" He chopped his hand into the other. "Let's do the other stuff and get it on the road map, but let's get this email out over the weekend. Who can help me put it together?" This decisiveness was informed by years of fierce in-the-trenches competition—companies like Flywheel, Sidecar, Hailo, and many others that were vanquished—driven by lightning-fast responses in situations like this. The Uber team monitored and responded to the health of their local city networks with speed and precision. And with that, the next step was clear.

The RGMs agreed to own it, and I would work with my team—which was accountable for the product/engineering side of driver referrals—to make changes to the structure and amounts. We committed to ship the changes before Monday. We took note of a number of other follow-ups due from the meeting, and we all decided to reconvene the group again next week. It was Friday and almost 10 p.m., and many of us had been working since early morning to prep for this meeting. I walked home, just a few short blocks away in the Hayes Valley neighborhood of San Francisco, and started my "Netflix and email" routine to close out the day.

This was my first experience with the North American Championship Series, and it turned into a weekly briefing, usually Friday midmorning. But sometimes it got scheduled at Tuesdays at 9 p.m., or Sundays at 2 p.m., when that was the only way to get everyone together. Although NACS was just one part of my role at Uber, it quickly became one of the most educational in how to think about starting and scaling network effects. For a multiyear span, I was lucky to be embedded in this critical team that operated Uber's biggest markets. Each week was different. At the NACS meetings, we shifted our attention nimbly each session from network rebalancing on the West Coast, to prioritizing product features to increase revenues, to launching new regions, and everything in between.

Uber was already hitting its stride when I joined but I had a front-row seat to the team that grew the business to 100 million active riders in 800+ markets worldwide, and $50 billion in gross revenue. It was an incredible experience, and I am proud of the work that we

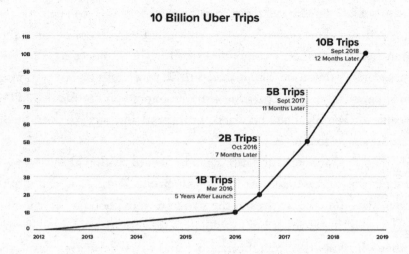

Figure 1: Number of Uber trips.[1]

did there. It didn't happen automatically—there were tens of thousands of people working hard to deal with network dynamics in hundreds of markets around the world, and we learned all the hard lessons from competing with fearsome local competitors who have their own strong network effects, too. I'm lucky to have been at Uber during a hypergrowth period, joining at the start of a so-called hockey stick curve—a curve that bent up as the business grew over 10x in a few years.

My time at Uber was an unforgettable experience. I got to see a startup scale to tens of thousands of employees, millions of customers, and billions in revenue. I saw new products start at zero and then rapidly scale up to dominate the market. It was a deeply educational journey, one that created many lifelong friendships—including people I still talk to every week. But by 2018, it was time for me to move on. The company had a tumultuous few years, a complete changing of the guard, and a new set of priorities that were less entrepreneurial than in the past. I wanted the opposite of that, and for my next chapter, I decided to go back to my roots: working with entrepreneurs to build the next big thing, but this time, as a venture capitalist.

Foundational Questions

In 2018, I began a new career after Uber, as a startup investor at Andrees-sen Horowitz. Started a decade earlier by entrepreneurs Ben Horowitz and Marc Andreessen, the firm made a splash when it launched, making a series of notable investments in startups including Airbnb, Coinbase, Facebook, Github, Okta, Reddit, Stripe, Pinterest, Instagram, and others. The firm built a foundation of nerdy street cred by hiring longtime Silicon Valley founders and executives who promoted a philosophy of hands-on operating expertise. The team began to refer to the firm by its shortened numeronym "a16z," a geeky reference to software development practices that often replaced long words like internationalization into i18n. The culture at a16z fit me perfectly.

Rejoining the startup world, this time as an investor, let me tap into a network of relationships and knowledge built over a dozen years in the San Francisco Bay area. Predating Uber, I had written and published nearly a thousand essays on topics like user growth, metrics, viral marketing—along the way, popularizing tech industry jargon like "growth hacking" and "viral loops." My blog would be read by hundreds of thousands, and due to this as well as the natural serendipity of the startup ecosystem, I came to become acquainted with a broad community of entrepreneurs and builders. I would come to serve as an advisor and angel investor to dozens of startups, including Dropbox, Tinder, Front, AngelList, and many others. All of this, combined with my expertise from Uber, would be the foundation to launch my career in venture capital.

Everything was different in the new role. Rather than commuting to Uber's offices in the chaotic center of San Francisco, I headed to the firm's idyllic offices near Stanford University. The a16z offices combine culture and invention—its hallways are lined with artwork from Rauschenberg, Lichtenstein, and contemporary artists, while its conference rooms are named after great inventors and entrepreneurs like Steve Jobs, Grace Hopper, Ada Lovelace, and William Hewlett. The work was very different from Uber's day-to-day as well—rather than going very deep into one sector, like rideshare, instead my purview was extremely broad.

Every day I was meeting with entrepreneurs to talk about their new ideas. In a given year, the firm might see thousands of startup ideas, many of which are new kinds of social networks, collaboration tools, marketplaces, and other new products—relevant to the examples in this book. Conversations with startups begin with a "first pitch" meeting, where the entrepreneurs introduce themselves, show the product, and talk through their strategy. These are pivotal meetings, because when they go well, the startup could eventually receive an investment in the millions or even hundreds of millions of dollars. It's high stakes.

Jargon thrives in these presentations: "Network effects." "Flywheel." "Viral loops." "Economies of scale." "Chicken and egg." "First mover advantage." These are some of the buzzwords and jargon that get thrown around in pitch meetings. And they are often accompanied with diagrams full of arrows and charts going up and to the right. The term "network effect" has almost become a cliché. It's a punch line to difficult questions, like "What if your competition comes after you?" Network effects. "Why will this keep growing as quickly as it has?" Network effects. "Why fund this instead of company X?" Network effects. Every startup claims to have it, and it's become a standard explanation for why successful companies break out.

But with all of these discussions and pitches, I realized I was getting confused, and I wasn't the only one. While "network effects" and its related concepts were often invoked, there was no depth to the idea. No metrics that could prove if it was really happening or not.

In my work with startups, and after a decade and a half of living in the San Francisco Bay area, I've heard "the network effect" used a zillion times in conversation. Sometimes over coffee, in meetings, or in investor discussions, but the concept was always discussed at a superficial level.

So how do you hear something thousands of times and still not quite understand it?

If network effects were a straightforward concept to understand, we would be in strong agreement on which companies have them, and which ones don't. We would know what numbers to look at to validate it was really happening. And we'd have a step-by-step understanding of how to create and build up network effects. And yet we don't. And it bothers me to a great degree, because it has become a critical topic in today's technology landscape. This is the journey that brought me to writing this book.

I began to research and to write *The Cold Start Problem* because I found my own understanding of the dynamics of networks to be unforgivably shallow for something so core to the technology industry. The network effect is something I've seen firsthand at Uber, and yet I lack the vocabulary and the frameworks to articulate the deep nuances.

There's a gap between the practitioners and the rest of the business world. For practitioners who work on specific networked products, the focus is on improving the mechanics within their very particular domains. Within rideshare, the discussion revolved around riders and drivers, reducing pickup times, surge pricing, and an accumulated set of specialized vocabulary and concepts that only apply to on-demand transportation. For a workplace chat tool, it's about channels and discovery and notifications and plug-ins. They feel unrelated, even though both product categories have deep network effects and are both ways to connect people. There should be a set of universal concepts and theories to talk about network effects, regardless of their product category.

We need to be able to answer the basics:

What are network effects, really? How do they apply to your business? How do you know if your product has them—and which other products don't? Why are they so hard to create, and how do you create them? Can you add a network to your product after the fact? How do they impact your business metrics, at the tactical level? Is Metcalfe's Law actually right, or should you apply something else to your strategy? Will your network fail or will it succeed? Does your competitor have network effects, and if so, what is the best way to compete with them?

Startup advice says, all that matters is to build a great product—after all, that's what Apple does. But why has it also been so critical to launch products in the right way? To get your product in the hands of influencers, or high school students, or aspirational technology companies—if B2B—if all that matters is the product? What's the right way to launch, and what's the sequence of ways to expand?

How do you build network effects in your product? How do you know when network effects are kicking in, and if they are strong enough to create defensibility? How do you pick the right metrics to optimize to achieve viral growth, reengagement, defensibility, and other desired effects? What product features do you build to amplify network effects?

When fraudsters, spammers, and trolls inevitably show up, what's the proper recourse? What have we seen other networks do in the past to combat the negative effects of a large, thriving network? And more generally, how do you keep scaling a network that's already working, especially in the face of saturation, competition, and other negative dynamics?

What happens when two networked products compete—what makes one player win over another? Why did we see big networks often succumb to smaller ones? How do you launch new networks across new geographies and product lines, particularly in competitive markets?

These are the most fundamental questions we can ask about network effects, and when you search for the answers—whether in books or online—there are only smatterings of actionable, pragmatic insights though there is plenty of high-level strategy. The best thoughts came from operators, at startups and bigger companies, who have been in the trenches and so that's where I started the process of writing my book.

I began by conducting more than a hundred interviews with the founders and teams that built Dropbox, Slack, Zoom, LinkedIn, Airbnb, Tinder, Twitch, Instagram, Uber, and many others. I asked them questions to learn about the earliest days, when it was just the cofounders and a handful of other people trying to take on the world. I also researched historical examples spanning hundreds of years—going back to chain letters, credit cards, and telegraph networks, and tying their success to modern innovations in Bitcoin, livestreaming, and workplace collaboration tools. All of this exposed a rich set of qualitative and quantitative data that forms the foundation of this book.

I found that people were repeating the same ideas and concepts, and observed that they were recurring throughout multiple sectors. You could talk to someone who spent their career working on social networks, and find that they had ideas that were equally applicable to marketplaces. Similarly, my time at Uber made me understand the dynamics in a network of riders and drivers, which informs my view of products like YouTube and its two-sided network of creators and viewers. Or Zoom, with its meeting organizers and attendees. Dozens of these recurring themes echo throughout the industry, whether we're thinking about B2B or consumer products.

The Definitive Guide to Network Effects

The Cold Start Problem is the culmination of hundreds of interviews, three years of research and synthesis, and nearly two decades of experience as an investor and operator. It takes much of the knowledge and core concepts swirling inside the technology industry and frames them in the context of the beginning, middle, and end of a network's life cycle. This is the core framework I'll describe via the major sections of this book, along with examples, and providing an actionable road map for your own products.

This is a critical topic. I've come to see network effects—how to start them, and how to scale them—as one of the key secrets of Silicon Valley. There are just a few dozen software products with a billion active users on the planet, and many of them share lineages of founders, executives, and investors who have unique expertise. This knowledge in turn has been developed in the tech community over decades of building social networks, developer platforms, payment networks, marketplaces, workplace apps, and so on. This community of elite talent collaborates and cross-pollinates, switching from one product category into another, bringing all of this knowledge together. I have seen this firsthand, and my interviews with founders and experts in writing *The Cold Start Problem* further illustrated the interconnectedness of these concepts.

Based on the foundational theories of network effects, I've taken these lessons and put skin in the game, focusing my venture capital investing at a16z toward products that have networks at their core. I find myself most captivated by new startups where connecting people lay at the heart of the product, whether for communication, socializing, work, or commerce. I'm now three years into the industry, and have invested over $400 million into more than two dozen startups in marketplaces, social apps, video and audio, and more. I've found my learnings about network effects to apply widely across the industry—everything from Clubhouse, which seeks to build a new audio social app, to Substack, which lets writers publish and monetize premium newsletters for their readers. And even video games, food pickup, or edtech.

My goal is to write the definitive book on network effects—one that is practical enough, and specific enough, to apply to your own product. You should be able to use its core framework to figure out where your product is on the journey, and what product efforts are needed to drive it forward. I've tried to lay out the entire life cycle—from the underlying mechanics of how to create network effects, how to scale them, to the best way to harness them—all from a practitioner's point of view, diving deep far beyond the buzzwords and high-level case studies that have been written.

The first phase of the core framework, naturally, is called the Cold Start Problem, which every product faces at its inception, when there are no users. I'm borrowing a term here for something many of us have experienced during freezing temperatures—it's extra hard to get your car started! In the same way, there's a Cold Start Problem when a network is first launched. If there aren't enough users on a social network and no one to interact with, everyone will leave. If a workplace chat product doesn't have all your colleagues on it, it won't be adopted at the office. A marketplace without enough buyers and sellers will have products listed for months without being sold. This is the Cold Start Problem, and if it's not overcome quickly, a new product will die.

This is all in the service of helping you, the reader, whether you are a software engineer, designer, entrepreneur, or an investor. Perhaps you partner with one of these companies I reference throughout the book, or are seeing technology reinvent your industry in the form of networks. Network effects are a powerful and critical force in the technology sector—as the entire economy is increasingly reinvented, it will become even more important to understand.

But let's not get ahead of ourselves—first, what's a network effect, anyway?

PART I

NETWORK EFFECTS

1

WHAT'S A NETWORK EFFECT, ANYWAY?

I n its classic usage, a network effect describes what happens when products get more valuable as more people use them. This is a simple definition, which I will deepen the framework of in later chapters, but it's a good starting point. For Uber, the more users joined the app, the more likely it would be for riders to quickly find someone to take them from point A to B. It also meant that it would be easier for drivers to fill their time with trips, increasing their earnings. While mobile apps like Uber can create network effects, the classic example of these forces came much earlier. In fact, it's educational to use as an example a technology product first introduced more than a hundred years ago and that we still use today on a daily basis: the telephone.

In 1908, there were fewer than 5 million phones for nearly 90 million people in the United States. Most of these phones were operated by the American Telephone & Telegraph Company. It was still a new technology, just a few decades old, but the company was thriving after being founded by Alexander Graham Bell, who invented and patented the first practical telephone. Today, of course, we would know the American Telephone & Telegraph Company under its modern name, AT&T.

The company's president at the time was Theodore Vail, who in his annual reports wrote unusually cogent, insightful, and philosophical observations about his business. For AT&T's annual report in 1900, Vail references the core concept of the network effect—but without the contemporary name:

A telephone without a connection at the other end of the line is not even a toy or a scientific instrument. It is one of the most useless things in the world. Its value depends on the connection with the other telephone and increases with the number of connections.[2]

Ultimately Vail's observation on the power of the network could be equally applicable to a telephone network, or a social network, or even the chat platform you use at work. Intuitively, it makes sense—if your friends, family, coworkers, or celebrities you know aren't using the same apps that you are, then the network is much less useful—or maybe completely useless. Whether it's a photo-sharing app where you'd want to see their photos, or a file-sharing service you use to access your coworkers' latest documents, you want the right people on the network with you. It's a simple idea, with profound implications for everything from product design to marketing to business strategy.

A subtler, but critical, point in Vail's statement is that there is a fundamental duality at play—first a physical product, the telephone—and then a second, the network of people and physical wiring that serve to interconnect the phones. I often refer to these two interchangeably, or together, in the form of "networked product"—but the distinction is important. A successful network effect requires both a product and its network, and that was true in the age of the American Telephone & Telegraph Company, and true today. For Uber, the "product" is the app that people run on their phones, and the "network" refers to all the active users at any given time who are connecting with Uber to drive or ride. (There's no physical wiring, in this case!) In contemporary parlance, the product is typically made of software whereas the network is typically made of people.

Both of these ideas—a duality of product and network, and the positive benefits of a larger network—would eventually make its way into the age of computers and software.

The Billion Users Club

Many decades after Vail's pronouncement about the network effect, innovation shifted from telephones into software. In this decade, software is eating the world, and its impact is measured in the billions.

The world's leading social network has over 2 billion daily active users. Consumers watch more than a billion minutes per day of video uploaded by millions of individual creators, businesses, and media properties. Our professional workforce, whether based in shiny downtown skyscrapers or out of noisy coffee shops, runs software to collaborate and share documents and files, all built on a multi-hundred-billion-dollar cloud software industry. The largest hotel chain in the world—facilitating over 100 million stays per year, generating billions in bookings per year—doesn't own any hotels at all. Instead, they've built a vast network of individuals who list their homes, and attract travelers who are looking for a place to stay. All of this is powered by apps built by developers who've published millions of apps running on 2 billion smartphones across the world, used by people living in remote villages or the world's urban centers.

These are among the world's most powerful technology companies, and they are united by the technology industry's most powerful market force: the network effect.

Network effects are embedded into many of the most ubiquitous and successful tech products around us, in different variations. Products like eBay, OpenTable, Uber, and Airbnb are examples of marketplace networks, comprising buyers and sellers. Dropbox, Slack, and Google

Suite are workplace collaboration products built from the network of your teammates and coworkers. Instagram, Reddit, TikTok, YouTube, and Twitter are networks of content creators and consumers (and advertisers!). Developer ecosystems like Android and iOS make it possible for consumers to discover and pay for apps, and the developers that build them.

In fact, just take a look at the companies that have made it into the "Billion Users Club." Apple has 1.6B iOS devices, while Google has 3B. Facebook has 2.85B users across their social network and messaging apps. Microsoft has over 1.5B devices running Windows, and another 1B running Office. In the Chinese technology ecosystem, the companies behind WeChat, TikTok, and AliPay all enjoy ecosystems numbering a billion users each. These are the tiny number of technology products that have reached incredible scale, and perhaps unsurprisingly, almost all of them leverage a network effect.

These are all very diverse products, with different value propositions, target customers, and business models, and yet they all share a common DNA—they have network effects so that their products become useful as more people use them. Just as telegraphs and telephones eventually connected billions of people around the world, so too do these products—to buy and sell, to work together, to communicate, and more.

When software connects people in this way, the network effect can be defined by breaking the term into its constituent parts—the "network" and the "effect."

The "network" is defined by people who use the product to interact with each other. For AT&T's telephone network, it literally consisted of the wiring that spanned between homes. In the digital age, for YouTube, the network is defined by software. It is the content uploaded by creators and the viewers that watch them—and the software platform sits in the middle, making recommendations, organizing the video with tags, recommendations, and feeds—so that the right videos are shown to the right consumers. We love using networks when the right people are on them, whether that means marketplace sellers who list the right products and services, app developers who are building our favorite games, or our favorite celebrities, writers, and friends. In turn, they participate in the network because we and millions of other consumers are on them. It's circular, because after all, they need an audience and a customer base, too.

These networks are counterintuitive in that they connect people, but don't own the underlying assets. Airbnb doesn't own its rooms, and the hosts are free to list their inventory on other networks—the value is connecting the guests with their hosts. Apple doesn't own the developers that publish apps to its app store. And YouTube doesn't own its creators, nor its videos. Although the networks don't own their underlying resources, it's the connection that matters. The entire ecosystem stays on because the value is in bringing everyone together. That's the magic.

The "effect" part of the network effect describes how value increases as more people start using the product. Sometimes the increasing value manifests as higher engagement, or faster growth. But another way is to think about it as a contrast—at its beginning, YouTube didn't have any videos, and neither viewers nor creators would find it valuable. But today, YouTube has nearly 2 billion active users watching a billion minutes of video per day, and this in turn creates engagement between creators and viewers, viewers and each other, and so on. People stay on the network and use it more, because other people are also using it more.

Given these definitions, how do you tell if a product has a network effect, and, if yes, how strong is it? The questions to ask are simple: First, does the product have a network? Does it connect people with each other, whether for commerce, collaboration, communication, or something else at the core of the experience? And second, does the ability to attract new users, or to become stickier, or to monetize, become even stronger as its network grows larger? Does the user face a Cold Start Problem where retention is low when there's no other users? Note that the answers to these questions aren't binary—generally not yes or no—but rather in shades of gray. And that's what makes network effects so much fun to study.

These are important forces. Network effects are key to some of the largest technology companies on the planet, which are in turn becoming the most valuable and important companies overall. You may see this list of "billion user" technology companies and find them aspirational— perhaps you're an entrepreneur who wants to build the next great startup, propelled and defended by network effects. Or perhaps you are part of the ecosystem of one of these giants, and need to better understand their motivations and strategy. Or maybe you are part of a larger, established player that is looking to compete in a sector defined by network effects. Whatever your motivation, it's critical to understand the underlying dynamics of these products—how they launch, how they grow and scale, and how they compete.

For companies that don't strive to understand these powerful dynamics, cautionary tales abound. I'll lay out, later in the book, how Instagram outcompeted an entire generation of photo startups that preceded it. Or how enterprise software—historically a sales-led, relationship-driven category—has been reinvented by new products using network effects to drive adoption within the workplace, whether that's WebEx versus Zoom, or Google Suite versus Office. As the technology industry grows, the power of network effects grows with it.

Launching New Tech Products Today Is Incredibly Challenging

At the same time as these tech giants have used the network effect to propel themselves into the stratosphere, it's not a great time to launch a new product. The technology ecosystem is downright hostile to new products—competition is fierce, copycats abound, and marketing channels are ineffective.

Given that, teams launching new products must consider the advantages of new networked products and master the knowledge and skill set to build and launch them. The mechanics of network effects provide a path for new products to break through, as they are often able to attract new users by word of mouth and viral growth, as well as increase engagement and decrease churn as the breadth and density of the network grows. When these types of services succeed, it is difficult for larger and more established companies to catch up. These techniques are evergreen, and especially critical during a time when the environment for new products is difficult. Why is it so difficult? We are now in a zero-sum era of attention with minimal defensibility for a vast swath of mobile apps, software-as-a-service (SaaS) products, and web platforms.

Recall that in 2008, iPhone apps platform launched with only 500 apps, and the ecosystem was wide open for entrepreneurial new start-ups. The home screen for phones came nearly empty—beckoning new users to install games, productivity tools, and photo-sharing apps. (And flashlight apps, and fart apps!) Developers had easy competition—they just needed to build experiences that are more interesting than activities like waiting in line or taking the subway, or more compelling than tedious meetings at work.

A decade later, this is no longer true. Starting with a few hundred apps at its start, the App Store now has several million apps, all competing for consumer attention. As a result, app developers are locked in furious competition. It's not enough to be a good, useful app—they have to actively take away attention from other hyperaddictive apps that have been optimized over years to engage users. It's a zero-sum game between the millions of apps in the Apple App Store and Google Play store. No wonder the top app charts now rarely change, and are mostly dominated by large, established products.

It's puzzling, because new startups have many advantages going for them compared to in years past, at least in the construction of software. Today, there's an ever-growing community building open source software that can be used instead of building or buying proprietary software, which was the norm a decade ago. Teams can utilize one of the new cloud platforms, like AWS or Azure, instead of operating their own data center. There's accountable, pay-per-click advertising to attract new users instead of spending unaccountably on traditional channels, like TV ads. There is off-the-shelf SaaS tooling, as an alternative to building substantial amounts of in-house tooling. There are app stores for efficient global distribution, allowing access to literally billions of new users. This all sounds great, but they are great for you as well as your competition. Most products these days are low technical risk—meaning they won't fail because the teams can't execute on the engineering side to build the products—but they are generally also low defensibility. When something works, others can follow—and fast.

Although software has been easier to build, growing products has not gotten easier. Networked products also have strong advantages in attracting new users, by leveraging their users to refer other users—this is critical as the channels to market to potential audiences have become highly competitive. Returning to the initial launch of smartphones, when there were fewer apps and app developers, marketing channels like mobile ads and referral programs were effective and affordable. Modern advertising platforms like Google and Facebook are auction based, and companies bid against each other for access to the same target customers. Thus, the fewer competitors the better, but predictably, this did not last. As apps learned to monetize effectively, and venture capital funding poured into the system, the advertising auctions grew more competitive. The channels that previously performed are now expensive, and as they mature and consumers acclimate to them, they click fewer ads and drive down response rates.

Network effects are one of the only protective barriers in an industry where competition is fierce, and defensive barriers are weak. While Instagram might be able to copy Snapchat's features like Stories or ephemeral photo messages in a few months, it's difficult to change the behavior of millions of consumers to switch over. Larger competitors are often able to copy the product, but find it difficult to capture the network. The engineering effort needed to create software is now relatively well understood, and furthermore, there is often an emphasis on simplicity, which can limit complexity and therefore cost.

These dynamics started in the consumer startup sector—within marketplaces, communication, social networks, where network effects have always clearly been important—but have infiltrated the software we use in the workplace as well. Knowledge workers increasingly have the same "it just works" expectations on enterprise software, as they do with the apps they use at home. Increasingly, this means the enterprise is becoming "consumerized" with software that is adopted by individuals, then spread within the company's network—with network effects. I'll talk later about Zoom, Slack, Dropbox, and other pioneers in this space, many of which have resulted in business outcomes into the many billions of dollars, as large as any consumer startup's valuation.

All of the above reasons—constrained attention from users, intense competition, limited marketing channels to access new users, network-based competitors, and unclear future application platforms—create intense pressure on the industry. There's a lot on the line. When a new product leverages a network effect to build an ecosystem around it, adjacent industries can be disrupted quickly. As technology reinvents industry after industry, the overall opportunity continues to get bigger. Technology will only get more ingrained in our daily lives. The intersection of these two pressures—one from competition, and the other from the immense market opportunity—makes it even more critical for us to get smarter about the impact of network effects in the technology sector.

I've talked about AT&T and the notion of network effects in telephones from 1908, and their importance today, but there's a missing piece that will help formalize our understanding: the dot-com boom of the late 1990s. While network effects were recognized as early as the turn of the century, our modern conception of it stems from the work done a few decades ago, at the start of the internet age.

2

A BRIEF HISTORY

The Dot-Com Boom

In 1995, at the dawn of the web, as millions of consumers began to experience the internet for the first time in all its dial-up glory, the world's first commercial websites began to emerge. These websites were built by startups and not just academic researchers, and they ushered in an age of technology-driven prosperity. Starting in 1995, the Nasdaq rose 400 percent, with dozens of startup IPOs within a few short years: Yahoo. Netscape. eBay. Amazon. Priceline. Today, many of these companies are still around, and worth billions.

In 1996, with the dot-com boom in full swing, just 20 million users had access to the internet, mostly via dial-up modems. When Theodore Vail had the insight in the early 1900s that the value of networks lay in the number of connections, the entire American Telegraph & Telephone Company network consisted of merely a few million telephones. Today, the size of networks is measured in the billions.

Even with these early, small numbers, there was tremendous excitement about the potential business value of these startups. A new generation of dot-com jargon proliferated, including terms like: "Winner-take-all." "First mover advantage." "Hockey stick curve." The theory was, if a startup became the first and biggest network—whether for connecting buyers and sellers, or users to content—it would become (theoretically) unstoppable. It would provide more value to its users, buy out its competitors, and otherwise dominate its industry, just as AT&T had done a century ago. No wonder, at its peak, AOL was valued at over $224 billion and was one of the most valuable companies in the world.

Of course, we look back and it all seems a little silly. That's why sometimes the "dot-com boom" is regularly called the "dot-com bubble"— many unwell startups IPO'd prematurely based on these ideas, then failed a few years later when funding dried up.

Yet the ideas that dominated dot-com thinking still exist. The tech industry still talks about winner-take-all markets and first mover advantages, when in practice, these are myths and in practical terms have been disproven. Look at the reality: there are weak advantages to being first, since the winning startup is usually a later entrant. And the winner usually doesn't take all, and instead has to battle a number of other networked products over control of different geographies and customer segments. So why the unbridled enthusiasm about network effects? Dig into the literature, and you'll see that one key theory popularized in the dot-com era presents an unabashed, but highly flawed view of network effects. That theory is Metcalfe's Law.

Metcalfe's Law

If you read the existing literature, it would only take a moment for Metcalfe's Law to come up as a core pillar in the study of network effects—it was popularized in the dot-com boom and used to justify the enormous valuations of startups at the time. Unlike Vail's quote, it offers a quantitative (albeit simple) explanation of the value of a network as more nodes join it. The law is defined below:

The systemic value of compatibly communicating devices grows as a square of their number[3]

Said plainly, each time a user joins an app with a network behind it, the value of the app is increased to n^2. That means if a network has 100 nodes and then doubles to 200, its value more than doubles—it quadruples.

Originally formulated in the 1980s by Robert Metcalfe, an early computer networking pioneer, this theory defines the value of a network as a mathematical function based on the number of connected devices (fax machines, telephones, etc.). It was originally derived from Metcalfe's experiences selling Ethernet, a pre-internet computer networking protocol.

In the late 1990s, it became popular to invoke Metcalfe's Law in the context of the new internet "dot-com" companies popping up in the industry to justify and mark up the valuations of "first movers" in the industry. The business implications of buying into this model of the world were profound. It meant you believed the 1990s dot-com startups were building the biggest new networks on the planet, and that the value would be exponential. Buy in early, and buy in soon, because the value of these startups would explode.

However, with the benefit of hindsight, it's not clear why Metcalfe's Law ought to apply to building internet websites. It doesn't say much about how to think about, say, buyers and sellers on eBay—are those users the same as "compatibly communicating devices"? Is eBay as equivalent to a computer networking technology as Bob Metcalfe's original invention, Ethernet? In the excitement of the dot-com boom, it didn't matter—this "law" was repackaged as the value of a website growing non-linearly as it added users, and became a foundational part of the discussion.

Metcalfe's Flaws

If you stopped reading right here in this book, you would have absorbed nearly all of the high-level strategic thinking that is commonly referenced for network effects. I covered a bit of history, defined a few bits of jargon, threw in a couple of case studies where a big network wallops a small one, a definition for Metcalfe's Law, and some strategic implications. And yet it is not even close to enough for those in the industry who seek to create, scale, and compete using this powerful force. Certainly not for the product managers, engineers, designers, and executives who need to map a strategy around network effects into their upcoming quarterly road maps!

Anyone who's ever actually built a networked product from scratch will tell you that unfortunately, Metcalfe's Law is painfully irrelevant. Although clever for its time, it has not aged well. Metcalfe's Law leaves out important phases of building a network, like what you do right at the beginning when no one is using your product. Nor does it consider the quality of user engagement, and the multi-sidedness of many networks—buyers and sellers, for example. Nor the difference between "active users" versus just people who have signed up, or the degraded experience of a product as too many users start to overcrowd a network. This is far beyond the simple model of "more nodes is better." Metcalfe's Law is a simple, academic model that fails the test of real-life messiness.

Meerkat's Law

If Metcalfe's Law is broken, what's better? It's one of the central goals of this book to put forth a better theory, and I think I've found one, built on the mathematics of animal populations. It starts with the study of meerkats—yes, you may have seen one, Timon, in the movie *The Lion King*, along with his friend Pumbaa the warthog.

A better theory for understanding network effects comes from my college years at the University of Washington in Seattle. In my senior year, I took a series of classes about the mathematics underlying the study of ecology, in particular those governing the populations of plants and animals. It is the math of social animals—like meerkats, sardines, bees, and penguins—that made me think of the network effect.

There are many types of social animals that benefit by living together—whether that's from coordinating hunting to finding mates to resisting predators. More nodes in these networks are better. However, if for whatever reason the population of these social animals declines, the benefits can quickly go away, making them more susceptible to collapse. But if the population grows too quickly, and there are too many animals living in too small a space, then overpopulation negates their advantages—which causes the population to plateau. Starting to sound familiar? Yes, it's true: social animals have network effects, too.

The Math of Meerkats

Meerkats are a perfect illustration. They are hypersocial animals living in the southern part of Africa, and when they live together in groups of thirty or fifty animals, they're called "mobs" or "gangs." Meerkats like to hang out in a gang because if one of them sees a predator approaching, they stand up on their two little hind legs and vocalize a complex set of predatory alarm calls to alert the group. They will bark or whistle to indicate if an aerial or terrestrial predator is nearby, and if this predator is low, medium, or high urgency. This helps keep the group safe.

These dynamics were first described in the 1930s by Warder Clyde Allee, a professor at the University of Chicago and a pioneer of American ecology. His paper "Studies in animal aggregations: Mass protection against colloidal silver among goldfishes"[4] observed that goldfish grow more rapidly and can resist water toxicity when they are in groups. Just as birds flock together to more easily confuse and resist predators, and mobs of meerkats warn each other of danger, goldfish share the same dynamics. This became an important concept in biology because it was the first to capture the notion that there was a tipping point—called an "Allee threshold"—where the animals would be safer and thus ultimately grow faster as a population. In other words, Allee's population curves describe a sort of ecological version of the network effect.

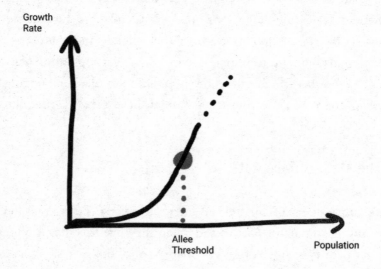

Figure 2: The Allee Threshold

When there are not enough meerkats in a mob to warn each other of danger, it's more likely an individual in the mob will get picked off by a predator. After that, it's a circular dynamic, because with even fewer meerkats, they are even less able to protect themselves, leading to a smaller and smaller population. This is an animal population under the Allee threshold—it tends to go toward zero.

The technology product metaphor here is obvious—if a messaging app doesn't have enough people in it, some users will delete it. And as the user base shrinks, it becomes more likely that each user will leave, ultimately causing inactivity and collapse of the network. This is what

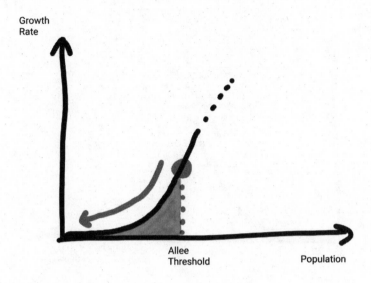

Figure 3: Collapse, if the Allee Threshold isn't met

happened to MySpace as Facebook began to take away its users, or when consumers and app developers moved away from BlackBerry and onto Google or Apple smartphones.

On the other hand, what happens when there's a nice, healthy mob of meerkats? They keep growing, reproducing, and perhaps creating multiple mobs. If you come in above the Allee Threshold, then the population will grow, because they can keep their mob healthy and protected. More meerkats then beget more, and even if predators occasionally pick one or two individuals off, as long as the overall population stays high, it will keep growing.

But that can't last forever, because there's only so many resources—like the meerkat favorites, bugs and fruit—to support a finite population. As the population increases, eventually there is a natural limit based on the environment—often called a carrying capacity. For social animals like meerkats and goldfish, overpopulation looks like this, starting flat, then hitting a tipping point before growing quickly and then saturating and falling once again:

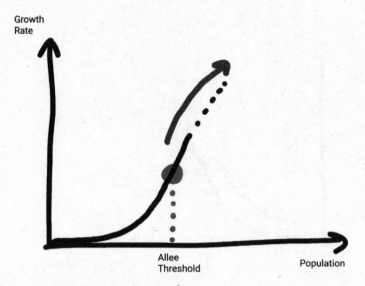

Figure 4: Growing past the Allee Threshold

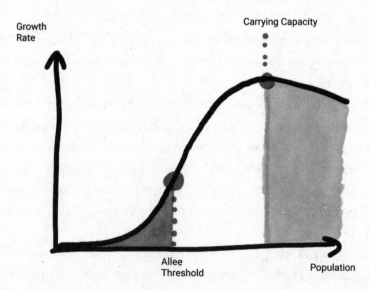

Figure 5: Carrying capacity as overpopulation develops

The network effect version of this in the technology industry happens when there is "overcrowding" from too many users. For communication apps, you might start to get too many messages. For social products, there might be too much content in feeds, or for marketplaces, too many listings so that finding the right thing becomes a chore. If you don't apply spam detection, algorithmic feeds, and other ideas, quickly the network becomes unusable. But add the right features to aid discovery, combat spam, and increase relevance within the UI, and you can increase the carrying capacity for users.

When Populations (and Networks) Collapse

When the oceans are overfished, the population of sardines, tunas, and other fish can tip over, collapsing in just a few short years. Technology products with network effects begin the same way—they become a bit less useful when friends leave, but then fully collapse once they dip below the Tipping Point the other way.

The ecological version of this idea can be seen clearly when visiting about an hour south of where I live in San Francisco, where there's a beautiful little town called Monterey, California. The town is famous as much for its abundant fishing as it is for being the hometown of classic American author John Steinbeck. In the early 1900s, when fishing became industrialized, a whole street of sardine canning factories were built, aptly named Cannery Row. The fishing industry of Monterey began to harvest hundreds of thousands of tons of sardines each year. Given it's a small fish, perhaps a few ounces at most, we are talking about something in the order of 5 billion sardines caught per year at the industry's peak.

The industry became a success, supporting a town of tens of thousands of people—until all of a sudden, it stopped. One year in the 1950s, the sardines mysteriously disappeared. The town waited patiently until the next year for the fish to come back—but they didn't. And the year after that, it was the same. And the same again, the year after. The sardines were gone. In the early years, a sardine catch totaled nearly 800 million tons—just a few decades later, it had collapsed to 17 tons.[5]

Overfishing, combined with complex animal population dynamics, spelled the end for the Monterey fishing industry. The canneries eventually shut down, and today the old factories serve as a wonderful tourist destination celebrating Steinbeck as well as the study of marine life at the Monterey Bay Aquarium. You can still tour the old canneries today, where signs and charts document the rise and fall of the Monterey sardines.

Sardines have network effects, and Allee's curves are useful in thinking about how networks can unwind and collapse. Just as crossing the "Allee threshold" is important for a school of sardines to switch from being low/negative growth into a self-sustaining population, when you harvest the sardines more aggressively, you can push them under the threshold.

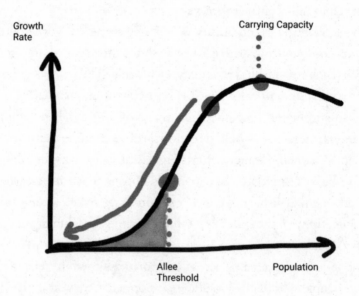

Figure 6: Collapsing back past the Allee Threshold

Just as sardines can collapse, so too can the networks of technology products. Why use a texting app that none of your friends are using?

Open an empty app enough times, and you'll quit, too. Pretty soon, the network effects unwind as it speeds toward collapse.

The Allee Curve at Uber

I studied Professor Allee's ideas on mathematical ecology at the University of Washington, but like much of what I learned in college, I promptly forgot them after graduating. Years later, I stood in front of a whiteboard at Uber's headquarters in San Francisco, trying to visualize how adding more drivers to a city would change the experience for riders. The more I thought, and sketched, the more a familiar curve emerged.

When there are very few drivers in a city, it takes a long time to get a ride—this is called having a high ETA (estimated time of arrival). As a result, conversion rates are low, because who has time to wait thirty minutes to get a ride? Thus, until you have a few dozen drivers—let's say fifty for the sake of this example—the value to the user is nearly zero. They won't really use the app, and drivers won't stick around, either, so the entire network will collapse on its own.

Once you pass the Tipping Point, however, things start to work. Riders start getting cars in 15 minutes, and it becomes somewhat inconvenient but still usable. Get it down to 10 minutes or even 5 minutes, then it's even better. The bigger the network of drivers, the more convenient it gets. The rideshare network in a city starts to see the classic network effect!

But eventually, the value of the network plateaus—there's a diminishing return to having more density of drivers. It doesn't matter if you can get 4 minutes versus 2 minutes versus having a driver instantly outside. In fact, it's kind of inconvenient, since you need a little time to get your keys and jump out the door to meet your driver.

Draw this curve out, and it looks something like this:

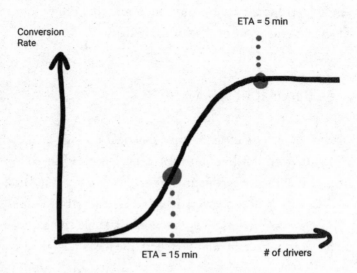

Figure 7: Uber's conversion rate based on number of drivers

Look familiar?

Meerkat's Law versus Metcalfe's Law

The math of meerkats that governs social animals applies to us, too. After all, humans are social animals, connecting with each other by sharing photos, selling collectible sneakers, sharing work projects, and splitting dinner expenses. Rather than hunting and mating, our networks help us with groceries and dating.

The same underlying dynamics unite groups of us and gangs of meerkats, and there's a lot of ideas to cross-pollinate between the two species. Just as a social network needs a minimum number of people on it to become engaging, so too does a mob of meerkats. Just as a messaging app will grow and grow but eventually saturate its market, so too does the growth of animals slow down as they begin to overpopulate their environment. While the terms are different, the core concepts and the math are the same:

The Allee effect → The Network Effect
Allee Threshold → Tipping Point
Carrying capacity → Saturation

In the upcoming chapters, while I use the vocabulary of business—network effects, Tipping Points, and market saturation—I credit the underlying ideas to Professor Allee and his mathematical models of ecology. Ecologists have created animal population models for centuries to predict how fast they grow, when they become overpopulated, and to predict their complex dynamics. I borrow these same ideas to describe how technology products might launch, scale, and defend their markets with network effects.

These ideas offer a richer theoretical foundation than the usual notion that technology products either have, or don't have, network effects. The tech industry can create a more granular and more precise set of vocabulary, which is needed to get down to the next level of analysis so that concrete concepts and metrics can ultimately be tied to product strategy.

What the industry needs is a unified framework that ties together a set of related concepts and vocabulary. This framework is the heart of *The Cold Start Problem.*

3

COLD START THEORY

The Framework

The central framework described in this book is a new way to think about network effects—split into stages, each with its own distinct challenges, goals, and best practices. My goal is not simply to describe what happens as a network grows and evolves, but to describe how to actually take action and propel a product from one stage to the other.

I call this framework *Cold Start Theory*, named for the first and most important stage in building network effects.

Cold Start Theory lays out a series of stages that every product team must traverse to fully harness the power of network effects. The curve represents the value of the network as it builds over time, and is shaped as an S-curve with a droop at the end.

There are five primary stages:

1. The Cold Start Problem
2. Tipping Point
3. Escape Velocity

4.   Hitting the Ceiling
5.   The Moat

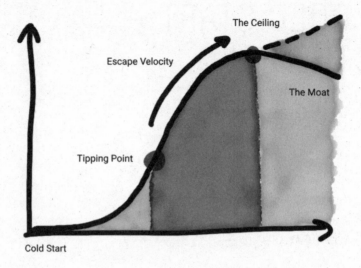

Figure 8: The stages of the Cold Start framework

Let me describe the framework, stage by stage, before jumping into a more detailed unpacking through the rest of the book.

1. The Cold Start Problem

Most new networks fail. If a new video-sharing app launches and doesn't have a wide selection of content early on, users won't stick around. The same is true for marketplaces, social networks, and all the other variations of consumer (and even B2B) products—if users don't find who or what they want, they'll churn. This leads to a self-reinforcing destructive loop. In other words, in most cases the network effects that startups love so much actually hurt them. I call these "anti-network effects" because these dynamics are downright destructive—especially in the early stage as a company is getting off the ground. Solving the

Cold Start Problem requires getting all the right users and content on the same network at the same time—which is difficult to execute in a launch.

This is the Cold Start Problem, and to solve it, I look at a series of examples—examining Wikipedia's most prolific content creators, the invention of the credit card, and how Zoom launched a killer product. From these case studies, I describe an approach that focuses on building an "atomic network"—that is, the smallest possible network that is stable and can grow on its own. For example, Zoom's videoconferencing network can work with just two people, whereas Airbnb's requires hundreds of active rental listings in a market to become stable. I look at the product idea at the heart of every network effect, and the similarities many startups have used to pick its features. I also ask, who are the first, most important users to get onto a nascent network, and why? And how do you seed the initial network so that it grows in the way you want?

2. Tipping Point

It takes an enormous amount of effort to build the first atomic network, but it's obviously not enough to just have one. To win a market, it's important to build many, many more networks to expand into the market—but how does this happen, at scale? Luckily, an important dynamic kicks in: as a network grows, each new network starts to tip faster and faster, so that the entire market is more easily captured. This is the second phase of the framework, the Tipping Point. I use Tinder as an example here, showing how their successful initial launch at the University of Southern California unlocked other colleges nearby. This was followed by cities like Los Angeles, then broader regions, and then entire markets—including India and Europe.

Imagine a network launch as tipping over a row of dominos. Each launch makes the next set of adjacent networks easier, and easier, and easier, until the momentum becomes unstoppable—but it all radiates from a small win at the very start. This is why we so often see the most successful network effects grow city by city, company by company, or campus by campus as rideshare, workplace apps, and social networks have done. SaaS products often grow inside of companies—landing and expanding—also jumping between companies as employees share products with partner firms and consultants. This is when a market hits its Tipping Point.

3. Escape Velocity

When a company like Dropbox, Slack, or Uber hits scale, it might seem like network effects kick in, and the next phase is easy. But it's not—to the contrary, this is when technology companies start to hire thousands of people, launch a series of ambitious new projects, and try to continue the product's rapid trajectory. The Escape Velocity stage is all about working furiously to strengthen network effects and to sustain growth.

This is where the classical definition of a "network effect" is wrong. I redefine it so that it's not one singular effect, but rather, three distinct, underlying forces: the Acquisition Effect, which lets products tap into the network to drive low-cost, highly efficient user acquisition via viral growth; the Engagement Effect, which increases interaction between users as networks fill in; and finally, the Economic Effect, which improves monetization levels and conversion rates as the network grows.

By understanding how these forces work, we can accelerate the systems that power them. For example, the Acquisition Effect is powered by viral growth, and a positive early user experience that compels one set of users to invite others into the network. PayPal's viral referral programs, or LinkedIn's recommendations for connecting are two examples of tactics that increase the power behind the Acquisition Effect.

The Engagement Effect manifests itself by increased engagement as the network grows—this can be developed further by conceptually moving users up the "engagement ladder." This is done by introducing people to new use cases via incentives, marketing/communications, and new product features. Uber did this via leveling users up from airport trips to dining out to daily commutes.

And finally, the Economic Effect—which directly affects a product's business model—can be improved over time as well, by increasing conversions in key monetization flows and ramping up revenue per user, as the network grows. For a product like Slack, for instance, a company is more likely to convert into a paying customer as more teams within it adopt the software. Or games like Fortnite that sell customized costumes and guns will monetize better as a gamer's friends join to play together.

Stitched together, all of these combine into a flywheel that can power networks into the billions of users.

4. Hitting the Ceiling

In many narratives about network effects, by the time a product has hit the Tipping Point, that's the fairy-tale ending of the company—it's won. Ask the operators inside a company, though, and you'll hear a different story: a rapidly growing network wants to both grow as well as tear itself apart, and there are enormous forces in both directions.

This is when a network "hits the ceiling," and growth stalls. This is driven by a variety of forces, starting with customer acquisition costs that often spike due to market saturation, and as viral growth slows down. Similarly, there's the Law of Shitty Clickthroughs, which drives down the performance of acquisition and engagement loops over time, as users tune out of stale marketing channels. There's fraudsters, overcrowding, and context collapse—all natural outcomes of a network that grows and matures. And many other negative forces that grow as the network grows.

In the real world, products tend to grow rapidly, then hit a ceiling, then as the team addresses the problems, another growth spurt emerges.

Then follows another ceiling. Then another cycle after that, each one often successively getting more complex to address over time as the problems become more fundamental.

I look at a series of case studies as major products hit periods of slowing growth: from the implosion of Usenet discussion groups in the early days of the internet, to eBay's slowing US business, to the origins of Nigerian prince scams. In each of these examples, sometimes they are easily dealt with and sometimes they destroy the network over time. The solutions are difficult—a successful product inherently comes with various degrees of spam and trolls. These are problems to be managed, not fully solved.

5. The Moat

The final stage of the framework focuses on using network effects to fend off competitors, which is often the focus as the network and product matures. While it is not the only moat—brand, technology, partnerships, and others can help—it is one of the most important ones in the technology sector.

However, there's a problem—using network effects to compete with competitors is tricky when everyone in the same product category is able to take advantage of the same dynamics. Every workplace collaboration is able to leverage network-driven viral growth, higher stickiness, and strong monetization as more users arrive. Same for marketplaces, messaging apps, and so on.

This dynamic drives a unique form of rivalry—"Network-based competition"—that isn't just about better features or execution, but about how one product's ecosystem might challenge another's. Airbnb faced this problem in Europe when a strong, local competitor called Wimdu emerged with a boatload in funding, hundreds of employees, and on paper, more traction in its home market. Airbnb had to fight off its European competitor by competing on the quality of the network, and scaling its network effects—not via traditional competitive vectors like pricing or features.

Because all products in a category likely have the same type of network effects, competition ends up being asymmetrical while leveraging the same forces. A larger network and a smaller network in any given market have distinctly different strategies—think of it as a David strategy versus a Goliath strategy. The upstart has to pick off niche segments within a larger network, and build atomic networks that are highly defensible with key product features, and, when applicable, better economics and engagement. The incumbent, on the other hand, uses its larger size to drive higher monetization and value for its top users, and fast-following any niches that seem to be growing quickly. I will also examine Uber and Lyft, eBay China and Alibaba, and Microsoft's strategy of bundling new products, to go deeper on how networks compete.

Five Stages

This is the Cold Start Theory. It is made up of five stages for creating, scaling, and defending the network effect, and aims to provide a road map for any new product team—at a startup or larger company—to leverage in their work.

Entrepreneurs will want to start at the beginning, since the Cold Start Problem is about the launch of new products and companies. On the other hand, teams working on established products will find the middle chapters most relevant—hitting Escape Velocity and optimizing all of your growth loops is the everyday activity of successful products trying to get to the next level.

Cold Start Theory is meant to apply to a large set of companies in the technology industry: video platforms, marketplaces, workplace collaboration tools, bottom-up SaaS products, social networks and communications apps, and more. Throughout the book, I also draw on historical examples—coupons, credit cards, and early internet protocols. There are surprising shared dynamics between archaic forms of communication that we used hundreds of years ago and the modern apps that we use today.

Along the way, I hope you come to see the patterns that underlie networks beyond technology products. Many of these ideas generalize beyond the world of mobile apps, as my friend Naval Ravikant, a noted investor and entrepreneur, has observed:

> *Humans are the networked species. Networks allow us to cooperate when we would otherwise go it alone. And networks allocate the fruits of our cooperation. Money is a network. Religion is a network. A corporation is a network. Roads are a network. Electricity is a network.*[6]

And furthermore, the stakes of building and controlling successful networks are high:

> *Networks must be organized according to rules. They require Rulers to enforce these rules. Against cheaters. And the Rulers of these networks become the most powerful people in society.*

Cold Start Theory aims to unify these ideas into one framework that is both universal and actionable. Along the way, each chapter lays out a new set of vocabulary to describe the challenges and goals of each stage—with examples, interviews, and research from iconic products from our industry.

Let's get into it. To begin our discussion, I begin with the first stage: the Cold Start Problem, the critical, early phase that lends its name to the book.

PART II

THE COLD START PROBLEM

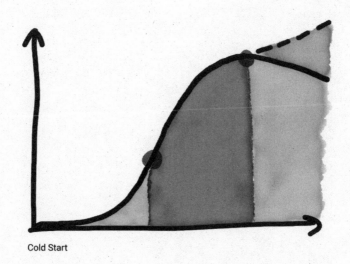

Cold Start

4
TINY SPECK

When you start a new product with network effects, the first step is to build a single, tiny network that's self-sustaining on its own. You just need one to get started. However, building even a single network is very hard. So I'm going to start by telling you the story of a product—and its network—that failed.

It took four years and ten months to go from founding the startup to shutting down its core product. It was a star team that had seen success in the past, building and selling a company for tens of millions, and as such, it did all the right things. It had an exciting launch, shipping a beta version with fanfare to users after two years, and worked closely with its users to add the right features, to fix bugs, and so on. Out of the gate, it raised $17 million from top investors, hiring forty-five very talented people to build a quirky, fun, delightful product. The startup was called Tiny Speck, and the product it was building was a multiplayer game called Glitch.

Judged by its description alone, Glitch may seem a little "out there." It was a multiplayer game in the browser, and the experience was set inside the heads of eleven giants, with names like Humbada, Lem, and Friendly, who had been dreaming about a new world that got willed into existence. The characters, background, and art looked like they were designed by "Monty Python crossed with Dr. Seuss on acid." Users walked around the game world, clicking objects in their environment, and learned skills like fox brushing, potion making, gardening, and teleportation.

Unfortunately, the initial reviews were not good: "[The game's] backstory, involving 11 giants who dreamed the world of the game into existence, is mostly stupid," said the AV Club. Users were not kind, either: "After all the pre-launch hype about changing the face of gaming forever, the game was dreadfully boring—you basically walk around and click on things. I described it to a friend as 'FarmVille where you don't get your own farm,'" said user dgreensp on internet discussion site Hacker News.

In the end, users didn't stick around—in an interview years later, the CEO of the company lamented about the poor retention: "Most people, like 97% percent who signed up, would be out of there within five minutes. The thing that killed it was just leaky bucket—I mean, just like very classic, you can put it into Excel in five minutes, and see that this is not going to work." Of course, as a multiplayer game, Glitch would only become fun when a lot of people were playing it and chatting with each other, and the product never achieved enough scale to unlock that social experience.

This is not a unique insight nor a remarkable outcome for a startup. After all, many new products go through a long journey only to end in failure—except one took a strange turn. Years later, Tiny Speck would relaunch with a second product—that product was called Slack. And now, you may know the end of the story, because as of this writing, Slack is used by over 20 million daily active users and by nearly a million businesses. It went from Tiny Speck, a startup that was going to be a complete loss, to Slack Technologies Inc., which eventually exited for $26 billion to Salesforce, all while generating more than $800 million in revenue. The company's CEO, Stewart Butterfield, and his cofounders, Eric Costello, Cal Henderson, and Serguei Mourachov, would successfully pull off one of the startup industry's most incredible reversals of fortune.

It is easy to imagine products like Slack, which have achieved "household name" status, as the epitome of overnight success—but networked products are usually not. In Slack's case, it took nearly four years to go from founding Glitch to giving up on this first product, with nearly all of the company's funding spent and employees laid off. It took another two long years to repeat the arduous journey of going from zero to one: to pick a new product, find beta customers, announce the new product broadly, rebuild the team, change the name to Slack, and raise funding for the new strategy. This was the opposite of an overnight success. In fact, I will describe to you in case study after case study that building a product with network effects can both be difficult and slow. But there is a pattern to their success that can be studied and repeated.

The question in Slack's case: What happened between the moment where the company formally started up Slack and the moment when it looked like it was really working? What can be learned? What can be replicated?

Luckily, Tiny Speck was backed by Andreessen Horowitz many years back—all the way at the beginning, at the formation of the company—by my colleague John O'Farrell, and he put me in touch with Stewart Butterfield and early employee Ali Rayl to give me the story. Here's what they told me.

First, let's go back to the beginning in 2009, when the team was still building Glitch. Stewart and his cofounders had attracted dozens of engineers from all over the place, including San Francisco and Vancouver (where the founders were initially based). Today we would recognize this as an important preview of a broader, more transformational trend around remote work. But at that point, remote work was just nascent, which meant that the tools supporting this type of work were also non-existent.

To help the team work together, they used a tool for chat with each other. It was not the kind of beautiful product that you and I would use today. It was all text. It had funny commands that started with a "/" because it was based on an old piece of technology, Internet Relay Chat

(IRC), originally built by Finnish university employee Jarkko Oikarinen. IRC was first created in 1988, during an earlier phase on the internet, when user-friendliness was not a priority. Thus, for novices, IRC was practically unusable, and as Stewart would later describe:

> *IRC pre-dates the Web by a couple years. And because it's so old, it misses a bunch of features that are now considered just standard.*[7]

IRC didn't have search. It didn't store old messages. It was confusing to find the right set of channels and people to talk to—you had to download one of many different IRC apps, connect to an IRC server, and join the right channel.

So the Tiny Speck team built a chat tool on top of IRC, building in the ability to store old messages and photos, and to make conversations easily searchable. This was the chat tool that glued some important workflows together, and in the early years, it wasn't even called anything, much less Slack. The service was hosted internally at irc.tinyspeck.com and nevertheless was very useful, as it allowed easy sharing of images, animations, and server logs. Many of the nontechnical employees weren't comfortable with IRC, and so instead, they were onboarded into the company's weird little chat app. This unnamed tool—early employee Ali Rayl called it a "frankentool" that sort of did everything—enabled team-wide collaboration, and became part of the core workflow at Tiny Speck.

When it was clear that Glitch was not going to work, the team needed a new idea. Stewart, Cal, and the cofounders decided that the next move was to work on what was right in front of them—to take the functional but unremarkable internal tool, and redesign it so anyone could use it. The tool soon was code-named Linefeed, at least for a few days. Other days, it was called Honeycomb, and other days Chatly.io, and a litany of other names.

Whatever it was called, the product that would become Slack was rearchitected to allow any company to use it, not just Tiny Speck. It was rebuilt with its own back end, not IRC. It supported searchable conversations, hosted photos and other assets easily, and automatically backed up conversations, solving all the issues IRC had. With these key features, "Slack" was picked to mean "Searchable Log of All Conversation and Knowledge." Although some on the board disliked the name, thinking it was strange for the users of the product to be called "Slackers," the product was soon launched.

The second step was a private beta-testing period with friends of the company, where Stewart would personally reach out, try to get them to use Slack, and iterate to add features and improve the experience. I asked Stewart if he was careful to target the initial base of customers, and he said:

> No, not at all. I just had friends at other companies and I would try to convince them to use us. We didn't have any teams for demand gen, field marketing, or anything else at the time—it was just me. Sometimes it would take dozens of meetings to convince people why it was cool.[8]

He had friends at startups like Rdio, Wantful, and Cozy, and eventually signed up forty-five companies in all. The teams that adopted tended to be other startups, for a very good reason:

> Technology startups adopted us early because they have the belief, whether naive or not, that software can better their lives. These startups were just like us—many of the early teams had fewer than 10 people, just like Slack.

Stewart and Ali Rayl, who ran customer experience, would personally handle all the feedback on social media and customer support tickets. Even once Slack publicly launched, Stewart personally handled the lion's share of 10,000 tweets per month and 8,000 customer support tickets.

Each of these beta customers formed an atomic network—a stable, self-sustaining group of users who can drive a network effect. Once an atomic network was formed in one of their beta testers, Slack would continually add users, become more useful, ramp up engagement, and ultimately become the de facto method of communication within their workplaces. The minimum number of people to be defined as a team, even today at Slack, is three. As long as you have three people, it can be stable. But it's even better if there's a larger team of fifty people in an organic unit—like a department—or an entire company of thousands that joins the product. Then it will just grow and grow.

The Slack team learned more and more as the product was tried with larger networks. "The pattern was to share Slack with progressively larger groups. We would say, 'Oh, that great idea isn't so great after all.' We amplified the feedback we got at each stage by adding more teams," Butterfield said, in an interview in *Fast Company*.

The team learned how groups of 120 people, like that at Rdio, would use a product and how it spread—from front-end developers to engineering and then to the entire company. Early on, a team of ten might only have a few channels. But a team of hundreds would suddenly create four different, mostly empty channels for activities like hiking, as Rdio did. It turned out that helping users discover channels was a problem. An even larger organization might need help with features like a "team directory" to figure out who worked at the company and what they did. Each increase in team size required a rethinking of the design, in order to form stable atomic networks that would grow.

Like many of the examples I'll visit later on, Slack is a network of networks. Within a larger company, a whole collection of atomic networks would spontaneously emerge and begin growing on their own. Stewart described to me how a large company might have tens of thousands of workspaces, each with its own set of channels. Each workspace might be a business unit or subsidiary, and each smaller team might independently have a ringleader or early adopter who set up the product, invited coworkers in, and started initiating conversations with others.

In later years, when the company added an enterprise sales team, they would target large customers who had adopted Slack across multiple parts of their company and ask if they wanted to go "wall-to-wall," bringing the entire company onboard in exchange for added security/ enterprise features as well as company-wide pricing. Enterprise sales became a huge accelerator a few years into the company's launch.

Many of these ideas for increasing adoption through viral growth are borrowed from consumer products. This is true not only for Slack but also for many of the new B2B products developed around their time period, like Zoom and Dropbox. These companies pioneered a new style of "bottom-up" growth, where individual contributors seeded a product's adoption within a customer company. Slack was early in this phase of the market, and had to invent many of the paradigms. Yet this was a team that understood the ingredients deeply. At the founders' previous startup, Flickr, one of the largest photo-sharing sites of the Web 2.0 era, they popularized what would become tagging photos and communal streams of content organized around topics and events. As a college student, Stewart was a passionate user of some of the earliest precursors to social apps for the internet: Usenet, which are old-school discussion forums; MUDs/MOOs, which are text-based virtual worlds; and of course IRC.

Eventually, Tiny Speck rebranded as Slack Technologies, and its new flagship product was launched to the world. In August 2013, when Slack debuted, 8,000 companies signed up to the wait list to try the product. Within two weeks, this grew to 15,000. By the next year, Slack would have 135,0000 paying subscribers and 10,000 new users signing up per day. Soon after that, a million daily active users, then two, then three, and so on. Stewart and the company—now 100 percent focused on Slack—would raise their next round in April 2014, fully completing their transition.

Slack has an incredible story, and there's much to learn across many dimensions. But for the purpose of this book, the journey from unnamed IRC tool to Linefeed to Slack is most remarkable in its demonstration of how to think about starting from zero: how they incubated a killer product, solving a problem that their own team acutely needed. And how Tiny Speck built individual stable networks, piecing together a network-of-networks at larger companies. This is one of the best examples of solving the Cold Start Problem.

Introducing the Cold Start

The book is named after the first stage because, quite frankly, it's the most important one. New products die when they flub their initial entry into the market, and their networks collapse before they even start. Every networked product, including Slack, starts with just a single network. The next few chapters are about how to build this first one, using the launch stories of Wikipedia, the original credit cards, Tinder, and Zoom.

First, I start with the principal dilemma, which I call "Anti-Network Effects." It's a myth that network effects are all powerful and positive forces—quite the opposite. Small, sub-scale networks naturally want to self-destruct, because when people show up to a product and none of their friends or coworkers are using it, they will naturally leave. What solves this? "The Atomic Network"—the smallest network where there are enough people that everyone will stick around.

These networks often have "sides," whether they are buyers and sellers, or content creators and consumers. Generally one side of the network will be easier to attract—this is the easy side of the network. However, the most important part of any early network is attracting and retaining "The Hard Side" of a network—the small percentage of people that typically end up doing most of the work within the community. For example, most of Wikipedia was written by a tiny percentage of prolific editors. A small group of drivers, about 5 percent of Uber's users, carry most of the load within the rideshare marketplace—riders are numerous but engage less frequently and deeply. To attract the hard side, you need to "Solve a Hard Problem"—design a product that is sufficiently compelling to the key subset of your network. Tinder did this for the most attractive users in its network, which I'll use as an example.

Not only does a product have to appeal to the hard side of the network, but as I discuss in "The Killer Product," the most successful network effects–driven apps are also sometimes dead simple. They eschew a long list of features and instead emphasize the interactions among people using the app. Zoom is just such an example. Although there was a long list of potential investors and industry pundits were skeptical of such a simple product, Zoom is a great example of a killer product that leverages network effects.

When the Cold Start Problem is solved, a product is able to consistently create "Magic Moments." Users open the product and find a network that is built out, meaning they can generally find whoever and whatever they're looking for. The network effects kick in, and the market hits its Tipping Point as users start coming to you.

5

ANTI-NETWORK EFFECTS

Successes like Slack capture our imagination—it's incredible to hear its origin story as a failed gaming startup and subsequent journey into a $27 billion exit. Yet for every successful launch like Slack, there are many more that are failures—and they usually stumble right at the start.

Anti-network effects are the negative force that drives new networks to zero. While the industry tends to focus on the positive results of network effects, at their inception, network effects are a destructive force, driven by a vicious—not virtuous—cycle where new users churn because not enough other users are there yet. For Slack, it doesn't make sense to use the product until your colleagues are also on the platform. For Uber, you can't use the service until there are enough drivers, who won't drive until there are enough rides. This first stage of creating a network is the hardest, and some will call it a "chicken and egg" situation or needing to "bootstrap" a community. I call it the "Cold Start Problem."

In the classic mythology of startup success, a small group of young founders are working away, perhaps in a loft in the warehouse district of a cool, coastal tech hub. They build a killer product, which creates a new way for people to interact, whether that's a communications app, a way to share documents, or a way to buy and sell a service. Whether they know it or not, the product has a network, and thus network effects. Of course, in this mythology, they launch the product to the world, and it's an immediate hockey stick. It generates incredible buzz in the tech press and in the wider internet community. Eventually it spreads around the world and is used by many millions of people.

This mythology conveniently skips the part of the story when the network is sub-scale and lacks activity. The reality is that new products are often greeted by a nice initial spike of users, but this falls to a trickle as the novelty wears off. Maybe there's another push, which again goes nowhere. People won't use their product unless their friends are on it. Features are feverishly added, marketing efforts are redoubled, but the network never gets off the ground, and the team ultimately is out of runway. They didn't solve the Cold Start Problem, and the result is failure.

The Cold Start Problem is the first challenge that new networks must face. Beating this initial challenge is very hard. Just look at the metrics: there are tens of thousands of social, communications, and marketplace startups but just a few dozen ones that have become large, independent companies. It's already hard to start a new company, but there is even more difficulty within the winner-take-all dynamics of these product categories.

Or take marketplace startups, as a subcategory of products. In a recent analysis by Andreessen Horowitz of the top 100 marketplace startups, just four of the top products drive 76 percent of all the gross revenue—there is immense concentration at the top. Other categories like social networking and collaboration tools are the same, where just a handful of products have built audiences of over a billion users. Yet these categories remain attractive because they produce the most valuable companies in the world, and they shape the technology industry in which we live and work. Understanding these dynamics is the key to understanding the future.

What's Enough?

For the first user of Slack within a workplace, the experience won't be great if there are zero other users. But what if they encounter one other coworker also using Slack—is that enough? Or two? How many do you really need? Stewart Butterfield, CEO of Slack, answered this question for me:

> *Slack works with just 2 people, but it takes 3 to make it really work. There are long-running 3 person groups that are stable— that's the minimum required to be called a customer.*

And how Slack users engage each other matters as well. It's not enough to sign up, but they also need to be chatting away over time. Eventually once they reach a threshold—for Slack it was approximately 2,000 messages—where they'll stick around and keep using the product:

> *"Based on our experience of which companies stuck with us and which didn't, we decided that any team that has exchanged 2,000 messages in its history has tried Slack—really tried it," Butterfield says. "For a team around 50 people that means about 10 hours' worth of messages. For a typical team of 10 people, that's maybe a week's worth of messages. But it hit us that, regardless of any other factor, after 2,000 messages, 93% of those customers are still using Slack today."[9]*

This idea can be generalized to a wide variety of products beyond Slack.

How many users does your network need before the product experience becomes good? The way to answer this is for companies to do an analysis on the size of their networks (on the X-axis) plotted against a set of important engagement metrics (on the Y-axis). For Uber, this chart showed that more drivers generally meant a lower waiting time, and thus more users—at least up to some point. Eventually, the difference between two minutes to get a car or one minute to get a car becomes diminishing returns. Facebook's famous growth maxim, "10 friends in 7 days," is an expression of the same idea.

Users who come in with more friends have higher retention, so you want to maximize it, at least up to a point of diminishing returns. Do enough of these analyses, and some interesting patterns will show up— you'll find the kink in the curve that tells you how much network density is needed to really spike up usage. Every product has this threshold, although some require higher numbers and some are lower. Zoom is also a workplace communications tool and has a low threshold requirement to form a stable network. Eric Yuan, CEO of Zoom, said to me:

> *You just need two people. One who wants to call someone else and have a conversation—that's enough for Zoom to be useful for both people and to have them keep using it.*[10]

Airbnb and Uber, on the other hand, are two-sided marketplaces that require more than one or two parties involved given the hyperlocal constraints. Here, choice matters a lot—you might want to browse dozens of different Airbnb listings or request cars from many different neighborhoods in the city. As a result, the numbers to get to a good product experience are much larger—for Airbnb, early employee Jonathan Golden said:

> *Cofounder Nate Blecharczyk is highly quantitative and had determined that 300 listings, with 100 reviewed listings, was the magic number to see growth take off in a market.*[11]

Uber tries to optimize based on getting customers their cars quickly, based on the metric of ETAs—their estimated time of arrival. Chris Nakutis Taylor, one of the early general managers at Uber, describes their importance:

> ETAs were always terrible to start. +15 min in some areas, especially in the suburbs. There was another key metric. Get ETAs down under 3 min on average as quickly as possible while covering the whole city.
>
> If you could get ETAs, unfulfilleds, and surge down quickly, you'll have a healthy market.[12]

William Barnes, another early GM who was one of the first fifty employees and launched Los Angeles, describes the early ad hoc calculation:

> The strategy was "let's get a bunch of cars on the road" and try and get their ETAs and the request conversion rate (the % who purchase a ride) to reasonable levels. In LA and other big cities, the goal was to try to get 15–20 concurrent online cars on the road at the same time. LA's launch was notoriously expensive because we worked hard to get that all in West Hollywood at launch.[13]

The higher the requirement, the harder it is to get started, but the more defensible the product is in the long run. In Uber's case, as much as critics have occasionally argued that the company lacks defensibility and network effects, today it maintains a big advantage on upstarts who can no longer solve the Cold Start Problem in the same way.

Conceptually, understanding that a product has a critical threshold is helpful, but practically speaking, what do you do with this metric? For new products, it's important to have a hypothesis for the size of your network even before you begin. Communication apps can be 1:1, so the network is small, and you can plan accordingly. Contrast that to products that are highly asymmetrical, with content creators and viewers, or marketplaces with buyers and sellers—these are likely to require a much bigger number to hit the threshold, and require a much bigger effort to get started. The size of an initial network helps determine a launch strategy.

The Antidote to the Cold Start Problem

Solving the Cold Start Problem requires a team to launch a network and quickly create enough density and breadth such that the user experience can improve in leaps and bounds. In Slack's case, you can think of it as how likely it is that the person you're looking for within your company uses Slack, and how likely it is they'll reply. If the network is small and sparse, you may not be able to message who you want, or when you do, because they use it infrequently, they won't reply quickly. Your coworker will just wonder why you didn't send them an email.

If you add more people, but add the wrong people, then it still won't be enough. You need the right people on the network. Ten people using Slack all from the same team is better than ten random people in a larger company. Density and interconnectedness is key.

Eventually, once you add enough users to the Slack network, it becomes the default way to reach out to someone in the office. You might use it for 1:1 messages, but start to also use it to share meeting agendas on conference calls, summarize outcomes, or a myriad of other use cases. Engagement, retention, and monetization all increase. It's not magic—it's not a black/white switch that takes you from a sub-scale network to a working one. Instead, it feels like a gradual series of improvements in the core metrics as the network fills in.

The solution to the Cold Start Problem starts by understanding how to add a small group of the right people, at the same time, using the product in the right way. Getting this initial network off the ground is the key, and the key is the "atomic network"—the smallest, stable network from which all other networks can be built.

6

THE ATOMIC NETWORK

Credit Cards

If you study the launch of products with network effects, you'll see that one of the most common threads is that they often start small, in a single city, college campus, or in small beta tests at individual companies—like Slack's story. Only once they nail it in a smaller network do they build up over time to eventually conquer the world.

If you can create one stable, engaged network that can self-sustain—an atomic network—then likely you can build a second network adjacent to the first one. And if you can build 1, and then 2, you can probably build 10 or 100 networks. Copy and paste many times, and you can build a huge interconnected network that spans the entire market.

For companies like Uber that exist both offline and online, it might seem obvious that a city-by-city approach is the right strategy. But there's a history of products like Tinder and Facebook growing from tight-knit college communities, as well as B2B companies like Slack that grow team by team within a larger company. There's a reason for this, and in this chapter I'll explain why, starting with one of the most important inventions in the past century.

Launching the First Credit Card

There is a fantastic example of the atomic network, not from the technology industry, but rather, from consumer finance: the invention of the first credit card, in 1958.

I first heard about the creation of the credit card from Alex Rampell, my colleague at Andreessen Horowitz focused on fintech. In an essay on the topic, Alex writes:

> Credit cards and payment cards are arguably the most valuable network in the world, with at least $1 trillion of publicly traded market cap. On September 18, 1958, it all began in the little town of Fresno, California.
>
> At the time, there were "charge cards," like Diner's Club, but there was no "credit" being extended. For consumers, lines of credit were either specific to a merchant (like Sears), or a burdensome process. If you wanted to get a loan, you had to go to the bank in person.[14]

Credit cards have network effects for the same reasons that marketplaces do: they aggregate consumers, merchants, and other financial institutions as a multi-sided network. Everyone in the network benefits, particularly the consumer, who can go shopping without carrying physical cash. Merchants and banks are happy, too. And the bigger the network gets—meaning more consumers, more places where credit cards are accepted, etc.—the more useful the network. This in turn drives new merchants and consumers to adopt it.

Bank of America invented the credit card, and picked Fresno, California, as its first test site. It would just focus on this single city—why?

> Fresno was chosen as the first test site partly because of its size— with a population around 250,000, it offered the critical mass the bank thought necessary to make a credit card work—and partly be-

*cause a staggering 45 percent of Fresno's families did some business
with the Bank of America.*[15]

To get the product into the hands of consumers, Joseph Williams
of Bank of America, who led this project, conducted the world's first
successful mass mailing of unsolicited credit cards. Alex describes this
further:

*On September 18, the bank mailed 60,000 Fresno residents a
BankAmericard. There was no application process. The card simply
arrived in the mailbox, ready to use. Credit card fees for merchants
were set at 6 percent and consumers received between $300 and
$500 in instant credit. There was a certain brilliance behind the
60,000-person drop: On day 1, cardholders simply existed. This
permitted Bank of America to sign up all merchants who didn't
already have proprietary credit card programs. BofA focused on
fast-moving, small merchants like Florsheim Shoes, not giants like
Sears. More than 300 Fresno merchants signed up.*

*Within three months, Bank of America had expanded its cus-
tomer base to Modesto in the north and Bakersfield to the south.
Within a year, it added San Francisco, Sacramento, and Los Angeles. Thirteen months after the initial Fresno drop, the bank had
issued 2 million cards and onboarded 20,000 merchants.*

The concept of an atomic network is immediately obvious here. Although Bank of America served all of California, they didn't focus on
trying to launch across the entire state at once, but rather, they focused
on Fresno, a town where they had a high degree of penetration. On top
of that, they focused on a moment in time—Bank of America issued all
the credit cards on the same day, so that there would be a tipping point
of people with the cards in their wallets, ready to use them. And after
getting the cards in the hands of consumers, they focused on a specific
segment of small merchants in the downtown corridor of the town, to

complete the other side of the network. These simultaneous moves combined to create the first atomic network for credit cards, starting one of the most valuable networks of all time.

The Atomic Network

Whether for credit cards, multiplayer games, or business collaboration software, the "atomic network" is the smallest network needed that can stand on its own. It needs to have enough density and stability to break through early anti-network effects, and ultimately grow on its own. I liken it to an atom because it is the unit upon which larger networks are ultimately built. If you can build one, and then another, you can build the rest of the network—this is the base unit to build everything else.

In Slack's case, the atomic network turned out to be pretty small. The threshold was just the team of people around you—under ten in a single company might be enough—and there would be enough chat activity to sustain user engagement. Contrast that to the credit card, which needed to launch in an entire city to make it work. After all, they had to sign a critical mass of retailers and consumers, and it makes sense to sign up most of a downtown commerce district as part of the strategy.

To build an atomic network requires a hodgepodge of different tools. Common themes emerge when you look at Slack's strong network launch as well as the successes across marketplaces, social networks, developer platforms, and dozens of other categories. Many of them are counterintuitive: The networked product should be launched in its simplest possible form—not fully featured—so that it has a dead simple value proposition. The target should be on building a tiny, atomic network—the smallest that could possibly make sense—and focus on building density, ignoring the objection of "market size." And finally, the attitude in executing the launch should be "do whatever it takes"—

even if it's unscalable or unprofitable—to get momentum, without worrying about how to scale.

Embedded within Slack's strategy, and the strategy of many early-stage networked products, is a series of short-term boosts—often called "growth hacks"—which are important in forming the initial atomic networks. In Slack's case, it was their incredible buzz within the early-adopter startup community, and their invite-only launch. There are other famous examples: The $5 referral fee that lit up the original Pay-Pal network, or Dropbox's demo video on Hacker News that created a huge line of folks excited to try the magical cloud-storage product. Or the "Uber Ice Cream" promotions letting people order soft-serve ice cream, on demand, via the rideshare app. In the early days, local newspapers and social media would often cover the ice cream promotion, which helped build out the rideshare network. Each of these growth hacks gave an important, quick lift that established an atomic network, kicking off future growth.

Once a single atomic network can be built, it becomes straightforward to build many others by repeating the same playbook. For Slack, an early-adopter team might start using the product regularly, until it starts to grow organically inside the company. Eventually the entire company upgrades to become paying customers. Rinse and repeat. Slack's earliest customers were other startups, but eventually, atomic networks started to form inside larger customers like IBM or other Fortune 500 companies. Once Slack could build a dense network that sustained a single team, it could eventually take over an enterprise.

Why Starting with a Niche Works

The atomic network is a complementary point of view to Clayton Christensen's Disruption Theory. These small networks often grow in niches, slowly growing to take over the entire market. Chris Dixon, my colleague at a16z, summarized the idea in an essay titled, appropriately, "The next big thing will start out looking like a toy."

> *Disruptive technologies are dismissed as toys because when they are first launched they "undershoot" user needs. The first telephone could only carry voices a mile or two. The leading telco of the time, Western Union, passed on acquiring the phone because they didn't see how it could possibly be useful to businesses and railroads— their primary customers. What they failed to anticipate was how rapidly telephone technology and infrastructure would improve (technology adoption is usually non-linear due to so-called complementary network effects). The same was true of how mainframe companies viewed the PC (microcomputer), and how modern telecom companies viewed Skype.[16]*

I think Chris is right, but I would extend this idea further into the target audience, too. Not only will the product initially look like a toy, but as a corollary to Disruption Theory, there is a huge benefit to picking a smaller and more targeted starting point. Nail this initial niche network, establish an atomic network, and grow from there. In other words:

> *The next big thing will start out looking like it's for a niche network.*

Networked products often look like toys, and moreover, toys for a weird niche. This is why they are easy to underestimate. The atomic networks are forming in niche audiences like teens or gamers, and picking up a lot of buzz, but it's not clear yet that it will be interesting to the mainstream. But that may soon change, as the network gets built out. In the meantime, you're not in the target audience, and that's okay.

Underestimating new products in this way is the number one way to make dumb predictions in the tech industry. It's what leads pundits to say a product won't work, isn't interesting, or has a small market size—followed by that product proving them wrong just a few years later. These erroneous predictions are understandable, because it's hard for a product to resonate when its network doesn't include you, your friends, or your colleagues. The addressable market will seem small, and it's not until relevant people join that the product will feel like it's for you. It's not that product changes are needed—it's that the network needs to fill out to the point where the people and content are relevant.

Picking Your Atomic Network

The first step to launching an atomic network is to have a hypothesis about what it might look like. My advice: Your product's first atomic network is probably smaller and more specific than you think. Not a massive segment of users, or a particular customer segment, or a city, but instead something tiny, maybe on the order of hundreds of people, at a specific moment in time. It was similar for Uber, whose networks we tend to talk about as "San Francisco" or "New York," but in the earliest days, the focus was on narrow, ephemeral moments—more like "5pm at the Caltrain station at 5th and King St." The general managers and Driver Operations had an internal tool, called Starcraft—referring to the real-time strategy game popular at the time—that allowed them to click on a group of cars, text them "Go to the train, lots of riders!" and direct them in real time.

Once rides start to consistently happen at these moments, then the discussion might shift to focus on the wider network defined by the 7x7 square miles of the city, then adding the suburbs of East Bay and Silicon Valley as the next step. Years later, a company might talk about entire countries or mega-regions, like EMEA or APAC, but in the early days, it's about something much more focused. It should be about building the smallest possible group.

Whereas our typical business verbiage revolves around aggregations of millions of people—that's usually what we mean when we talk about "markets," "segments," and "demographics"—the language of launching new networks should be focused on groupings of a handful of people, with the right intent, in the right situation, at the right time. This is true in dating apps, marketplaces, but even in workplace products. The wedge begins with "The Q2 planning cycle in the Product team at Chase Bank."

The more users you need to get to an atomic network, the harder it is to create. There are networked products with small minimum size requirements, for example the telephone, a communications product like Snapchat, or Zoom for videoconferencing. This makes it much easier to get started—because as long as you can get each new user to find a friend that's already on the network, or to invite a friend, then it'll work. No wonder these are some of the stickiest, fastest-growing products, too. But there are drawbacks, too, because what's easier for you will be easier for your competitors—they just need a few users to get started as well, which is why there are so many messaging apps and chat features inside larger products.

Let's look at the other end of the spectrum on network size. There are enterprise products like Workday (a financial HR management tool) that require the company to implement them before there's any value. Here, a viral growth strategy is difficult, because it's not enough to dribble in a few users at a time. If you need hundreds of users on the same platform at once, company-wide coordination is needed. In this situation, a top-down enterprise sale that gets a company to mandate usage for everyone might work better.

The Power of Atomic Networks

Growing city by city, campus by campus, or team by team is a surprisingly powerful strategy. It leads to dense, organic connections of users that strengthen network effects across multiple dimensions: Engagement goes up, because users are more likely to find other relevant users. Viral growth goes up when prospective users of a product see that their friends and colleagues are all using the service. In the earlier example of Bank of America's credit card launch, focusing on one city at a time made it more likely that customers would find local merchants that accepted this novel new method of payment. Contrast that to when you peanut-butter your efforts across a whole industry or geography—the active parts of the network rapidly dissipate as anti-network effects kick in, because a network of 1,000 random users of Slack will have less retention than 1,000 users all inside the same company.

The concept of atomic networks is powerful because if you can build one, you can probably build two. Each one often becomes easier, because each network can be intertwined with the next—Slack's success within one company can help it become successful in another, as employees move about and introduce the product to new workplaces. Facebook's early campus launches became easier over time as students' friends at different schools began to demand the product more and more. Build a few atomic networks, and soon you can copy and paste them into many, many markets.

There's a big question at the heart of all of this: What does it take to build an atomic network in the first place? And why is it so hard? To answer this, I'll start with an important sub-segment of every network that has to be made happy in order for it to function.

7

THE HARD SIDE

Wikipedia

Even at the start of an atomic network, there is an important and surprising dynamic at play that only increases over time: there is a minority of users that create disproportionate value and as a result, have disproportionate power.

This the "hard side" of your network. They do more work and contribute more to your network, but are that much harder to acquire and retain. For social networks, these are often the content creators that generate the media everyone consumes. For app stores, these are the developers that actually create the products. For workplace apps, these are the managers that author and create documents and projects, and who invite coworkers to participate. For marketplaces, these are usually the sellers and providers who spend their entire day attracting users with their products and services.

Sometimes the hard side is obvious, but I encourage you to think deeply about which side is which, because it can be nuanced. For instance, large-scale job listings marketplaces are inverted compared to most other marketplaces. The companies looking to hire—the buyers—are the hard side, whereas the supply of talent is generally easier to acquire.

You might look at a product and think its network doesn't have sides. Sometimes this is referred to in the industry as one-sided networks, like messaging apps and social networks. But even in these cases, there are active, extroverted users who initiate conversations and organize get-togethers, and there are those who don't. Nearly every network has them, and the hard side must all be happy for the network to function. When they work, they generate what academics often call "cross-side network effects"—when more users in one side of the network benefits the other side of the network. At Uber, more drivers help lower prices and ETAs for riders, and more riders helps drivers successfully earn fares.

Needless to say, acquiring the hard side of the network and keeping them happy is paramount to standing up an atomic network. To understand the motivations of these users, let's describe one of the largest networked products ever built—Wikipedia.

The Volunteers Who Built Wikipedia

Wikipedia is one of the largest websites on the internet, often ranked #8 or #9 depending on the month, just above Amazon and Netflix, and well above eBay and LinkedIn. It generates over 18 billion page views and 500 million unique visitors a month, with articles across an enormous variety of topics. It's a networked product, with visitors looking for content and editors contributing articles. And the editors have contributed a ton—since Wikipedia's founding in 2001, more than 55 million articles have been written on the site. Wikipedia itself lists some facts about its size in comparison to paper encyclopedias:

Currently, the English Wikipedia alone has over 6,308,342 articles of any length, and the combined Wikipedias for all other languages greatly exceed the English Wikipedia in size, giving more than 29

billion words in 55 million articles in 309 languages. The English
Wikipedia alone has over 3.9 billion words, and has over 90 times
as many words as the 120-volume English-language Encyclopædia
Britannica.[17]

It may surprise you to know that all of Wikipedia—with more than
55 million articles—was written by a small group of users. Not just
small, actually, but tiny. Even though there are hundreds of millions of
users, there are only about 100,000 active contributors per month, and
when you look at the small group of writers who make more than 100+
edits in a month, it's about 4,000 people. As a ratio, it means that active
contributors represent only 0.02% of the total viewer pool.

The motivations of these contributors are worth studying. Within
the most hyperactive group of editors is a contributor named Steven
Pruitt, a records and information officer for US Customs and Border
Patrol Protection. Steven edits Wikipedia in his spare time—but when
I say spare time, it's almost like a part-time job. CBS News covered his
contributions to Wikipedia in 2019, as the editor with the most edits on
English Wikipedia:

> *Steven Pruitt has made nearly 3 million edits on Wikipedia and*
> *written 35,000 original articles. It's earned him not only accolades*
> *but almost legendary status on the internet.*
>
> *Pruitt was named one of the most influential people on the*
> *internet by* Time *magazine in part because one-third of all English*
> *language articles on Wikipedia have been edited by Steven. An in-*
> *credible feat, ignited by a fascination with his own history.*
>
> *Pulling from books, academic journals and other sources, he*
> *spends more than three hours a day researching, editing and writing.*[18]

And how much does he earn by doing this? Nothing. He's a volunteer editor. While it might seem strange to some of us to spend hours

per day writing on Wikipedia, when you look across user-generated products, this is actually the norm, not the exception. There are nearly 100 million riders on Uber, but just a few million drivers. There are two billion active users on YouTube, but just a few million upload videos. Even think about all the people who write documents and make presentations versus those who just view or make small edits. This relationship exists everywhere.

The Easy Side versus the Hard Side

Why is there a hard side at all? Hard sides exist because there are tasks in any networked product that just require more work, whether that's selling products, organizing projects, or creating content. Users on the hard side have complex workflows, expect status benefits as well as financial outcomes, and will try competitive products to compare. As a result, their expectations are higher, and it's difficult to engage and retain them.

The good news is, the hard side of the network creates a ton more value. At the extreme, you can look at a platform like Valve's Steam, which lets users buy and download games—this is a kind of two-sided network where the hard side of the network is game developers. The best game developer on the platform might build a single piece of content that is downloaded millions of times and require tens of millions of dollars of investment and hundreds of people to create. In a less extreme example of value creation, the best Uber drivers will work many times more hours than the average driver (who is part-time), but the difference is not as stark as with a digital good like content or an app. In both cases though, the game developers and drivers have to put in a lot more effort than the consumers of both services. Consumers are generally the easy side of a network, and are typically cheaper and easier to attract and retain.

Because the hard side is so critical, it is imperative to have hypotheses about how a product will cater to these users from day one. A successful new product should be able to answer detailed questions: Who is the hard side of your network, and how will they use the product? What is the unique value proposition to the hard side? (And in turn, the easy side of the network.) How do they first hear about the app, and in what context? For users on the hard side, as the network grows, why will they come back more frequently and become more engaged? What makes them sticky to your network such that when a new network emerges, they will retain on your product? These are difficult answers, and require a deep understanding of the motivations of your users.

The motivations of the hard side depend on the product category—content creators have different goals than marketplace sellers. Those who use workplace collaboration tools have yet another set of motivations. Understanding these diverse points of view makes it easier to serve them.

The Hard Side of Social Content Apps

Content creators are the core of a wide class of networked products that at their foundation is about creating, sharing, and consuming content. These are some of the largest and fastest-growing products in the world, with billions of monthly active users, like TikTok, Twitch, YouTube, Instagram. As I discussed earlier, Wikipedia falls into this category, too—and they are a tiny slice of a much larger network of users.

In a widely read essay called "Creators, Synthesizers, and Consumers," Bradley Horowitz, now a vice president of product at Google, described the 1 percent of users who create versus everyone else:

- 1% of the user population might start a group (or a thread within a group)
- 10% of the user population might participate actively, and

actually author content whether starting a thread or responding to a thread-in-progress

- 100% of the user population benefits from the activities of the
above groups (lurkers)[19]

This is often called the "1/10/100" rule, and it's no surprise that the
1 percent of highly engaged users is extremely valuable. For YouTube,
Instagram, and other content-sharing platforms, there is a "power law"
curve where the 20 percent of top influencers and content creators end
up with the vast majority of engagement. They attract millions of followers, and make content that generates tens of millions of views.

This describes what happens, but it doesn't describe why. More recently, Evan Spiegel, CEO and cofounder of Snap, described his understanding of the content creation pyramid for Snap and Instagram,
versus TikTok:

*You can imagine a pyramid, if you will, of internet technology or
communications technology, where the base of the pyramid—the
very broad base—is self-expression and communication. And that's
what Snapchat is really about. Talking to your friends, which is
something everyone is comfortable doing. They just express how
they feel.*

*As the pyramid gets narrower, you have the next layer, which
is status. Social media in its original construct is really about status,
representing who you are, showing people that you're cool, getting
likes and comments. Those sorts of things. And that's less accessible
to the broad base of humanity, and has a narrower base of appeal.
[There's a] more limited frequency of engagement, because people
only do some things that are cool once a week or once a month, and
not every day.*

*At the top of the pyramid, which I think is represented by Tik-
Tok, is really talent. People who have spent a couple hours learning a new dance, or think about a funny new creative way to tell*

a story. They're really making media to entertain other people. I
think that's even narrower. . . . [20]

In Spiegel's pyramid, people have emotional needs—whether that's
self-expression, status, or communication—and create different forms
of content to achieve them. Sending an ephemeral photo is easy, particularly a selfie on the go, which anyone can do. But spending hours to
learn a new TikTok dance is difficult, and not everyone can do it. The
more difficult the work needed to be part of the hard side of a network,
the smaller the percentage of users who will participate.

For Snapchat, there is the simple value proposition of communicating with your friends, and deepening your relationship with them over
time—that's the utility. Yet across many other platforms, particularly
"broadcast" apps where you share videos or photos widely, the value
proposition is displaying your status. No wonder our Instagram feeds
are photos of travel adventures, cars, concerts, working out, and so on.
Users become addicted to the "social feedback loop"—you publish content, and others see it and engage in the form of likes, shares, and comments. When this feedback is positive, it drives the creator to generate
even more content.

The social feedback loop is a core concept because the creator/
viewer network is so ubiquitous as a network structure. We also see
this structure in categories beyond content sharing. We can see these
motivations among individuals who organize group chats in WhatsApp,
events on platforms like Eventbrite, writers who publish email newsletters, reviewers who love to curate their favorite restaurants on Yelp, and
so on. Within these platforms, just ask yourself, "If a piece of content
was created, and no one saw it, would the creator be disappointed?" If
the answer is yes, then social feedback is a key value. The combination
of tools, aggregation of audience, and a networked product is what is
needed to unlock the hard side of these networks—it's all about the
content creators.

Content creators are just one example of the hard side. There's also hard sides that exist within marketplaces, workplace collaboration tools, multiplayer games, and other categories. Each set's motivations are idiosyncratic to the category—sellers on a marketplace might focus on creating revenue, whereas multiplayer games might be oriented around status and fun. It's important to focus on this tiny slice of users so that messaging, product functionality, and business model are all aligned to serve them. Without this group, the atomic network will collapse—a social network can't exist without its content creators, and a marketplace can't exist without its sellers.

Wikipedia's Teeny, Tiny Hard Side

The hard side of Wikipedia's network is minuscule—a mere 0.02 percent of highly motivated users create the content for the rest of the network. It's not the 1/10/100 pyramid that I quoted earlier, but something even more extreme. Attracting and retaining content creators is paramount. Their motivations might seem unusual—it's certainly not economic, as Wikipedia editors are not paid. Nor is it utility, since there are easier and simpler ways to publish content online. It would be easy and superficial to attribute their efforts to boredom, but it's not likely that.

Instead, using the frameworks presented in this chapter, I'll make an educated guess: similar to Instagram and YouTube's content creators, Wikipedia's content creators are likely motivated by the community itself. Social feedback, status, and other community dynamics encourage editors to keep creating content. Wikipedians, as they call themselves, can show their expertise in a topic by maintaining comprehensively written pages, and people within the community will thank and appreciate them. This provides status. They can make edits to correct others, which offers another form of status and satisfaction. There's teamwork and a feeling of camaraderie, which create bonds that retain users over months and years. Steven Pruitt, the wildly prolific Wikipedian, might have just a normal job during the day, but in the evenings and weekends he is one of the most important contributors to one of the largest web-sites in the world.

The hard side of a network is important to understand, not just for Wikipedia, but for any new product seeking to launch its atomic net-work. Without this critical group, an atomic network will struggle to get off the ground. You might go so far as to say they are the most important group of users to start with, and it's important to have a thesis for why your product will appeal to them starting on day one.

8

SOLVE A HARD PROBLEM

Tinder

The hardest problem to solve in creating the first atomic network is, well, attracting the hard side. Focus on attracting content creators to a new video platform, or sellers to a new marketplace, or the project managers inside a company to a new workplace app. The other side of the network will follow. The question is, how?

The answer is by building a product that solves an important need for the hard side. Let's look at online dating, which evolved over time to better solve the matchmaking problem that has bedeviled humanity since the beginning of time. Dating apps are network effects–driven products that grow city by city, and the more folks that join the network, the better the chances that people will find matches. But at the genesis of online dating, the experience was generally terrible, especially for the hard side of the network.

The Problem of Too Many Love Letters

Online dating was invented at the beginning of the web, in the early 1990s. It was designed like newspaper classifieds, where men and women browsed large databases of profiles, and could message each other if they were interested. Match.com and JDate were successful pioneers in this category, which worked despite its flaws. The classifieds-based design created a poor product experience since the popular members—particularly women—would become overwhelmed with a large number of messages, and they would struggle to reply. At a bar or club, potential suitors might be dissuaded if they saw a line of people waiting to talk to an attractive man or woman, but online, there was no such signal. So in turn, the experience for everyone else also ended up poor, because it seemed like no one would write them back.

The lesson is, unsurprisingly, that attractive people—particularly women—are the hard side of the online dating network. A few years later, the next generation of online dating would emerge, led by products like eHarmony and OKCupid. These products used quizzes and matching algorithms so that the system could decide who got which matches, and how often. This ensured women got fewer messages, and hopefully more of the right ones. And the men got more replies, too, so that it didn't feel like it was devolving into a copy-paste messaging exercise.

It wasn't until 2012, at the beginning of the explosion in mobile apps, that yet another generation of dating apps would emerge. These apps, exemplified by Tinder, would innovate even further for the hard side of the network. I talked to Tinder's cofounder, Sean Rad, about how Tinder innovated on the previous generation of products. He described the combination of new ideas:

The older dating sites made it feel like you were doing work, like you were inside the office. You'd go and do work emails during the day, then go home and write more messages at night. Only to pro-

spective dates rather than work colleagues. Tinder was different—it made dating fun. You could sign up without filling in a bunch of forms. It's visual, you just swipe back and forth, and you could take five minutes to do it while you were waiting in line or something like that. It's a form of entertainment.[21]

The other problem was how to wade through all the replies. In real life, you're often introduced to potential romantic partners through friends, or you have a shared context—like work or school—to help filter. For online dating, the most attractive members of a network need some additional signals to help sort through their matches. Tinder did this by integrating with Facebook, and Sean also explained how the app was able to build trust:

Tinder started by making everyone connect their Facebook, so that we could show the number of mutual friends you had, which built trust. We also made it so that you could only be matched with people who lived around you—we used the GPS location from your phone, which was new. These were people with mutual friends living around you, the sort of person you might meet in real life! Connecting with Facebook also made sure you would never be shown to friends, or vice versa, if you were worried about that. This all created trust. Tinder also had built-in messaging so that you didn't have to give out your number. If the conversation didn't go anywhere, you could just unmatch without worrying about getting harassed.

And of course, the mechanic of swiping itself is a way to make sure people don't feel overwhelmed. Whereas men tend to swipe right (that is, to indicate interest) on about half of women's profiles—about 45 percent to be exact—the ladies in the product swipe on only 5 percent of profiles they see. As a result, women mostly match with the guys they select. However, if they feel like they are in too many conversations, they can stop swiping for a while and just focus on the messaging of their existing matches. All of these insights made Tinder a much better experience for the most important side of their network, solving one of the most important obstacles in the Cold Start Problem.

The Hard Side for Marketplaces Is Usually the Supply Side

Marketplaces tend to revolve around their sellers. I've seen the difficulty of managing the hard side for rideshare firsthand. For Uber, in any given market, so-called power drivers constitute 20 percent of the supply but create 60 percent of the trips. These are some of the most valuable users on the planet, as they are the core of Uber's business.

Uber's drivers are just one example of a broader set of workers that drives most marketplace companies. For marketplaces, the hard side is usually the "supply" side of the network, which refers to the workers and small businesses who provide the time, products, and effort and are trying to generate income on the platform. They use digital marketplaces as a side hustle, selling collectibles or coaching sessions. They often do this as an alternative to hourly jobs, of which there are nearly 80 million in the United States. These are folks often living in the middle of the country, working in retail jobs that turn over 100 percent year over year, and are struggling for additional income. Marketplace startups often provide these opportunities to this group.

To solve the Cold Start Problem for marketplaces, often the first move—as it was for Uber—is to bring a critical mass of supply onto the marketplace. For a marketplace like eBay, you start with sellers of collectibles. For a marketplace like Airbnb, you might start with people with a few extra rooms in their place. For a social platform like YouTube, it might be video creators. For a more esoteric category, like GitHub, it's helpful to bring on some prominent open-source projects and key developers. But once the supply has arrived onto the network, it's time to bring in demand—the buyers and users that will form the bulk of the network. Once that's working, though, it becomes all about supply again. Thus the order of operations, at least for most consumer-facing marketplaces, is "supply, demand, supply, supply, supply." While supply might be easy to get onto the network early on through subsidies, eventually it will become the bottleneck. The hard side of a network is, by definition, hard to scale.

Uber had to get creative to unlock the hard side of their network, the drivers. Initially, Uber's focus was on black car and limo services, which were licensed and relatively uncontroversial. However, a seismic shift occurred when rival app Sidecar innovated in recruiting unlicensed, normal people as drivers on their platform. This was the "peer-to-peer" model that created millions of new rideshare drivers, and was quickly copied and popularized by Lyft and then Uber. Jahan Khanna, co-founder/chief technology officer of Sidecar, spoke of its origin:

> It was obvious that letting anyone sign up to be a driver would be a big deal. With more drivers, rides would get cheaper and the wait times would get shorter. This came up in many brainstorms at Sidecar, but the question was always, what was the regulatory framework that allows this to operate? What were the prior examples that weren't immediately shut down? After doing a ton of research, we came onto a model that had been active for years in San Francisco run by someone named Lynn Breedlove called Homobiles that answered our question.[22]

It's a surprising fact, but the earliest version of the rideshare idea came not from an investor-backed startup, but rather from a nonprofit called Homobiles, run by a prominent member of the LGBTQ community in the Bay Area named Lynn Breedlove. The service was aimed at protecting and serving the LGBTQ community while providing them transportation—to conferences, bars and entertainment, and also to get health care—while emphasizing safety and community.

Homobiles had built its own niche, and had figured out the basics: Breedlove had recruited, over time, 100 volunteer drivers, who would respond to text messages. Money would be exchanged, but in the form of donations, so that drivers could be compensated for their time. The company had operated for several years, starting in 2010—several years before Uber X—and provided the template for what would become a $100 billion+ gross revenue industry. Sidecar learned from Homobiles, implementing their offering nearly verbatim, albeit in digital form: donations based, where the rider and driver would sit together in the front, like a friend giving you a ride. With that, the rideshare market was kicked off.

Nights and Weekends

The key insight in the stories of Homobiles or Tinder is—how do you find a problem where the hard side of a network is engaged, but their needs are unaddressed? The answer is to look at hobbies and side hustles.

There are millions of content creators, app developers, marketplace sellers, and part-time drivers that power the hard side of networks. They are smart, motivated, early adopters who are finding opportunities to make themselves useful. They are the developers behind the open-source movement who have built Linux, WordPress, MySQL, and many of the other technologies that underpin the modern internet. They are the millions of eBay sellers that have created jobs and companies by buying and selling goods that people want. For photo-sharing and messaging products like Instagram and YouTube, they stem from the countless amateur photographers and videographers who like to record travel, special occasions, architecture, beautiful people, and everything else.

What people are doing on their nights and weekends represents all the underutilized time and energy in the world. If put to good use, this can become the basis of the hard side of an atomic network. Sometimes the army is built on people with excess time, but sometimes it is built on people with underutilized assets as well. Rideshare networks, for example, fundamentally depend on the underutilization of cars, which generally sit idle most of the time besides the daily commute and the occasional errand. Airbnb is built on the underutilization of guest bedrooms and second homes, combined with the time and effort of the hosts. Craigslist and eBay are built on letting people sell their "junk"— the stuff that they don't value anymore—to new owners who might value it more.

Usually the hard side will continue to use Airbnb or TikTok because that's where the demand is, and thus, they are locked into the positive network effects on those platforms. However, the trick is to look closer— to segment the hard side of the network and figure out who is being underserved. Sometimes this is a niche, like a passionate subcommunity of content creators for makeup or unboxing that might be better served with additional commerce features. It could be a low-production-quality, amateur part of the community, like those who are doing #whateverchallenge of the week, who would benefit from basic video editing tools. For networks that are derived from underutilized assets, it might be the niche of those who like to have new side hustles every weekend to make money online. Or perhaps there is a new platform shift coming soon that feels niche, but might upend the entire ecosystem.

The idea is to start with these underserved segments—whose users may not be very attractive customers on their own—and to apply Clayton Christensen's disruption theory. New products often disrupt markets by starting on the low end, providing "good enough" functionality, and growing from there into the medium, and eventually into the core market of the incumbents. Recently, the opposite trend has emerged—products like Uber and email company Superhuman, have started at the top of the market as a luxury product, and worked their way down.

When we combine disruption theory with network effects, it makes even more sense—atomic networks often start at the low end in terms of functionality, in a niche market. But once an atomic network is established, the hard side of the network is willing to extend their offerings and services to go into the next vertical. This attracts an incrementally higher-end opposite side, which in turn spurs the hard side to extend even further—and the cycle continues! Airbnb may have started with airbeds, but the same hosts that might be willing to rent out an airbed might be willing to rent out their room, or their entire apartment. This changes the potential nature of the supply in the marketplace, attracting a higher-end demand side, which in turn attracts higher-end inventory. No wonder today, Airbnb hosts a wide variety of high-end offerings, from luxury penthouses to boutique hotel rooms. In that way, network effects can play a key role in disrupting new industries—creating the momentum for a low-end atomic network to slowly build out into higher-end offerings over time.

The Hard Side of Dating Apps

Let's go back to online dating for a moment—when viewed as networked products, the apps bring together two sides in a romantic context. In that way, Tinder, Bumble, Match, eHarmony, HotOrNot, and other dating apps reflect something that existed as a human behavior for eons. It's long been a hobby of amateur matchmakers to introduce their single friends to each other. There is a deep need for this service—but also skill required to do it successfully. In the modern age we have digitized dating, using algorithms to match people, dating profiles to easily swipe through thousands of people at once, and real-time messaging to make communication easier.

Importantly, these improvements help attract and maintain the most desirable members of a dating network—the hard side. The matchmaking algorithms need to find them equally attractive matches, and the profiles they browse through must help them decide between princes and frogs. The in-app messaging experience has to cater to their needs, with an option to get out of conversations quickly if needed. Without these types of features, desirable people will churn from the product, degrading the network and worsening the experience for everyone else.

While dating apps—and really, all networked products—need to find a value proposition for the hard side of the network, what about all the other users? Well, it's a high bar, but you need to nail the experience for them, too. You need to build a "killer product."

9

THE KILLER PRODUCT

Zoom

W hen I first started Zoom, people thought it was a terrible idea."
I sat across from Eric Yuan, CEO of Zoom, chatting over
Mediterranean food served in a nondescript restaurant at a San
Jose hotel near the Zoom offices. Eric described the early days:

> Zoom was originally called Saasbee. When Saasbee was first get-
> ting started, I sent a pitch deck to my friends and angel investors
> asking them to invest. Many of them decided to fund me just
> because they knew me and didn't care much what I was working
> on. But if they looked at the deck, they always hated the idea and
> wouldn't fund it![23]

Yet in the ensuing years, Zoom's idea would turn out to be a killer
one. The product idea matters. In the past few chapters, I have mostly
focused on building an atomic network, but have not directly addressed the product idea at the center of it all. What makes an idea for

a networked product good versus bad? And why was Zoom's initial idea so non-obvious?

Zoom was founded in 2011 and ten years later, as I write this book during the COVID pandemic in 2021, it has become essential to enabling remote work for millions of professionals. It happened very quickly—the product grew from 10 million yearly meeting participants at the end of 2019 to over 300 million just a few months later. This catapulted Zoom's valuation to $90 billion.

I first got to know Eric over lunches and coffees spanning several years that I worked at Uber, because we were a large early customer. I wanted to spend time with him since the product was so impressive. Uber ran our highly distributed global workforce of tens of thousands of employees on Zoom. Whatever office in whatever continent you were in—I personally spent time in the Uber offices in Sydney, Amsterdam, New York, and San Francisco—the conference rooms and all-hands spaces would show upcoming Zoom meetings. They displayed a list of meetings in a familiar blue background, on iPads mounted on the walls. It was an essential part of Uber's work culture.

Yet at the beginning, people didn't get the idea behind Zoom—why? According to Eric, it just seemed too simple, literally. An easier-to-use videoconferencing product wasn't an obvious idea when products like WebEx, GoToMeeting, Skype, and others had already conquered the market. Zoom didn't have more features per se, but in fact had the most important feature of all: the "it works" feature.

Zoom's value proposition reinforced the network effects within a team and between companies, by enabling frictionless meetings. It allowed attendees to join with a single click of a link, rather than entering meeting codes and dialing numbers. The high-quality video meant that successful adoption by a few people in a workplace would quickly expand virally to more teams within the office. Beyond that, there was an ecosystem of vendors and consultants working with Zoom. In other words, the frictionless usage created a design where its network effects were stronger. It was more easily able to acquire users onto its network, and it kept the ongoing engagement high. Zoom is a networked platform that has both a killer product and the mechanisms to build the network around it. They are intertwined, in a way where one reinforces the other.

It's easy to think of Zoom's simplicity as a competitive advantage, but this kind of simplicity is actually hard to implement in practice. Customers request endless features while competitors emerge with a longer list of functionality. Yet I observe that it's a distinctive quality of networked products that they often do one thing well.

What makes Zoom special, and how should one go about picking a great idea for a networked product? How are these ideas different from a traditional software product?

Networked Products versus Everything Else

Networked products are fundamentally different from the typical product experience—they facilitate experiences that users have with each other, whereas traditional products emphasize how users interact with the software itself. They grow and succeed by adding more users, which create network effects, whereas traditional products grow by building better features and supporting more use cases. It's why products like Twitter and Zoom and others often seem so simple, and are critiqued as "features not products" that seem trivial at first. They have one magical core experience. Contrast this to traditional products, which often win the "checkmark contest" bake-offs common in enterprise software purchases, but lose in the contest of actual product engagement from their end users.

Networked products must balance the needs of multiple sides of a network—not just buyers, but sellers, too. Not just content creators, but viewers as well. And the most important features in networked products often revolve around how users find and connect with each other, whether that's photo tagging, sharing permissions, or "People You May

Know." This is what lets users connect with relevant people and content on the platform, whether that's your favorite video game streamer, the right project area for your team, or something else. This is a concept missing from traditional software products, where the richness and complexity of the experience depends on who's on the network rather than the feature set.

Unlike its predecessors, Zoom's simplicity unlocked new atomic networks—after all, you just need two people. This then allowed the company to expand from videoconferencing's prior use cases of webinars and sales calls into constant, multiple-times-per-day usage. Zoom's simplicity is a strength when it comes to the company's ability to grow its network. When the product concept and value is simple to describe, it makes them easier to spread from user to user, much like the "meme" coined by noted biologist Richard Dawkins in one of my favorite books, *The Selfish Gene*. You can copy and paste a Zoom link—it's just that easy.

It's no surprise that compelling networked products often sound like a meme. The idea seems to be really basic, as it allows you to take one or two main actions. The entire product experience exists on just a handful of screens, with a small set of focused features. For example, Snapchat lets you send photos to friends. Dropbox is a magical folder that syncs your files. Uber lets you hit a button to get a ride. Slack is a chat product for your coworkers. YouTube lets you watch videos. They're very simple to use, but also easy to describe to your friends and coworkers as well.

The dead simple nature of these products means that they are often criticized for lacking technology differentiation or defensibility. It's rare to see patents or even deep intellectual property as part of the core strategy. In fact, when I meet with consumer startups, an entrepreneur bragging about patents is a turnoff. Sometimes this is a mistake—the polished, simple interface of a product actually belies deeply technical underpinnings. This was the case with Zoom's investment in video codecs, compression, and more. But often, this perception is true. Twitter's initial engineering team was often criticized for being inexperienced, resulting in the infamous "fail whale" error screen in the early years. Both Snapchat and Facebook were built by college students. Uber's app was initially outsourced to Mexico, so that when later engineers joined the company, they needed to be issued Spanish-to-English dictionaries to understand the comments and source code. In these cases it isn't until later, as the product hits scale, that the engineering teams are upgraded.

This trend of viral, easy-to-use products first started in the consumer space, but over time has taken over the enterprise software landscape as well. Some products, like Dropbox, are initially envisioned as consumer companies until later they become so popular in workplaces that the strategy shifts to the enterprise. Others, like Slack, are enterprise products started by entrepreneurs with consumer software backgrounds. In recent research by a16z examining the hottest "bottom-up" enterprise startups, most were started by founders from consumer companies like Airbnb, Uber, Yahoo, and so on. The same skills that can create successful networked products in the consumer sector can be applied toward the enterprise categories.

This cross-pollination of skill sets helps product ideas and features jump from one sector into another. It's been observed that there is an "internet software supply chain" that unites different customer segments and geographies. One example is the direct line that can be drawn through the history of emojis—they were invented on Japanese mobile phones in the 1997, adopted by teens on instant messenger and SMS, emerged into the mainstream via smartphones, and now appear on "consumerized" enterprise products like Slack. Livestreaming, video formats like Snapchat/Instagram Stories, and on-demand marketplaces are all at various points in the great software supply chain—one that connects niche consumer trends into widespread usage across enterprise and the mainstream.

Zoom had many of these same consumer-driven characteristics in the product from the start. Although the early team came from the enterprise world, in the very early days the company, then called Saasbee, had aspirations to succeed at consumer group calling as well. The product experience felt very minimalistic. And although there was strong technology underneath—after all, Eric built and ran much of the engineering team at WebEx—it was in the service of frictionless user experience. Yet many early investors balked at the fact that Zoom was tackling what they perceived as a solved problem. The commonality between all these networked products is that they offered novel ways for people to interact, and over time, the network became the defensibility.

In other words, the ideal product to drive network effects combines both factors: The product idea itself should be as simple as possible—easily understandable by anyone as soon as they encounter it. And at the same time, it should simultaneously bring together a rich, complex, infinite network of users that is impossible to copy by competitors.

Zoom, of course, is a fantastic example of this ideal.

Why Networked Products Love to Be Free

It feels like a paradox that many of the most valuable products in the world have a business model that emphasizes "free." Social networks and communication apps are free, and SaaS products tend to be freemium. Marketplace companies are free to browse and use, though obviously buying services or products cost money. This is part of their shared DNA because it affects how rapidly killer products can spread. Eric's thinking on Zoom's frictionless experience for attendees extended into the pricing. He explained:

> I wanted Zoom to be free, at least for the basic experience, so that people could see why it was so much better. I first thought, maybe it should be limited based on participants. Maybe 3 attendees could join, but once there were 4, you'd have to pay. But that didn't feel right. I studied Dropbox's pricing strategy and wondered, why did

they start charging at 2 gigabytes instead of 1? As I thought about it, I realized, it gave you time to use Dropbox more, and the more you used it more likely you will hit the cap and starting paying. I wanted Zoom to be the same way, so I set the limit to be 40 minutes per meeting but you could get the full experience of the product. That way, if the quality was good and you liked it, then you'd eventually pay.

Even from the early days, these key product decisions made a big impact on Zoom's trajectory. The product combined an easy-to-use app that allowed meetings to form quickly, had a value proposition that was simple to describe, and was free to use, at least initially. Eric mentioned that the inbound customers started right away:

During the beta release, the product was just a download button on a webpage. But the people at the Stanford Continuing Studies Program tried it, and wanted to pay! I didn't know what to charge yet, so they eventually just gave us a check for $2,000. It happened around Christmas that year, and I still have a copy of that check that I kept for myself.

After the first customer, the viral growth continued:

Several other colleges in the area were the next set of customers. The product engaged customers and they would reach out wanting to pay. Ever since then, there's been a lot of leads. I didn't have a marketing team for the first 4 years!

This strategy of making Zoom a freemium business meant it was easier for the network to grow. Offering a free tier is a recurring theme for many networked products: some are ad-supported (as video and social media platforms are), others have premium features unlocked by subscription (as with more workplace/B2B products), and others are powered by microtransactions (as with marketplaces, games, and live-streaming platforms).

This is a recurring theme across business models because of the Cold Start Problem. Charging customers directly is a straightforward way to generate revenue, but it adds friction for every new user to join the network. It's hard enough to build an atomic network; why make it even harder by erecting barriers? Without being able to build out a network quickly, growth channels like virality are more muted. If Zoom charged every user with no free tier, it might have generated more revenue in the short run, but would likely have needed to spend more on marketing and sales to compensate.

Freemium is an essential part of Zoom's appeal and ability to grow. And once Zoom had the right ingredients—a simple, killer product—its business model then provided the revenue and business model to leverage viral growth.

New Shifts in Behaviors and Computer Platforms

Zoom is just one example of a killer product emerging at just the right moment as the world changed. Videoconferencing emerging into the mainstream was a combination of widespread broadband, remote work, and professional work, all accelerated by the pandemic. Other times, the world changes when a new computing platform emerges that resets customer behavior. In previous decades, this was kicked off with the introduction of the personal computer with a text-based command line interface. Soon after that, the Macintosh brought the graphical user interface to the world. After that, we got the internet and web browser, followed by our current generation of smartphones. In future years, it might be voice gadgets, AR/VR, the metaverse, or something else entirely.

New technologies allow for new customer behaviors. There are new interface paradigms, like swiping or tapping with your finger, that allow

for new product ideas. This creates a mad scramble among big companies and startups alike—in the great reset driven by a new technology
shift—to figure out what people want and quickly build the next killer
product. Sometimes this looks like Microsoft Office's desktop apps
evolving into web-based products like Google Suite, Notion, or Airtable.
Similarly, dating websites like Match were subsumed by easy-to-use,
swipeable interfaces like Tinder, and Flickr was replaced by Instagram,
which tightly integrated to mobile phones and social networks.

These computing shifts bring us some of the most obvious new
killer products. When the smartphone arrived with a high-resolution
camera, built-in location, and the App Store, we got a long string of hits
like Snapchat, Uber, and TikTok. When the web came along, we got the
search engine, ecommerce, marketplaces, and more. The era of Windows and Macintosh computers brought us Office, desktop publishing,
and a slew of use cases for the personal computer. In other words, when
there's a new platform shift, the companies that build the killer products often create some of the most valuable companies in the industry.

Importantly, these new shifts also create huge opportunities for
startups. In a platform reinvention, everyone—incumbent or upstart—
needs to start over, and faces the Cold Start Problem. In the shift from
websites to mobile, for instance, products needed to be squeezed down
to a much smaller user interface that could be operated with big, clumsy
fingers and not the dexterity of a small mouse pointer. New ideas could
be implemented that took advantage of the unique technology of the
phone: cameras, location, notifications, and so on. You couldn't just
translate your website into a mobile app; you had to think mobile-first.

Zoom rode on many of these technological trends. Zoom benefited
from the rapid acceleration of high-speed internet that makes widespread use of videoconferencing feasible. It is adopted alongside a number of products by end users in a "bottom-up" motion, where office
workers can just pick and choose whatever services they want to use,
rather than accepting whatever IT is imposing on them. The company's
choice of a simple, freemium business model made it the right fit to grow

virally. And while Zoom was already a mature, valuable company by the time the coronavirus struck in 2020, all of the above factors certainly put Zoom in place to explosively accelerate. Any workplaces or contexts where Zoom was still facing the Cold Start Problem—where it wasn't working yet—instantly jumped onto the service.

Of course, the killer product is just one ingredient in solving the Cold Start Problem. It was also important for Zoom to quickly figure out its first atomic networks, finding that organizations like the Stanford Continuing Education Program, and small Bay Area colleges could each adopt the product independently. Get one to adopt, and others would soon follow, as people using the product would naturally spread it to others. Once the killer product and the first atomic networks are built, then a company starts to create "Magic Moments."

10

MAGIC MOMENTS

Clubhouse

I t becomes obvious when a product has solved the Cold Start Problem—the experience starts to really work. When you open a workplace collaboration app during a meeting, all the relevant tasks are in there, and your coworkers are chatting away about next steps. Or when you open a social app, engaging and entertaining content is there on your feed. You have notifications because your friends have already commented on your new photos. A marketplace app might start to feel like it has everything, like it's fully comprehensive. Search for any product, and dozens of relevant listings show, and they're cheap, high quality, and shippable same day.

When the network is fully filled out, active, and people are connected in the right way, then the product experience can really shine. This is the Magic Moment, when a product can deliver its core value—whether that's connecting people for work, entertainment, dating, games, or otherwise. A product that hasn't yet solved its Cold Start Problem will fail to deliver any magic in its early days. Often, the network will seem empty, like a ghost town. But once the network forms, the Magic Moments start to happen all the time—that's when the product is ready to expand. That's when you know the Cold Start Problem has been solved.

I saw this transformation firsthand as an early user of Clubhouse, the audio-first social app. The product was launched in 2020 by Paul Davison and Rohan Seth, and when I signed up for its beta test, it had a tiny number of users—officially, I was #104. Clubhouse started as a simple app that let you log in and speak to other users, all in a single "room." Often, it would just be Paul in the room, so that I could drop in, chat with him along with some other friends, and that was it.

In its earliest days, Clubhouse hadn't yet solved the Cold Start Problem—when you opened the app, it was often empty. There would be no active conversations and no one to talk to—not even Paul could be in there 24/7. The product, at the time, also lacked key features. It didn't even have user profiles or a network where you could follow other users. Adding all the social features and supporting multiple conversations in different rooms at once all happened later.

But there were little bursts of magic: sometimes I'd drop in and start having one of the most wonderful conversations with friends I hadn't seen in months—after all, it was during the COVID pandemic year. Or I might just listen to others having a fascinating chat about robotics, Bitcoin, the history of technology, or some other nerdy topic. I was hooked. When the product had just a few thousand users, I led a16z's Series A investment in Clubhouse, and joined its board of directors. It was during my second year as a venture capitalist, and I valued the company at what seemed like an outrageous sum—nearly $100 million—when it was just two employees.

Less than a year after its launch, Clubhouse would be adding millions of users a month. A large, diverse group of networks began to form in every geography. Whenever I opened the app during my evening routine, there would be multiple Clubhouse rooms going that I'd want to join—a few celebrities in one room, some political pundits in another. A new reality TV show, in audio form. Plus an a16z-hosted room or two on startups and technology. The Magic Moments started to happen all the time so that every time you opened the app, there was something worth listening to. Clubhouse quickly became a top-10 app in over twenty countries, and achieved a valuation of $1 billion, then $4 billion, all within a year of our initial investment.

This is an amazing trajectory—what happened? And more important, why did it happen?

The Clubhouse Story

It might seem like an accident that Clubhouse launched in 2020, where in the midst of the pandemic, the drive to connect with other people was such an important part of our lives. Yet it wasn't pure luck, as Clubhouse was one of many iterations in new audio app ideas by Paul and Rohan, who were excited by the trends in podcasting and audio devices.

Before Clubhouse, there were other apps focused on connecting people through audio. Years before, Rohan had worked on Phone-a-friend, an app to connect groups of friends over audio. Then together, they worked on Uncalendar—to fill spare moments with quick catch-up calls—and then later and more substantially, Talkshow, which made it much easier to produce podcasts. People could quickly start a podcast, record with hosts, edit, and publish, all in the same app. Talkshow had all the tools in one place. Yet because of the nature of podcasting, it was still awkward and hard to use. When I asked Paul and Rohan why it didn't work, they described the hurdles:

> *Talkshow was too heavyweight for the creators. You'd say, "Come to my Talkshow" and people ended up treating it like a podcast. The resulting content felt super scripted, and the recordings ended up sounding like a low quality podcast. The content never felt unique enough to consume. The app was too targeted at hosts, and it never felt like it could become a place to just listen to podcasts.*[24]

In other words, the product wasn't quite there, and didn't nail the experience for the hard side—the podcast hosts. It took a lot of setup and a lot of work to get to anything that felt like a Magic Moment.

Paul and Rohan learned from the experience and asked themselves the key question: how do you get to something magical faster?

After working for months on Talkshow, the duo realized that they needed to radically simplify. To make sure creators had a lightweight experience, it would be ideal to easily create content with people already hanging out in the app—that way, it avoided the coordination problem of getting your friends into an app at the same time. Clubhouse wasn't recorded, so the expectation was more like a phone call and less like a podcast—this made it lower-pressure to talk. And for users who didn't want to talk, there was an easy "lean back and listen" experience from day one. Even after the app was released, nearly a year of work went into adding user profiles, the ability to follow people, a feed to discover rooms, and so on.

Great products take time to figure out, and Clubhouse is no different. It was an overnight success that took years.

Early on, the initial atomic network formed among tech early adopters—friends of Paul and Rohan—who numbered in the thousands. I was part of this first wave. This small group was already enough, creating Magic Moments consistently as friends in the tech industry connected with each other during the pandemic. But it was the next fifty thousand or so people that brought Clubhouse into mainstream culture. The Black creative community—centered on entertainment and media hotspots like Atlanta, Chicago, New York, and Los Angeles—started to join the network in a major way in mid-2020. This was propelled by musicians, comedians, influencers, and creators hosting shows on a regular basis. Some of this activity was directly catalyzed by a16z, but much of it also happened organically. This unlocked the next set of users by late 2020 growing to millions of people globally.

By then, the experience of opening up the Clubhouse app became magical—not just for me, but for millions of people around the world. The product started to put up retention and engagement numbers as high as anything I've seen—comparable to Instagram or WhatsApp.

It's also undeniable that Clubhouse was launched at a moment in time that took advantage of shifts in technology and consumer behavior—the latter, of course, shaped by the COVID-19 pandemic of 2020. Bubba Murarka, an early Facebook employee and a close friend, was one of the earliest investors and advisors to Clubhouse. He saw the early chapters of the company up close, working with the team from its founding, and watching them iterate on the early versions of the product, all the way to its explosive launch.

It was Bubba who first introduced me to Paul many years back, and he had this observation about Clubhouse's earliest days:

> *Audio content consumption was already a daily habit for everyone, but it was getting even bigger. AirPods, Alexa devices, and in-car software like CarPlay were creating tens of millions of hours of new listening time. Podcasts were going mainstream and getting bundled into products like Spotify and Audible. When Clubhouse launched, there were magic moments left and right for the early community. It took all the benefits of audio content, like the lean-back, passive experience that lets you engage while you cook, do chores, and drive, but also made it 100x easier to create the content. You just talk, like a phone call. Everyone talks! Clubhouse arrived when we were looking for human connection while locked down and grappling with COVID-19 pandemic. Audio content, and particularly, the human voice, filled an important void at a time we needed it. Clubhouse brought us together.[25]*

Combine a killer product, with a release at the right time, and the Cold Start Problem was quickly solved.

The Opposite of the Magic Moment

The Magic Moment is a nice concept, but it would be even more useful if you could measure it. The way to best do this might be surprising—you start with the opposite of magic, the moments where the network has broken down, and you start solving the problem from there.

At Uber, we called these moments Zeroes. A zero at Uber was the worst experience you could have, when a rider opens the Uber app with the intent to pick an address and pick up a ride—but there aren't any drivers in the area! This is a zero. When the point of the product is to interact with other participants in the network, a zero means that its value can't be fulfilled, which means users will bounce and possibly never come back again. It's obvious when there are not enough users, listings, or videos to make a product engaging.

This isn't a problem just for Uber or for other marketplaces—each product category has its own version of a zero. For a workplace collaboration tool, like a wiki, it might be stale or missing documentation needed for work that no one's filled out. For Slack, it might be that the user you're hoping to message hasn't yet signed up for the app—that can be demotivating, leading you to go back to email. For a social network, a zero might be when a user joins and none of their friends or favorite content are yet on the service—causing them to spend their precious attention elsewhere. For demand-driven products like the Airbnb, Yelp, or eBay, a zero might be defined as when no listings are returned for something where the potential customers search.

A zero is a terrible experience, but even worse, it's not easily solved. Adding just more one driver to the Uber network doesn't ensure zeroes won't happen, nor does adding one more colleague to a Slack workspace. To consistently ensure that people never experience zeroes, the network needs to be built out substantially, and it needs to be active, too! Drivers on a network have to respond when there's a ride request and if they aren't actively using the app, it's an unfulfilled request—just another form of a zero. Or when you send a message in Slack, the person has to actually reply—if they've signed up but haven't installed the apps, that won't work.

The real cost of a zero is not just at the moment where it's experienced, but rather, the lingering destructive effects afterward. Users who get "zeroed" often churn and worse, they come to believe the service isn't reliable. It's not possible to sustain a strong network when a large percentage of users are churning, but unfortunately, by definition new networks default to having many zeroes. Until this destructive force is dealt with, the network can't get off the ground.

Thinking about zeroes and unfulfilled requests was such a useful concept at Uber that we baked it into many of our more common dashboards, split by city and region so we could understand how often it was happening. I encourage product teams to develop their own form of this metric, laid out as a dashboard of networks—whether that's divided by geography, product category, or whatever else makes sense. Within each, it can be useful to track the percentage of consumers that are seeing zeroes. If it's too high a number, that category of users is experiencing anti-network effects, and it will never break through.

After the Cold Start Problem

When a networked product nails its launch, its users can have consistently great experiences whenever they use the app. All Magic Moments, with minimal zeroes. This is a function of both the right features and the right network—not just one without the other. I described the first few months of Clubhouse's launch where this came together quickly, but it still took an atomic network of thousands of users and the right set of product features. All of this was informed by years of tinkering in social networks and audio. Had a key feature been left out, like the ability to spontaneously invite people as speakers, the launch might have fizzled. But the same would have happened if the company picked the wrong network, starting with an inappropriate audience in a faraway geography. Both the right product and the right network are needed.

When a networked product finally starts to generate Magic Moments, it feels really good. Often, this is called "Product/Market Fit"—here's Marc Andreessen's description of when a product gets there:

> *You can always feel when product/market fit isn't happening. The customers aren't quite getting value out of the product, word of mouth isn't spreading, usage isn't growing that fast, press reviews are kind of "blah," the sales cycle takes too long, and lots of deals never close.*
>
> *And you can always feel product/market fit when it's happening. The customers are buying the product just as fast as you can make it—or usage is growing just as fast as you can add more servers. Money from customers is piling up in your company checking account. You're hiring sales and customer support staff as fast as you can. Reporters are calling because they've heard about your hot new thing and they want to talk to you about it. You start getting entrepreneur of the year awards from Harvard Business School.[26]*

Of course he was talking about getting to product/market fit more generally, but for networked products, I would take this description and infuse it with network goodness—users are inviting other users, and sharing content from your product across the internet. You search on Twitter, Reddit, and other social media and it's chock full of your loyal users talking about how good your product is. Engagement goes up as people find more utility from it, and as more users join.

If it sounds easy and automatic, it is anything but. The Cold Start Problem doesn't stop once a networked product has established its first atomic network—it needs to be continually solved by the network as it grows. Even once an atomic network is thriving, the networks intertwined with it—whether you think of that as industry sector, geography, demographic, or otherwise—still need to solve the Cold Start Problem as well. Even if there are enough users in the IT department of a company to enjoy Slack, it may not be enough for someone to join from the marketing team. All those users will churn unless enough density is built across the organization, network by network. And once you get a particular office location, colleagues will start joining from other cities. The Cold Start Problem doesn't need to just be solved once; it needs to be dealt with over and over.

And as soon as a team can build one of these stand-alone networks, they're ready to build more—many more—and try to take over the entire market.

PART III

THE TIPPING POINT

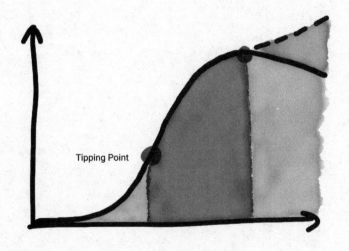

Tipping Point

11

TINDER

To take over the world, it's not enough to build a single atomic network—you have to scale from one to two to many, many more. Only once you get scale do the broader network effects we desire— viral growth, increased stickiness, and strong monetization—start to kick in. Sometimes this happens city by city, and sometimes it happens team by team. When this becomes repeatable, the network will hit the "Tipping Point," when a product can quickly grow to take over the whole market.

In buses, subways, and trains around the world, a familiar scene plays out during the rush hour commute: rows of twentysomethings sit quietly, headphones in, eyes glued to their phones. You could be sitting across from them, or even ten seats away, yet it'd be obvious what app they're on because of the unique gesture they keep making with their thumbs: Swipe, swipe, and swipe. Swipe again. Then another swipe, but in other direction. They're on Tinder, and in the span of their trip, these young commuters might swipe through a couple dozen potential romantic prospects before their commute ends and it's time to pack up. Around the world, this scene repeats itself, and when you sum up all the activity, it's a big number: at the time of this writing, tens of millions of people use Tinder and they swipe more than 2 billion times per day, leading to a million dates per week. That's what love looks like at scale.

Tinder is a radical exception to the generally accepted observation that online dating is a poor market to launch a new product in. Dating apps are notoriously hard to start and even harder to scale—this category has the Cold Start Problem in spades. Dating is a hyperlocal affair where even if people live in the same city, they may want to be in the same part of town to want to meet up. Don't ask two single people, one in San Francisco and the other in Oakland, across the bridge from each other, to get together. Or the LA equivalent, Santa Monica versus its east side counterpart, Silver Lake. A dating app's network needs a lot of density to be successful, and even if one market works, you need to be in multiple geographies at once to hit scale. Even then, if you gain success in one demographic—let's say, 40+ year old Christian singles—you have to restart the network in each new demographic. Dating networks are naturally high churn—when happy couples pair off, they leave the platform, so that more success leads to more churn.

During my Uber days, I was introduced to Sean Rad, Tinder's co-founder and CEO. He was trying to figure out the question of how to grow Tinder's reach to the entire world, after it had already gotten popular in the dense urban markets in the United States. Sean and I immediately hit it off, and I agreed to become an advisor to Tinder. During some of their most critical years of growth, I would fly down to their offices in Los Angeles to riff on business metrics, product strategy, and user growth. After a session at the office, we'd meet at Soho House or occasionally grab a drink at Chateau Marmont near their offices in West Hollywood, where I'd hear more about the backstory about the company. By then, Tinder had reached millions of users, but the team was unusually small given its impact—just eighty people.

The challenge at that point for Tinder wasn't to launch on new college campuses—they knew how to do that. It was how to capture the entire market, to get to hundreds of millions of users across all of its core geographies. The company hit its Tipping Point, and the entire market was rapidly shifting into the Tinder way of online dating—mobile first, swiping left and right, with built-in messaging. Soon, it would grow to over $1 billion in revenue, and redefine the market.

How did this happen? In my conversations with Sean, I learned the incredible story behind one of the biggest tech successes in the past decade.

USC Campus, 2012

"It all started with a single party at USC," said Sean, talking about the early days of Tinder when it first launched in 2012.

> *Back then, the app was really simple. It showed a series of dating profiles, but when we first launched it, the swiping wasn't in the app yet.*[27]

At the time, the number of users was tiny, and the app was built by a scrappy team of a half dozen people. The cofounding team of Sean Rad, Justin Mateen, and Jonathan Badeen had put something together they called Matchbox, not Tinder. There was no swiping— instead there was a green heart button to "like," and a red X to "pass." You'd tap the button to move forward. It was only later that the left and right swipe would be added, almost as an afterthought by Badeen, the iOS developer at the time. Jon described to me how he landed on the swiping insight:

> *I had a deck of cards at my desk, and would play with them while I coded. I'd fiddle around with them between coding, and decided one day I'd add it in as a fun feature. It felt good to swipe left and right, but at first, it wasn't meant to be the main way people would use the app.*[28]

Once this iconic gesture was added, there was no turning back.

But there was a problem—the initial growth of the product was slow. Sean and Justin turned up the hustle, texting all the friends in their address books. About four hundred people trickled in slowly to try out their new app, but as you can imagine, that only sort of worked—there weren't enough users. It was a slog, because of the Cold Start Problem.

Launching a product like Tinder is hard. It requires you to simultaneously attract multiple segments of users, at the right proportions, at the same time. At least in the heterosexual version, it is a two-sided network of men and women that must be built and scaled up in exactly the right ratios. Not too many ladies, and not too many guys, either, at similar levels of interests, demographics, and attractiveness, to ensure that everyone has enough matches.

Furthermore, online dating is not typically a product that takes advantage of viral growth—although culturally things may be changing, many folks still find it a bit embarrassing to tell their friends they're using a dating app. And if your product is successful, and matches the right people, then ironically you have two very happy people who then quit using your app—although they may tell all their friends how they met in the first place. All of these dynamics make new products in this category very hard to start, and even harder to scale.

The answer to this conundrum was the University of Southern California, which in many ways was an ideal place for Tinder to get started. Nestled in the heart of gritty south Los Angeles and spread over a 300-acre campus, USC hosts over 19,000 undergraduate students, with a very active social scene, centered on the sororities and fraternities in their Greek system. By starting in a small niche, Tinder could launch to both men and women that wanted to meet each other, all in about the same age range, 18–21, the common context of the same geography and school, and similar interests—including going to parties.

Both Sean and Justin had gone to USC, and more important, Justin had a younger sibling going to the college at the time. And they concocted a plan: Tinder would work with Justin's younger brother to throw a birthday party for one of his popular, hyperconnected friends on campus, and use it to promote Tinder. The Tinder team would do all the work to make it an incredible party. The day of the party, students from USC were getting bused to a luxurious house in LA, where everything had been set up to pull you inside.

Sean described how it worked:

There was one catch with the party: First, you had to download the Tinder app to get in. We put a bouncer in the house to check that you had done it. The party was great—it was a success, and more importantly, the next day, everyone at the party woke up and remembered they had a new app on their phone. There were attractive people they hadn't gotten to talk to, and this was their second chance.

The college party launch tactic worked. For the Tinder team, this one party created the highest ever one-day spike of downloads, however modest it might seem in retrospect. It's not just the number that matters here, but that it was "500 of the right people"—Sean would explain to me later. It was a group of the most social, most hyperconnected people on the USC campus, all on Tinder at the same time. Tinder started to work. Matches began to happen, as the students who met each other from the previous night started to swipe through and then chat. Amazingly, 95 percent of this initial cohort started to use this app every day for three hours a day.

The Tinder team built one atomic network, but soon figured out how to build the next one—just throw another party. And then another, by going to other schools, and throwing even more parties. Each network was successively easier to start. Tinder quickly reached 4,000 downloads, then 15,000 within a month, and then 500,000 just a month after that—first by replicating the campus launch, but then letting the organic viral growth take over. In a flurry, Sean, Justin, and the team brought this tactic to throw parties at fraternities and sororities at other campuses all over the country.

By April 2013, Mateen told the *Huffington Post* they had launched at ten college campuses, saying, "We believe in top-down marketing, so we went to highly social people and had them promote it to their friends and it grew from there."[29] The app, by virtue of its location capabilities— users could only see other users within a specific distance—allowed the team to curate their initial audience to popular, influential college students. Later, the team would come to believe that upon getting 20,000 users in a single market, the app would fully hit Escape Velocity and grow to take on that region completely.

If you put Tinder's path onto the Cold Start framework, launching at a party at USC was the solution to the first stage, but the second was about scaling that success from campus to campus:

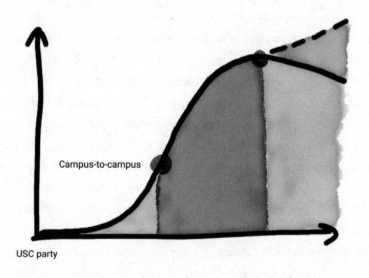

Figure 9: Tinder

This second phase was the Tipping Point—Tinder had hit a point of repeatable growth, since once the team knew how to create one atomic network, and a second, then it was repeatable from there. These growth tactics continued to scale, and the team iterated to make them more effective. There were Valentine's Tinder parties, cocktail Tinder parties, sorority Tinder parties, and more—and it kept working. At Tufts University, less than a year after the launch, more than 80 percent of the Greek system had signed into the service and 40 percent of the entire undergraduate population was on it.

The team scaled by recruiting a large team of ambassadors who were highly connected on campus, and executing the same strategy until they leveled up from campuses to cities to international regions. In India, the focus was on call centers, whose dense communities were the equivalent of Greek life on college campuses. For Europe, people in the United States would invite their friends overseas, and connectivity got the product launched.

Tinder's network grew quickly. Within two years, it became one of the top 25 social networking apps in the App Store. Five years after that, it found a business model, becoming the highest-grossing non-gaming app, beating Netflix and Spotify. It spread throughout the world, and is today offered in more than forty languages in virtually every country.

Tinder defied the odds in a market that historically has been very tough for startups. For every Tinder, there is a HowAboutWe, Tagged, Speeddate, and dozens of other dating startups that see some success but never hit scale. And yet Sean Rad, Jonathan Badeen, and the early team at Tinder—a group of twentysomethings who were first-time entrepreneurs—figured it out in 2012. They took a college birthday party and turned it into a repeatable, scalable effort that went from colleges to cities to countries and the world. With it, they created an iconic new product, along with a universally recognized gesture for modern romance.

Introducing the Tipping Point

The key to Tinder's start was discovering a repeatable strategy that took them from USC to other colleges, then absorbing the metropolitan areas, and then country to country. This is when the market hits the second phase of our theory, the Tipping Point. This is where momentum starts to go in your direction, and strategies should be oriented around tipping over entire markets, rather than launching individual atomic networks one at a time. The next few chapters use examples from LinkedIn, Instagram, Reddit, and the invention of coupons.

To begin the discussion of the Tipping Point, I'll start with a prominent strategy, "Invite-Only," that is often used to suck in a large network through viral growth. Another method to tip over a market is with a "Come for the Tool, Stay for the Network" strategy. Take Dropbox, for instance, which is initially adopted by many people for file backup and keeping files synced up between work and home computers—this is the tool. But eventually, a more advanced and stickier use case emerges to share folders with colleagues—this is the network. And if that doesn't work, some products can always just spend money to build out their network, with a strategy of just "Paying Up for Launch." For many networked products that touch transactions like marketplaces, teams can just subsidize demand and spend millions to stimulate activity, whether that's in paying content creators for your social network, or subsidizing driver earnings in rideshare. If the hard side of the network isn't yet activated, a team can just fill in their gaps themselves, using the technique of "Flintstoning"—as Reddit did, submitting links and content until eventually adding automation and community features for scale.

In the end, all of these strategies require enormous creativity. And to close out the Tipping Point section of the book, I introduce Uber's core ethos of "Always Be Hustlin'"—describing the creativity and decentralized set of teams, all with its own strategies that were localized to each region. Sometimes adding the fifth or one hundredth network requires creativity, product engagements, and tactical changes. In the goal of reaching the Tipping Point, teams must be fluid to build out a broad network of networks.

12

INVITE-ONLY

LinkedIn

S orry, you need an invite to sign up to this app." No one will be happy to see a message like this. It might seem like a counterintuitive way to launch an app, particularly during the Cold Start phase, when new users are so desperately needed. Why turn down users who want to try your product?

Yet this constraint is at the heart of the so called "invite-only" strategy for launching a product. And for Gmail, LinkedIn, Facebook, and many other networked products, it has worked. Why?

Some have espoused the invite-only tactic as a method to generate hype, since potentially a buzzy new product might cause people to head to social media to ask their friends for invites. Others say the value of invites comes from a method of limiting audience growth so that teams can fix bugs and scale a product's infrastructure, before going to market more fully. Yes, these are all true, but they miss the most important reason to have invites in a product with network effects. Invite mechanics work like a copy-and-paste feature—if you start with a curated network, and give them invites, that network will copy itself over and over automatically.

This is exactly what happened for LinkedIn—the startup was

initially founded in 2002, and had to solve the problem of spreading among professional users. At the time, combining social networking and a professional context was controversial and non-obvious—it wasn't clear that the same social features mostly being applied for a young, college demographic would also work in a professional context. Would people want to share photos, update their statuses, and send invites, but with their coworkers? And furthermore, did people want to create profiles on a website that some used for job-hunting? At the time, many argued no. However, with nearly 700 million registered users and a $26 billion sale to Microsoft, I think we can say the answer was yes. At the start, it was not so obvious.

I spoke with Reid Hoffman, LinkedIn's cofounder and early CEO, about how they thought about this go-to-market challenge. It was clear that Reid personified his signature product in every way. He was gregarious and charismatic, telling stories about the early days and how he brought his personal friends and mentors onto LinkedIn.

We also quickly connected on a personal note—I immediately recognized the Orca whale carving he had behind him on the wall on our video call. Turns out, Reid had relocated temporarily during the COVID pandemic to the San Juan Islands, a beautiful chain of islands near Seattle, my hometown. It was one of my favorite childhood places to visit, and it turned out Reid loved the area as well. After comparing notes on the Pacific Northwest, we got into the main topic: the early story of LinkedIn.

From the earliest days, Reid's theory about professional networks was that, yes, there was a spiderweb of connections, but there was also a hierarchy. Reid described LinkedIn's early network:

> There are people like Bill Gates who are at the top of the professional hierarchy. He gets more requests for intros than he can deal with, and everyone who knows Gates will be asked for intros to him. At the launch, LinkedIn wouldn't have made sense for people like Bill Gates. But there's a mid-tier of successful people who are

still building and hustling, who get fewer requests for intros but will actually take the meetings. This middle rank of people is where LinkedIn really worked.[30]

To seed the initial network of this middle tier of the hierarchy, the product was designed to be invite-only.

On the first week of LinkedIn's launch, employees and investors of the company could invite as many people as they wanted, but you couldn't sign up from just the website. We intentionally seeded the network with the mid-tier of successful professionals that wanted to take time to connect.

The invites went out to this part of the talent hierarchy, but not only that, the positioning of the product had to be right. It was important, according to Reid, that LinkedIn never explicitly described itself as a "job seeking" product. This was a concern because there was a bit of a stigma appearing on a site when your coworkers or boss might see, and thus, it was safer to avoid the label. LinkedIn thus adopted a more flexible positioning as a professional networking service. You could have a profile and connect with people and yes, searching for a new job was part of the functionality, but it was one of many features in the product. This means when someone got an invite to LinkedIn, they would be more likely to sign up and then invite others.

LinkedIn saw explosive growth even from the first week, simply powered by their invite-only functionality. It started from the address books of the founding team, but then the members who joined started to invite their own. This is the copy-and-paste mechanism in motion— take LinkedIn's curated initial network, give them invites to join a killer product, and watch the network scale with more like-minded individuals. This is superior to a centralized PR-based launch, which can fizzle out and become diluted by different geographies, industries, and demographics. Invite-only mechanics amplify a networked product that is already useful for the first few dozen users. Past this initial set, the invites will attract a dense network that will grow and grow. Lee Hower, on LinkedIn's early team, describes how the invites exploded early on:

> *Reid and the rest of the founding team all sent invites to our professional contacts on launch day. We asked all those folks to try the v1 product and invite their professional contacts. In total that was maybe a couple thousand individuals. . . . Virtually all of the people who signed up in the first week were part of the startup ecosystem (so predisposed to try out new products) and had a direct or indirect connection to the LinkedIn team (therefore more willing to check out a colleague/friend's new project).[31]*

The invite-only requirement didn't last long for LinkedIn. By the second week, the core network was already strong, and the decision was made to then open up membership for people who heard about LinkedIn in the news. Users could now sign up without an invite. The initial group of well-connected, aspirational Silicon Valley entrepreneurs and investors were helpful. They created the buzz that brought in an even more important audience, a broader base of users that Reid calls the LinkedIn "true believers." While the Bay Area tech community would continue to trickle in over time, the true believers were highly engaged, spread all over the world, and grew exponentially.

Within a few weeks, it was clear that LinkedIn had hit the Tipping Point—the product was engaging users, and was valuable beyond the early-adopter tech community. Many other networks from around the world started to join, too, and soon, LinkedIn would come to define the professional networking category. While the battle to become the dominant global social network comprised a dozen products like MySpace, Facebook, Hi5, Tagged, Bebo, and others—the professional network category was mostly uncontested. LinkedIn tipped the market faster than competitors could emerge, and ultimately won its category.

LinkedIn is just one example—of course, invite mechanics aren't unique to it, and invites have become part of the standard playbook for bringing new products to market. Famously, Facebook initially required a harvard.edu email address to sign up, both defining an atomic network where everyone trusted each other, and also providing an explicit way to think about school-by-school launches. Years later, Slack would employ a similar tactic, using corporate email domains as the way to define who should join what network. These are all clever, and while invites-only strategies are often described as taking advantage of the fear of missing out—FOMO—that's not the core driver. When a new product carefully curates a network, followed by implementing invites so that it can copy and paste similar networks, then it can grow to take over the market.

The Welcome Experience

Invite-only mechanics provide a better "welcome experience" for new users as well. To explain why, imagine arriving at a large dinner party. A good friend welcomes you at the door, and as you step in, you see acquaintances, close friends, and a number of new people who've been curated to be absolutely fascinating. If that's the ideal experience for a dinner guest, it's also an apt metaphor for the best possible entry into a new product experience. Invite-only products can facilitate this, because every new user that signs up is already connected to at least one person—their inviter. For products like Slack or Zoom where you only need a few people to make it useful, having the guarantee of at least one connection is a giant step toward solving the Cold Start Problem.

Mathematically, it tends to work even better than that—the most connected people tend to be invited earlier, and in turn they tend to invite other highly connected people. The connected bring in the more connected. This results in a dinner party of social butterflies—which is hugely beneficial in launching a new network. I've seen this firsthand when working on invite features for social apps and for Uber. You often ask users to import email and phone contacts as part of the invite process, often presented as a "Find Friends" screen while signing in.

It's fascinating when you analyze the initial networks. The earliest users tend to have large contact lists, often way into the thousands, and tend to invite people with similarly large lists. Over months and years, the late adopters of the product might have just a few hundred connections. The end result of this mathematical property is that early adopters can be instantly connected with dozens of their friends and colleagues right away. Again, it's a dinner party of social butterflies.

LinkedIn also refined their invite mechanics over time. Early on, the product started with just the basics—asking users to connect with each other with big blue buttons that said "connect." But it was clear from the data that making connecting a primary action would spur engagement throughout the app—and so it became a central action. New users were asked to import their email contacts to invite more people. After each connection request, users were shown screens of even more suggestions. New users who appeared in other people's contacts—even if they skipped importing it themselves—had suggested connections right after sign-up. The web of connections was mined to suggest "People You May Know"—a feature still in use today that helps build density of networks, thus driving strong network effects. All of these tactics helped amplify growth. The denser the LinkedIn network, the more likely it was for new users to have a great initial experience.

Hype and Exclusivity

Invite-only mechanics are also closely associated with creating buzz on social media. People with an invite to an exclusive product will post praise, critiques, and other commentary. People without an invite will ask for it, prompting discussion and sometimes controversy, driven by scarcity and exclusivity dynamics. This in turn attracts more attention and engagement. It works!

Gmail first launched as an invite-only product on April Fool's in 2004. It offered a gigabyte of storage at a time when others were offering megabytes of storage. The original idea wasn't to create hype, but rather something more practical—the infrastructure running Gmail couldn't support a fast ramp on the number of users, so an invite-only strategy was utilized:

> *Gmail ended up running on three hundred old Pentium III computers nobody else at Google wanted. That was sufficient for the limited beta rollout the company planned, which involved giving accounts to a thousand outsiders, allowing them to invite a couple of friends apiece, and growing slowly from there.*[32]

However, it soon became clear the product was going to be a hit—George Harik, one of the first ten employees at Google said:

> *Once it was clear that Gmail was the real deal, the invitations became a hot property. The limited rollout had been born of necessity, but "it had a side effect. Everyone wanted it even more. It was hailed as one of the best marketing decisions in tech history, but it was a little bit unintentional."*

People began to buy and sell invites to Gmail:

> *Bidding for invites on eBay sent prices shooting up to $150 and beyond; sites such as Gmail Swap emerged to match up those with invites with those who desperately wanted them. Having a Hotmail or Yahoo Mail email address was slightly embarrassing; having a Gmail one meant that you were part of a club most people couldn't get into.*

It might seem silly to fight for early access, but there are permanent benefits for getting on in the first few months. Earlier users could grab the username that they wanted. An address like frank@gmail.com might be claimed right away, whereas a late-comer might have to be happy with frankthetank2000@gmail.com. Social networks have a similar incentive, where early users can claim short, pithy usernames that might eventually become status symbols. And decades ago at the start of the web, an early-adopter decision to buy a domain like Insurance.com or VacationRentals.com might be life-changing, as they would later be sold and resold for tens of millions of dollars.

You might ask, if invite-only is so great, why isn't it used more often? There are good reasons. It's often seen as risky, because it can kill the top-line growth rate of your product. It requires you to build a lot of extra functionality, so that people who newly sign up are connected properly with people around them. A lot of people might show up without an invite and get turned away. From the lens of a company doing a Big Bang Launch, why limit your numbers? If there aren't enough new users showing up and interacting with others, the network might be too small—you might hit the Cold Start Problem.

However, invite-only launches have been a key feature of many products precisely because for networked products, there are huge advantages. It allows the early network to gel as a community, develop a high density of connections, and grow organically via virality.

Curating a High-Quality Network

"Rate us 5 stars!" says the app. By now, we've all seen a screen like this in our favorite apps.

Product categories like marketplaces, dating, app stores, and food delivery ask us to review and rate (with a five-star scale!) because they are categories where trust, safety, and high quality are key to the experience. Part of this is picking the people on the network, but the other is teaching users how to interact with each other and enforcing these "rules" within the product. Quality begets quality. Networked products in these categories can be magnetic to consumers on the quality vector, which is why companies often handpick them—another form of invite-only tactics—to curate the initial network.

Ubercab—as it was initially called—started out as a black car service, with an app where you could hit a button and a limo would show up. The cofounders and senior executives would personally meet and onboard every driver in person before adding them onto the network. At the time, the young startup was dealing with licensed, professional limo drivers, but nevertheless the team decided it was important to explain the expectations for how the service worked, how to communicate with riders, how to deal with problems, and so on. As a bonus, it increased the rate of sign-up to activation—getting drivers on the road and taking trips. Although high-touch onboarding isn't always scalable, it establishes cultural norms and a high-quality network that sets the tone for new users, and so sometimes the trade-off makes sense. To further reinforce and scale these processes, in-product features can be added, with reviews, customer support, and ratings that allow further drill-downs—like a one-star that triggers options to flag bad driving, a bad route, etc.

Of course, in-person interviewing doesn't scale. A more scalable version would just do it all in software, which is eventually what Uber implemented. There are big advantages to an in-app wait list experience. For example, Robinhood, the commission-free online brokerage, had a hot and widely anticipated launch, and launched by signing users up to a wait list. On the back end, the team slowly let people in, pacing the growth so servers weren't overwhelmed. The Robinhood mechanic asked wait list users to tweet or post to social media in order to jump ahead, ultimately bringing a million users in before a widespread release. Another variation of this is to ask users on the wait list to fill out detailed information about themselves, including their potential use cases, giving the teams a way to let a curated, small trickle of users in to form the initial network.

How Invite-Only Products Curate Their Networks

Invite-only is a powerful strategy. When executed well, the people in an initial atomic network become a magnet for even more users. It allows a network to copy and paste itself many times over, attracting more and more adjacent networks over time.

Just as creators of new products spend endless hours designing the experience, creators of networked products have an additional task: curating the right people so that the experience of a new member joining the community, marketplace, or other network is just right. A good product designer wouldn't allow a random set of feature ideas to be added to the final version of a new app, and in the same way, a mindful designer of networks wouldn't allow a random set of users to initially join.

Had LinkedIn started with an undesirable set of users, it likely would not have become a magnet for the true believers that continued to onboard their friends over time. Had Tinder begun somewhere besides USC—let's say in a small rural town—it wouldn't have been able to build campus to campus, and then large cities and then on from there. It would have changed the whole strategy.

For networked products, the curation of the network—who's on it, why they're there, and how they interact with each other—is as important as its product design. Starting with a deliberate point of view on who's best for your network will define its magnetism, culture, and ultimate trajectory.

13

COME FOR THE TOOL, STAY FOR THE NETWORK

Instagram

Come for the tool, stay for the network" is one of the most famous strategies for launching and scaling networks. Start with a great "tool"—a product experience that is useful even for one user as a utility. Then, over time, pivot the users into a series of use cases that tap into a "network"—the part where you collaborate, share, communicate, or otherwise interact with other users.

To outline one of the best examples of this strategy, I'll begin at the dawn of the App Store.

When the iPhone was first released, there weren't many apps. In the first two years, about 50,000 or so apps were published—a far smaller number than the several million apps that exist today. But even within these apps, some were starting to break out. One app in particular—I'll leave its name up to you to guess—was designed and coded up by two young entrepreneurs who had a passion for photography in September 2009.

What did the app do? Well, it popularized a style of mobile photos that has since become ubiquitous. The app promised to take almost any photo and apply hip, vintage photo filters to transform them into something beautiful and shareable on social media. It quickly gained millions of installs, was featured in the *New York Times*, and landed a number of effusive early reviews. Here's an example from the Pocket-Lint blog, quoting Mario Estrada, early community manager:

Within the first month it started growing hype and making it to the top 10 apps in a few countries. Then we started seeing pictures pop up on Facebook and realized that we needed to embrace this community and create a contest for people to submit their images. The response was incredible and I think that's when we realized this was bigger than us.[33]

A killer app, released at the dawn of a new platform. It had millions of users, and was far ahead of any of its competition—it was bound to be a huge success, right?

This app was—drumroll, please—called Hipstamatic.

No, not Instagram! Hipstamatic was created by two friends from Wisconsin, Ryan Dorshorst and Lucas Buick, and showed the enormous appetite people would have for mobile photography in the coming years. In 2010, in its inaugural "Apps of the Year," Apple selected Hipstamatic as one of four apps—alongside Flipboard, Plants vs. Zombies, and Osmos.[34] It was loved by consumers, too—people enjoyed the retro feel of the photos this app produced, and as one of the first apps on the iPhone, this recognition only further propelled it into millions of downloads.

Yet some of Hipstamatic's design choices were odd and added friction. The app required you to interact with a virtual camera, swiping through a virtual set of lenses, and required multiple taps to see a filter's effect on your photos. In the *New York Times* article mentioning the app, it described how "[t]he Hipstamatic app forced him to wait about

10 seconds between photos, so each one had to count."[35] It cost $1.99, so users had to spend money to use the app. And most important, Hipstamatic was a tool. After applying filters to your photo, it was simply saved to your camera roll. You had to post it on other social networks yourself. All of these issues created an opening for a massive new competitor to emerge.

In the same year that Hipstamatic saw so much success, Kevin Systrom and Mike Krieger were working from an office on Pier 38 of San Francisco, incubating Burbn. The startup had been backed by Andreessen Horowitz and other investors in 2010—predating my time at the firm—in a $500,000 seed round. They were hard at work building a browser-based app for checking in at locations, making plans with friends, and importantly, sharing photos. It was rich with functionality, but it was becoming clear that there was a problem.

Many months into Burbn, Kevin and Mike realized the product was getting too complex, and going to run straight into Foursquare—a location-sharing app that was rocketing into success at the time. It was time to refocus. The team looked at the best features of the product, oriented around photos, and stripped everything else out. Kevin Systrom would recount the reinvention of the app:

We wanted to focus on being really good at one thing. We saw mobile photos as an awesome opportunity to try out some new ideas. We spent 1 week prototyping a version that focused solely on photos. It was pretty awful. So we went back to creating a native version of Burbn. We actually got an entire version of Burbn done as an iPhone app, but it felt cluttered and overrun with features. It was really difficult to decide to start from scratch, but we went out on a limb, and basically cut everything in the Burbn app except for its photo, comment, and like capabilities. What remained was Instagram. (We renamed because we felt it better captured what you were doing—an instant telegram of sorts. It also sounded camera-y.)[36]

Importantly, Instagram was built with a network from day one. It had user profiles, a feed, friend requests, invitations, and many other features of a modern social product. It added a popular feed to aid in discovery within the network, and added the constraint of perfectly square, 640x640 pixel photos. It had features to share to Facebook, but importantly, each shared photo would include a link that pointed back to Instagram, which drove viral growth. The photo filters within the app were implemented in a more direct, less skeuomorphic way than Hipstamatic, so that tapping on a filter would let you instantly preview its effect. And also importantly, Instagram would be a free app.

The team took the goodness that Hipstamatic had proven, and added network effects—and the result was spectacular. Instagram launched on October 6, 2010, to the App Store, and at the end of the first week, it had been downloaded over 100,000 times. Within another two months, it had hit a million, and it just grew from there.[37] To this day, it is still one of the fastest-growing apps ever created.

Interestingly enough, in its first few months, it was not the social features that were important. Six months after the app's launch, an article on Techcrunch by analytics firm RJ Metrics analyzed data from Instagram's APIs and concluded that 65 percent of users were not yet following other people on the network. Instead, the engagement was oriented completely around photo editing, noting that "Instagram's 2.2 million users upload 3.6 million new photos per week (or 6 photos per second)."[38] In other words, Instagram was being used first as a tool—a free Hipstamatic with a better design. The network would come later.

After this initial launch, Instagram would grow faster and faster. As its audience grew, celebrities began to show up—for example, in 2011, tennis player Serena Williams and singers Drake, Justin Bieber, and Britney Spears would all post their first photos. Popular Instagram accounts of cute dogs, travel destinations, and models would eventually turn into the "influencers" that would define the platform. These influencers, celebrities, companies, meme accounts, and many others would all join to create content, building network density and increasing engagement. Eighteen months after its launch, Facebook acquired the company for $1 billion in stock and cash.

While photo filters kicked off Instagram's rise, it would not sustain. Similarly, over time, the "tool" part of the product—the photo filters—have waned in importance, as users often post photos with the "#nofilter" tag. A recent analysis has shown that the vast majority of photos—82 percent[39]—had no filter used at all. Eight years after its initial launch, network effects had fully taken over for the utility of photo editing—it's more network, and less tool. Looking backward, this is widely seen as one of the best tech acquisitions in history, as Instagram would likely be worth several hundred billion as a stand-alone entity. It has more than a billion active users and generates $20 billion in revenue as part of Facebook. Not bad.

How Great Tools Help Tip Entire Markets

While Hipstamatic built a great tool, it was Instagram that used network effects to win the market. The Instagram versus Hipstamatic story is perhaps the canonical example of a strategy made famous by Chris Dixon's 2015 essay "Come for the tool, stay for the network." Chris writes:

> *A popular strategy for bootstrapping networks is what I like to call "come for the tool, stay for the network."*
>
> *The idea is to initially attract users with a single-player tool and then, over time, get them to participate in a network. The tool helps get to initial critical mass. The network creates the long term value for users, and defensibility for the company.[40]*

There are many other examples across many sectors beyond photo apps: The Google Suite provides stand-alone tools for people to create documents, spreadsheets, and presentations, but also network features around collaborative editing, and comments. Games like Minecraft or even classics like Street Fighter can be played in single-player mode where you play against the computer, or multiplayer mode where you play with friends. Yelp started out effectively as a directory tool for people to look up local businesses, showing addresses and phone numbers, but the network eventually built out the database of photos and reviews. LinkedIn started as a tool to put your resume online, but encouraged you to build up your professional network over time.

"Come for the tool, stay for the network" circumvents the Cold Start Problem and makes it easier to launch into an entire network—with PR, paid marketing, influencers, sales, or any number of tried-and-true channels. It minimizes the size requirement of an atomic network and in turn makes it easy to take on an entire network. Whether it's photo-sharing apps or restaurant directories, in the framework of the Cold Start Theory, this strategy can be visualized. In effect, a tool can be used to "prop up" the value of the network effects curve when the network is small.

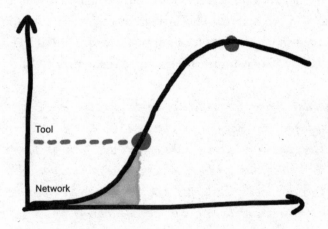

Figure 10: Come for the Tool

Conceptually, you can imagine the S-curve of a network effect—low when the network is underneath its critical mass, then high once it passes through. Having a tool, in effect, overlays a dotted line on top of this S-curve. The tool acts as a backstop to the value of the product, making it useful even when no one else is on it.

At the intersection of the tool and network, eventually, a pivot has to happen. Mechanically, this happens in multiple ways: This could be as simple as Instagram's decision to open the app to a home screen feed of photos from other users. As a tool, it might be more efficient to show its photo-editing interface first, but Instagram emphasizes the network to show the feed, popular photos, and people recommendations. A big notifications icon with a red number on it filled with likes and follows further emphasizes the network feature. In the workplace, an example might be an office worker that uses Google Docs to author a memo. Sharing the document as a link is easy, and coworkers will then add comments, suggest changes, and make edits themselves—these are the network features.

The tool-to-network shift is a specialized strategy—not every network is built this way. Tinder had no single-player mode, nor do communication apps like WhatsApp or Slack—these are products that need their atomic networks to quickly form, which is why smaller critical mass thresholds are better. Marketplaces are generally networks, not tools, from the start. But for a large class of products centered on content creation, organization, and reference, it can be a winning strategy. When it works, the tool can help take on an entire network, and once atomic networks start to form, the entire market will come over.

Underlying Patterns for Tools and Networks

There is a broader pattern at play. Examine Instagram's strategy, as well as products like YouTube, Google Suite, and LinkedIn, and you begin to see a pattern. Each provides a tool oriented around content editing and hosting—whether that's a video, photos, resumes, or documents. The tool is combined with a network that allows people to interact with the content and by extension, other people.

Group a few other products that have a tool/network pairing, and some clusters start to emerge:

Tool, network

Create + share with others (Instagram, YouTube, G Suite, LinkedIn)

Organize + collaborate with others (Pinterest, Asana, Dropbox)

System of record + keep up to date with others (OpenTable, GitHub)

Look up + contribute with others (Zillow, Glassdoor, Yelp)

Each of these different approaches has its own nuances: Organization tools begin with new, clever ways to collect links, files, tasks, and forms of content to make them more easily searchable and browsable. Project management tools like Trello and Asana help you track to-do items using a variety of useful interfaces, including the popular "kanban" layout inspired by the Toyota lean production system. Same with Dropbox, which magically syncs all the folders and files you've organized across your different devices. Pinterest started by providing a tool for organizing recipes, home ideas, and other items into different pinboards, with a unique layout so that scanning a large collection is easy. These are valuable for individual use, but as someone is organizing a collection of items, it's natural to assign tasks to other people, or to tag them, or to invite them to also add to the space.

The "systems of record" approach comes from building a tool—like GitHub's source-code version control services—that becomes deeply embedded into a business or workflow, becoming the authoritative and comprehensive version for whatever you're tracking. For example, GitHub lets individual developers manage their source code, making it a core part of their development environment—this is the tool. The network is then formed by inviting other software engineers to build on the project as well. OpenTable started in 1998 as a reservation management system for restaurants, which at the time were using pen and paper to track their guests. Once enough leading restaurants used it to manage their business, they flipped into a network by allowing customers to book directly on OpenTable. A consumer example might be when people with Android phones start using Google Photos to manage, store, and back up all their photos—comprehensively, not just the best ones they share to social media—which then flips to a network as they set up shared photo albums.

You've probably used Yelp and Glassdoor as tools for a reference on information, like the address and phone number of a restaurant, or the sector or headquarters of a company. Almost always, this data is licensed from elsewhere, or in Zillow's case with their "Zestimate," is algorithmically created from licensed data, to provide a base of content that is immediately useful. However, each of these flips into a network as people are able to add to the listings with their own photos, notes, and other forms of user-generated content. As users find the sites more valuable, it can further flip into becoming a marketplace as the restaurants on Yelp claim their listings and start allowing reservations or deliveries. Glassdoor and Zillow have added tools for the other side of their networks, in the form of recruiting tools and real estate agent lead generation features as well. Famously, of course, Google also executed this strategy by providing search and adding an advertising marketplace.

Why This Strategy Works, and When It Doesn't

Building a tool/network combo is a powerful approach, but it doesn't always work. Pivoting users from tool to network can be hard. Sometimes only a small percentage will make the transition, since it requires them to change their behavior—to click on a notification, or a new piece of user interface, introducing them to the network—and then they have to stick. A lot of people can get stuck on just the tool. Not every feature can be a social network.

It's this two-step move that makes "come for the tool, stay for the network" a tricky one to pull off. The tight coupling of tool and network matters. At one end of the spectrum, the tool and network are divergent—you are just bundling one popular tool with a completely separate and unrelated networked product. This is hard because the conversion rate from tool to network might be low—there are thousands of photo apps that tried to add feeds, profiles, and social features after Instagram showed the way. On the other end of the spectrum are tools and networks that are highly integrated, like Dropbox's folder-sharing functionality, which defines its network. This type of integration is so elegant that it would feel like an obvious missing functionality if it didn't exist—users would likely drive the product toward a network, not away from it. This type of conversion from tool to network tends to be high.

But when this strategy works, it can be highly effective. It aids in the Tipping Point of a market because it is much easier to spread a tool than a network—after all, the latter suffers from the Cold Start Problem. Spread a tool far and wide, and then grow it properly, and it might start to build networks upon networks around the tool. Continue executing, and the entire market might follow.

Building a tool is just one approach—not every strategy to push a market toward the Tipping Point involves a two-step approach of utility, then a network. Next I will discuss how, for some products, you can just go at it direct: use money. Pay up for the launch, and subsidize usage of the network until it starts to work. It's expensive, but it can work.

14

PAYING UP
FOR LAUNCH

Coupons

One of the common criticisms of fast-growing startups is "Is it ever going to be profitable?" This was a continual criticism of Uber, which grew quickly early on but burned billions of dollars per year before its IPO. Amazon too lost money in its first seventeen straight quarters. Standing up a network can be expensive—very expensive.

Yes, of course you eventually want to figure profitability out. But for networked products, in the earliest stages, sometimes it makes sense to spend—often wildly—to pay up for growth. The goal is to get the market to hit the Tipping Point, driving toward strong positive network effects, and then pull back the subsidies. The result, if executed properly, should be a fast-growing, high-monetization product.

There are many forms of financial incentives, but I'll start with the humble coupon as an example—yes, the grocery store coupon that's snail mailed or included in a newspaper and that gives you a dollar or two off a toothpaste or box of cereal.

Coupons were invented in 1888 by John Pemberton and Asa Candler, cofounders of the Coca-Cola Company. The early coupons for Coca-Cola showed the classic cursive logo in the center, with the headline "This card entitles you to one glass of Coca-Cola" and along the sides, it encouraged you to go to any dispenser to redeem the coupon. This is one of the first nationwide campaigns to brand something that historically had many regional varieties. The campaign was a huge success, and within the first two decades of its existence 8.5 million free drinks for one in nine Americans had been redeemed. Coca-Cola was soon flowing in every state across the country. It was such a powerful tool that many other companies—especially in consumer packaged goods—began to adopt it.

Where coupons intersect with network effects is in the problem of getting a particular company's new products into grocery stores. Grocery stores are a physical embodiment of a multi-sided network, after all—shoppers on one side, and food producers on the other—but with the physical limitations of retail shelving space. As a result, if consumers aren't asking for a new product, grocery stores aren't going to carry it, and if grocery stores won't carry it, consumers can never try it. It's a classic chicken-and-egg problem.

Coupons presented a solution to the problem, and marketing legend Claude Hopkins used them to their full advantage, as he describes in his 1927 memoir, *My Life in Advertising*. He writes about solving this for his client, Van Camp's Milk, which made a powdered milk:

So I devised a plan for making Van Camp's Milk familiar. In a page ad, I inserted a coupon, good at any store for a ten-cent can. We paid the grocer his retail price. For three weeks we announced that this ad would appear. At the same time we told the story of Van Camp's Evaporated Milk. We sent copies of these ads to all grocers, and told them that every customer of theirs would receive one of these coupons. It was evident that they must have Van Camp's Milk. Every coupon meant a ten-cent sale which, if they missed it, would go to a competitor. . . . The result was almost universal distribution, and at once.[41]

The clever part about this is that while it was standard by this point to advertise products in newspapers, by focusing the effort on the hard side of the network—grocers—it bootstrapped the entire network. Coupons were effectively a subsidy by Van Camp's milk to the grocers, so that they would stock the product long enough to decide to carry it themselves in the long run. And it worked.

Once Hopkins showed that this worked in creating one atomic network, the effort could be repeated in building the second, third, and so on:

> *We proved out this plan in several cities of moderate size. Then we undertook New York City. There the market was dominated by a rival brand. Van Camp had slight distribution. In three weeks we secured, largely by letter, 97 per cent distribution. Every grocer saw the necessity of being prepared for that coupon demand.*
>
> *Then one Sunday in a page ad, we inserted the coupon. This just in Greater New York. As a result of that ad, 1,460,000 coupons were presented. We paid $146,000 to the grocers to redeem them. But 1,460,000 homes were trying Van Camp's Milk after reading our story, and all in a single day. The total cost of that enterprise, including the advertising, was $175,000, mostly spent in redeeming those coupons. In less than nine months that cost came back with a profit. We captured the New York market.*

Of course, powdered milk is not an app or an operating system or a document editor. But we can learn from Van Camp's successful effort to bootstrap a multi-sided network, because the same ideas that worked centuries ago still work in other contexts.

A similar two-sided network problem exists with rideshare. In launching a new city with riders and drivers—which side do you start with first? The hard side is the default place to start, and Uber began—similarly to Van Camp's Milk—with a subsidy to the driver side. The beginning of this started with buying listings in the Craigslist Jobs section, offering $30/hour guaranteed payment, regardless of how many trips they did. They just needed to leave the app on. The common wisdom was, "If you have a chicken and egg problem—buy the chicken."

Hourly guarantees were a quick but expensive solution to the Cold Start Problem. It burned cash like crazy, and unfortunately wasn't sustainable as the market grew and more drivers needed to be recruited. To combat this, the Uber operations teams needed to execute a "commission switch"—going from guarantees to their usual business model of driving for fares and taking a percentage. To encourage this, executives set up an internal leaderboard to see how fast operations teams could execute this playbook—each city would quickly launch a market, start paying hourly guarantees, gather a critical mass of drivers and riders, and flip to a sustainable fee-based model. Friendly competition among the teams helped turn this crank faster and faster. This is the Tipping Point in action.

The next part of scaling the initial traction was to recruit a lot more drivers. This is where the power of leveraging the network helped tremendously using referral programs. The Uber driver app would ask drivers to participate in their referral programs ("Give $200, get $200 when a friend signs up to drive") to create leverage on their Craigslist spend. Of course, the flexibility and earnings potential of Uber also spread purely through word of mouth, as drivers told their friends. The combination of referrals and word of mouth—both methods relying on the network—drove almost two-thirds of Uber's drivers to sign up. As enough drivers came onto the roads, the teams would begin to address the demand side, working toward a city launch.

Over time, many different financial structures were used to achieve different goals in managing the hard side—in addition to hourly guarantees, driver referrals, and Uber's infamous surge pricing, over time structures like "Do 10 trips and get an extra $1 per trip" (called internally, DxGy) were built. Hundreds of people on the Marketplace team—composed of data scientists, economists, engineers, and others—would manage these levers to shift the balance of supply and demand in the hundreds of markets around the world.

Financial Levers for Growth

Subsidizing the hard side of the network works across marketplaces and many other categories—you see Netflix, Twitch, and others in media often guaranteeing payments to content creators for this same reason. In B2B, you could think of a freemium business model as a way to lower the friction for content creators and organizers within a workplace, who then spread it among their colleagues. There is a cost for servicing free users, of course, but the premium users more than make up for it. Sometimes in marketplaces they are set up as an earnings guarantee or a subsidized revenue share percentage, and sometimes in other business models as an up-front payment or discount to the pricing—either way, these are all different paths to the same thing.

Using money as a growth lever can feel like a dangerous move, and it should only be executed at the right time. While establishing an initial network, it usually doesn't make sense for an underresourced startup to throw a lot of money around to get started. Instead, teams are often better to focus on basics, like figuring out the right target market, and creating the initial product features. You need to nail the killer product, and prove that you can gain an atomic network, before reaching for the financial lever.

But once a team can reliably launch a product's initial atomic networks, financial levers can rapidly accelerate the speed in which the market hits the Tipping Point. These levers are implemented in different ways—sometimes these look like referral programs, or up-front advances or guarantees, or differentiated tiers of pricing. What they all share is allowing the team behind the network to juice its growth by using dollars rather than building features.

These levers are particularly powerful for networked products that are close to the money—payment networks like Venmo, cryptocurrencies, marketplaces and social platforms like Twitch that allow creators to make money. Because these products are often already in the middle of financial transactions, it can be straightforward to compel all the active participants in a network to add more to the network, whether that's by referring more users or spending more time in the product. Financial levers can be a powerful force to rapidly accelerate a market toward the Tipping Point.

Crypto and Its Use of Economic Incentives

Cryptocurrencies like Bitcoin present a fascinating variation on "paying up to launch," creating and sharing the economics of a network rather than directly using a company's cash reserves to subsidize. Bitcoin was originally invented in 2008 by someone—their identity still unknown—using the pseudonym Satoshi Nakamoto, describing the protocol in a succinct, nine-page paper: "Bitcoin: A peer-to-peer electronic cash system." The paper was sent out within a cryptography mailing list, followed by the release of an open-source implementation of Bitcoin a few months later. Today, Bitcoin's market capitalization is over $100 billion, calculated by multiplying the number of Bitcoins in existence by its current price—it's one of the most successful launches of a network in decades. And the network effects are so powerful that an ecosystem of millions of Bitcoin buyers act in concert based on the design decisions of one still unknown programmer.

It's the ingenious design of the Bitcoin protocol that creates economic incentives for all parties to cooperate. For the holders of Bitcoin, there is a mathematically guaranteed scarcity of the cryptocurrency at any given time, expanded gradually for the next hundred or so years. The argument from cryptocurrency advocates is that, in contrast to traditional currencies issued by governments, it is impervious to inflation—no one party can just print more, for example, when the economy is doing badly. In the back end, Bitcoin's design was driven by a network of decentralized "miners" that do the work to maintain the protocol, by processing transactions. They are rewarded with Bitcoin each time, incentivizing them to participate in the network.

At the beginning, Bitcoin made it attractive to join the network. At its inception, miners received very large rewards that then tapered and shrank over time. Both miners and holders of Bitcoin knew the exact level of scarcity dictated by the protocol, and treated it as a hedge against inflation. You could also think of cryptocurrency as a bet toward more economic and government instability, nationalism, and closed economies, which are all unfortunate trends happening now globally. The promise was, participate in Bitcoin early, and receive huge upside in return—which has proven out, with several billionaires minted by simply holding on to their cryptocurrency as prices went up.

Bitcoin and other cryptocurrencies are just one implementation of the idea of shared economic upside in a network. I've also seen a new pattern of startups offering network participants everything from stock options, to consulting fees, to investing rights, just to bootstrap the initial network. It's particularly effective for influencers, creators, developers, and the hard side of the network. That way, the company is aligned with its network—if the network grows and succeeds, its individual participants also win.

Partnerships with Larger Companies

Sometimes the concept of "paying up" is less about financial spending and much more about taking time and effort—as smaller companies have to do when they partner with larger players. These partnerships are often asymmetrical, where the smaller player must customize and build product for their partner, in exchange for access to distribution or revenue. Usually this doesn't work, but there are a few key examples where it has—starting with Microsoft. I focus not on the Microsoft of decades ago, but back when they were a startup in the 1970s.

Yes, Microsoft was a startup at one point. It rose from humble origins in Albuquerque, New Mexico, its original offices in a strip mall occupied today by T-shirt and jewelry shops. Led by childhood friends Bill Gates and Paul Allen, the company started by building tools for the entry-level programming language BASIC (literally, Beginner's All-purpose Symbolic Instruction Code) in the 1970s, but it was their subsequent entry into operating systems that created Microsoft's dominance. At the time, the budding technology industry thought much of the profits would be generated on selling the actual hardware of personal computers, and when IBM entered the PC industry in 1981, the company struck a deal to license Microsoft's Disk Operating System (DOS). Just like today's iOS and Android, DOS served as an essential piece of software that intermediated IBM's hardware components and the applications, like word processors, spreadsheets, and games, that developers built. The OS brings together a network effect of users, developers, and hardware manufacturers—but IBM didn't understand at the time.

This is where the IBM/Microsoft partnership worked, as a solution to Microsoft's Cold Start Problem. The way the partnership was set up, all the application developers and users who wanted to use the IBM personal computing platform would need to adopt MS-DOS. Yes, Microsoft had to build a custom OS to have it run on IBM. But also, critically, in the deal, Microsoft retained the right to sell DOS to hardware manufacturers besides IBM, and so later when a wave of manufacturers reverse-engineered IBM's designs and launched their own so-called IBM-compatible PCs, they used Microsoft's operating system, too.

Eventually dozens and then hundreds of PC manufacturers showed up, alongside thousands of software startups large and small that targeted MS-DOS as their primary platform. Application developers and users would interact with programs running on Microsoft's DOS regardless of where they bought their PC, ultimately commoditizing PC hardware makers and shifting the power. Much of that power went to the operating system.

It was in the chaotic creation of the personal computing industry that Microsoft's network effects were born. Although there were alternative ecosystems in the 1980s like Amiga, OS/2, Apple's Macintosh, and others, the nature of operating systems meant that they had strong network effects that would propel the Microsoft ecosystem forward. The network that constituted Microsoft's ecosystem could be thought of as three sides—users, developers, and PC makers—with each side attracting the others. Users (and their workplaces) bought PCs that ran MS-DOS (and later, Windows) because Microsoft's software ran the most applications and had the most choices for hardware, including the cheapest PCs. Developers preferred to build applications for the Microsoft platform because it had the most users, the best tools, and well-established distribution. And PC makers licensed Windows because users demanded it. All of these factors, in various ways, contributed to acquisition, engagement, and economic network effects for the different sides of the network.

We know how this story ends—the bigger the Microsoft ecosystem, the more valuable it would become. Eventually the company would dominate nearly 80 percent of the market for operating systems, establishing the monopoly that would allow it to go after adjacent markets. Through the years, critics have often accused the company of prevailing repeatedly and almost unfairly over competitors—including well-established companies with thousands of employees like WordPerfect, Lotus, Ashton-Tate, Stac, Novell, Netscape, AOL, and Sun—by leveraging its network effects. While Microsoft didn't invent the browser, spreadsheet, or word processor, years later it would come to control each of these markets.

But at the company's start, it was the crucial partnership with IBM that helped Microsoft reach a Tipping Point to ultimately control the most valuable network in the computer industry. They had to create a custom product to get it started, but used that work to parlay a presence on billions of PCs, at a time when network effects were mostly unknown and underappreciated.

Why Unprofitability Is Sometimes Smart

All of the examples in this chapter—coupons, Uber, crypto, Microsoft, etc.—involve the use of up-front efforts to bootstrap the network. One critique of subsidizing networks in this way is that it's like "selling a dollar for ninety cents." Yes, it would be ideal to be able to grow a network with positive unit economics from day one, but sometimes it's just not possible. Or it might be too slow. A new networked product is better off taking on the risk of subsidizing the network up front, and then improving the economics over time.

This is the reason why lack of profitability—while controversial—is often a smart way to accelerate a network past the Tipping Point. Once you are able to create a few atomic networks, you might want to buy your way into an entire market. For marketplaces, low prices for buyers and high earnings for sellers are both key value propositions. The same is true for social products, whether in communication or content-sharing, where it's important for content creators both to achieve an audience and earn revenues. The launch plan might require a heavy bit of up-front subsidy, whether that comes in the form of buying content initially or by guaranteeing payments in a marketplace.

At scale, it's almost always the goal to reduce incentives once the market has been won. If the entire addressable market is active on your platform, you'll no longer need to spend on acquisition costs. If you are the dominant player in the market, you may not have to spend on discounts aimed at competitors, or you may be so efficient at your spending that your competitors have to leave the market. What looks like unprofitability in the short term might lead to dominance in the long term, if the market reaches a Tipping Point in your favor.

15
FLINTSTONING
Reddit

In the classic 1960s animated sitcom *The Flintstones*, we see a prehistoric family sitcom set in the city of Bedrock. The show follows Fred and Wilma Flintstone and their loving family, complete with a pet dinosaur, a cave house, and a job that requires Fred to wear a tie. Memorably, there's a car made of stone, furs, and timber—started up by a flurry of Fred's legs—which rolls the family to their destination. Yabba dabba doo!

"Flinstoning" is a metaphor for this car, except in software, where missing product functionality is replaced with manual human effort. Early product releases often go into beta while lacking simple features like account deletion, content moderation tools, referral features, and many others. In lieu of these features, the product might simply offer a way to contact the developers who will handle it manually for you, using tools they have in the back end. Once they get enough inquiries, eventually the feature gets built out and users can do it themselves. In the meantime, a Flintstoned product launch lets the developers get the app out into the market and get feedback from customers.

Flintstoning can be a method to help bootstrap content or to handhold new users initially. For example, on user-generated video platforms, the initial library of videos and content might be uploaded by its founders, as YouTube did early on. For workplace collaboration tools, the team might offer onboarding and practically embed themselves within a client, offering custom software development and more, to make a particular project successful. Once these initial networks are formed, the Flintstoning techniques evolve toward automation as the momentum builds. The goal is just to manually fill in critical parts of the network, until it can stand on its own.

Reddit is a perfect example of how Flintstoning can be used early, and how it evolves from manual work into automation at scale. Cofounders Steve Huffman and Alexis Ohanian employed the technique when they first launched Reddit more than a decade ago. Today, Reddit is self-described as the "Front Page of the Internet" and is consistently one of the world's largest websites, with hundreds of millions of users organized into 100,000+ active subreddit communities, sharing millions of links. But the startup had a modest launch in 2005, when it initially consisted of a simple home page with a list of links each day, submitted by its users. By Reddit's users, though, I mean just two—at that point, it was Steve and his cofounder, Alexis Ohanian—before other visitors started to slowly trickle into the community.

a16z is an investor in Reddit, and over the years, I've gotten to know Steve and the team. I would visit him in person, once or twice a quarter, often with Marc Andreessen, to hear the latest on the business. Reddit's offices are in downtown San Francisco, with a playful interior decorated with various versions of the company's little alien mascot, Snoo. On my most recent visit, Steve and I sat on a sofa in his office, where he reflected on the early days of solving the Cold Start Problem:

> No one wants to live in a ghost town. No one wants to join an empty community. In the early days, it was our job each day to make sure there was good content on the front page. We'd post it ourselves, using dozens of dummy accounts. Otherwise the community might dry up.[42]

All of these dummy accounts looked and acted like real users, but it was Steve and Alexis controlling them. And while in the early days it might require a lot of manual searching and posting of content, the two became more clever over time. They began to build software to help them scale this activity—which Steve describes:

I wrote some code that would scrape news websites and post them with made-up usernames. That way, it looked like there was an active community. Problem was, it still needed my attention—about a month after launch in July of that year, I went camping with my family and didn't submit any links. When I checked Reddit, the homepage was blank! Whoops.

On one hand, the automation to scale their Flintstoning worked—Steve's code helped find and submit interesting content from a number of different websites. But on the other hand, it was still dependent on him being involved and checking in. Nevertheless, it tided the Reddit network over until it was able to have enough organic content creators for Steve to lay off the dummy scripts entirely.

Flintstoning the Hard Side of the Network

Reddit's use of Flintstoning is similar to the strategy used by companies like Yelp and Quora—to fill in the hard side of the network, which were also content creators. Study the pattern of Flintstoning across industries and you'll see the focus tends to be on replicating the hard side of the network with employees, contractors, and other direct efforts.

For food-delivery apps, signing up restaurants is difficult as they mostly exist as millions of small businesses, and they are often skeptical of new technology. And why would they work with you before you have demand? Services like DoorDash and Postmates Flinstoned by showing a large selection of restaurants, regardless of whether those restaurants had actually signed up. When customers ordered, the apps would send couriers to pick up the food, unbeknownst to the small, local businesses! They would just act as customers, grab the food, and deliver to the users who ordered it. Later on, once the demand had been proven the food apps would form direct relationships with restaurants.

There are B2B examples, too. B2B marketplaces exist in real estate, freight, labor, and many other large multibillion-dollar industries, spawning billion-dollar startups like Flexport and Convoy. Incumbents often exist as operationally intensive brokerages with a ton of employees that mostly operate by pencil, paper, and fax machine to help match corporate customers with trucking carriers, commercial real estate, or whatever other services they might need. The goal is always to build software to replace all the pen-and-paper workflows, but early on, it's easier to just do it the old-fashioned way. High-tech upstarts often employ Flintstoning by throwing employees at it—acting as a traditional brokerage—while slowly automating the most repetitive tasks. Eventually, the workflow is automated that the marketplace becomes more of a tech company, but the first few years are just people powered.

Sometimes these types of companies are called "cyborg startups," because they combine humans (who are executing tasks manually) with a team of software engineers who automate as much as they can over time. In cases like these, customers might initially interface with a thin layer of software, but in the back end, there's a rapid flurry of running legs to make the prehistoric car go.

Automation Can Scale Flintstoning

The downside of Flintstoning is that it feels like it's overly manual. You start by throwing people at the problem, but can it scale? I argue that it scales further and longer than you might think. Flinstoning can be thought of as a spectrum:

- Fully manual, human-powered efforts
- Hybrid, where software suggests actions to take, but people are in the loop
- Automated, powered by algorithms

A fully manual version of Steve Huffman's Reddit launch would have been to submit links by hand, and to hire a team of contractors to create content. That was effectively what Steve did himself at the beginning. It might seem inefficient, but companies like Yelp and Quora relied on employees and other staff to build their library of reviews and Q&A respectively, so it can be done. And as I mentioned earlier, B2B brokerages like Uber Freight can start in this way, too, where humans take the lead and software automates inefficient steps.

If the manual efforts work, technology can be layered on to create leverage. A hybrid model like Steve's approach with Reddit can make sense—he had scrapers and bots identify high potential content, but there was a human in the loop to decide what to actually post. For a marketplace product, you might still have human brokers who help match supply and demand, but start adding in tooling to increase efficiency. This represents the middle of the spectrum.

A fully software-driven automated approach might have been to start with bots that would fully gather and present high-relevance content in an algorithmic feed. Perhaps the closest example to that is TikTok today, which uses algorithms instead of explicit upvoting and downvoting by users, to figure out what content is shown. Famously, PayPal built bots that would automatically buy and sell items on eBay, but insist on transacting only with PayPal—it became a way to convince eBay sellers to sign up for the service.

The Extreme—Platforms and Their Applications

How far can Flintstoning go? At the extreme of the strategy, a network might hire entire teams and build entire companies to fill in for the hard side of the network. Imagine if, instead of Reddit's founders submitting content, it was teams of people organized into studios creating content all day long. While this seems like a wild hypothetical, it's one of the core strategies of the video games market, as demonstrated by Nintendo's launch of the Switch console.

In 2016, Nintendo aimed to launch an innovative new console that could double as a handheld as well as plug into a TV. But consumers won't buy a console just to have it—they buy it to get access to new, must-have video games that generally accompany the launch. Ideally, outside game developers will build for the new platform, but they often don't know how to take advantage of the new functionality, nor do they have an incentive when they can build for a preexisting console that has a much larger user base.

To break through this Cold Start Problem, Nintendo spared no expense in the Switch launch, simultaneously releasing the latest installments of their classic Mario and Zelda franchises—each have sold tens of millions of units. In an ultimate Flintstoning move, these games were built by Nintendo specifically to help support the Switch's launch. This strategy is a Nintendo staple from prior generations. The original Nintendo launched more than three decades ago with seventeen games, some developed by the company and by external developers—Nintendo Switch would do the same.

Mario Odyssey and Zelda: Breath of the Wild were built by internal studios within the company, each with its own creative directors and game designers. Imagine having hundreds of people Flintstoning to launch a new network—that's what happens in the world of new consoles. The strategy worked, and within the first few years the Switch hit 70 million units, making it one of Nintendo's most popular products ever.

The games industry calls this "first-party content," and it can be a serious investment. Over the years, Microsoft Xbox has taken this strategy to an extreme, buying a large number of studios and bringing them in-house. This isn't a small outlay of cash—Microsoft now owns nearly a dozen video game studios, including Mojang, the maker of Minecraft, which they bought for $2.5 billion in 2014. It might seem expensive, but this is what's needed to win in the video game console market. Sometimes, you just have to do it yourself.

Reddit didn't pursue this type of strategy, but it could have. There could have been a world where Reddit built many internal studios—one for their "cute" sub-Reddit community, another for sports, yet another for music—and hired full-time moderators as employees of those studios to create the necessary content. While this isn't a common strategy for social networks, it's also not crazy. In recent years, we've seen players like YouTube in video and Spotify in podcasts begin to license and create more first-party content to accelerate their services.

Exit Strategy

Flintstoning can be phased out over time. In that way, it can be thought of as a close cousin to the "come for the tool, stay for the network" approach. The Flintstoning approach focuses on artificially propping up the hard side of the network with highly manual efforts, whereas the "come for the tool" props it up with software. Like the Tools approach, it's important to have an exit strategy with Flintstoning. With the former, a networked product must be designed to switch users from single player to multiplayer mode. With the latter, the product must switch from manual (and company-supported) to automated.

Eventually, a marketplace with Flintstoned sellers must make way for organic sellers that drive the network efforts we all seek. A new PlayStation game console has to make third-party game developers successful, so that an ecosystem can form. Had Reddit increased the number of accounts controlled by Steve and his code, they would eventually have drowned out the organic content creators that emerged over time. Because the value proposition to social content creators often revolves around status and feedback—in the form of likes, comments, and so on—it's important that the bots don't soak up all of this engagement.

In other words, once the Cold Start Problem is solved, it's important to let the network grow and stand up on its own—and turn off Flintstoning entirely.

This is exactly what happened to Reddit once it broke through. Steve explained:

> *After I'd been posting links every day for a while, one day I was hanging out in Boston and didn't submit anything into Reddit. I was worried I'd left an empty homepage, but when I pulled it up, it was full of links! I clicked on the usernames of the people who'd posted that day and saw that yes, they were real people.*

By that point, Reddit had hit a few thousand users, and it was self-sustaining—it didn't need Steve to post links. Later, as traffic grew, the home page was eventually split into three subreddits: Politics, Programming, and NSFW. Then eventually Sports and a few other categories. But the pattern repeated itself, where each subreddit—think of this as Reddit's network of networks—needs at least a thousand subscribers to self-sustain. The Flintstoning strategy had sustained the network long enough to begin tipping over category after category, eventually driving Reddit into one of the most important online destinations on the internet.

16

ALWAYS BE HUSTLIN'

Uber

In 2015, Uber decided to have a team retreat—it would be an unusual one, if only for its size. More than four thousand employees from Uber's global offices would all fly into Las Vegas, as discreetly as possible given the number. It was in celebration for a major milestone: hitting $10 billion in gross revenue, just six years after the company had been founded. This was one of several milestones the company had celebrated in previous years as another stop along the exponential growth curve—first at $100 million, then $1 billion, and now $10 billion—also known as 10 to the 8th power, 10 to the 9th power, and then 10 to the 10th power.

As a result, the retreat was branded "X to the X," with a subtle logo of two white Xs in a diagonal. This "X to the X" logo was printed on T-shirts, water bottles, and signage throughout the conference area, so that the typical Vegas tourist wouldn't spot the thousands of Uber employees who were in town. For the most part, the secrecy was maintained—there were minimal photos posted to social media, and the only press that got alerted was British gossip magazine the *Daily Mail*.

The team retreat would be a mixture of entertainment and work, just as Uber itself aspired to be. The agenda would alternate throughout the week, with formal events during the day—covering all aspects of the business, from international to product strategy to pricing—followed by social events at night at nightclubs throughout Vegas. The second night of the retreat, dance music legends David Guetta and Kygo played. The third night, the surprise was a private concert from Beyoncé, who danced and sang for hours, catering to thousands of Uber employees. To this day, I still have water bottles, T-shirts, and hundreds of private photos from the event—it was memorable, maybe the high-water mark in terms of raw team morale.

"X to the X" celebrated a major victory for the company, but out of the thousands of people at the retreat, one team deserved the most credit. They constituted the largest portion of the company and had made the biggest impact over the years: Operations, made up of the thousands of "boots on the ground" that launched new cities. They grew riders and drivers the hard way—coordinating street teams that handed out discount cards next to train stations—and reacted to the constant treats of regulation and competition. Travis would regularly say to the product teams, "Product can solve problems, but it's slow. Ops can do it fast." As a result, Uber saw itself as an "ops-led" company, and it was this team that best embodied the startup's entrepreneurial and creative culture. The hustle within the Ops team was renowned, and one of the foundational elements of Uber's success.

The Importance of Creativity

The Tipping Point for a market can be accomplished with some of the grand strategies I've discussed—subsidizing markets, making the product invite-only, building tools, Flintstoning, etc.—but that's all built on raw creativity and entrepreneurship. Creativity is important because there are often brief moments of opportunity that can cause a market to quickly tip, if you try the right idea. This is like Twitter launching during the SXSW conference, where a critical mass of users was attending. Airbnb employed a similar strategy during major local events, as Jonathan Golden, an early product leader, noted:

> We also latched onto local events that were bigger than us whenever possible. Online campaigns such as "Make $1,000 in one weekend renting your apartment to Oktoberfest attendees" instead of more generic campaigns like "Rent your apartment to strangers" dramatically improved supply-side conversion metrics. And because one of the most powerful ways to bootstrap supply is to guarantee demand, we encouraged employee travel to unreviewed listings.[43]

Usually, these types of stunts and hacks are neither scalable nor repeatable. A funny viral video might work once or a few times, but it can't be the only lever to drive growth over the long terms. Eventually, highly scalable efforts like SEO, paid marketing, viral growth, and partnerships have to kick in. However, in the early days, when the focus is on tipping each new additional network, everything helps.

The Uber Ops team provided a steady stream of this creativity. Every new city launch in the early days was a Cold Start Problem, and the city teams were structured to be autonomous and decentralized, able to react quickly to new ideas on the ground. The goal was to tip over the entire market, one network at a time. For example, the launch team would often execute a playbook that would enlist a local celebrity to be "Rider Zero"—the first Uber rider in the market—alongside local press coverage. The Ops team also came up with special promotions like Uber Puppies and Uber Kittens—a way to request a truck full of puppies or kittens, depending on your preference—to show up at your office for an hour at a time. Or Uber Ice Cream, where a soft-serve truck would arrive. On the supply side, the Ops team would call local limo service companies one by one, stand outside major local events to pass out flyers, and text drivers to get them to start driving, among dozens of other highly manual tactics.

Going from a single network into a network of networks requires hustle and creativity. Uber started in major cities like San Francisco, New York City, and Los Angeles, and found that each one required dramatically different tactics. New York was a licensed market, where limos operated by professional drivers reigned, and Uber competed with the subway. LA is a sprawl of a city, and unlike San Francisco and New York, everyone has a car. It wasn't clear that Uber would be successful in each city. But after a few dozen cities were launched, the playbook became clear. Each new market became easier and easier, as the Tipping Point kicked in.

Hustle as a System

Uber Ice Cream is fun, but the real magic comes from creating an innovative, bottom-up organization that can create endless variations of ideas like this. The Ops team culture rewarded experimentation, and after ice cream came Uber Puppies, Uber Mariachi Band, Uber Health (for flu shots), Uber Lion Dance (to celebrate Chinese New Year!), and dozens of other variations from around the world. The Ops teams would "holidize" their efforts, aligning special dates with product features that promoted growth. A driver referral program like "Give $200, Get $200" could be bumped up and turned into a New Year's branded "Start your new year right—Give $300, Get $300" campaign. In-app notifications celebrating July Fourth, Thanksgiving, Christmas, and other holidays could keep the messaging fresh and response rates high.

Unusually, in the early years the San Francisco–based engineering and product teams would really play a support role. They created customizable levers within the app, giving the city teams tools and controls to manage their own markets. City teams could create new "vehicle classes" within the app, so that ideas like Uber Moto, Uber Helicopter, and Uber Pitch (for startups to pitch investors!) could be launched. For San Francisco's Pride Parade, the car icon within the app had a rainbow trail behind it, to signify the special day.

In the end, you might ask—did Uber Ice Cream really help? As an individual stunt, it may not have had a massive impact on the company. But I argue that within the framework of taking a market from zero to the Tipping Point, these types of quick, clever tactics played a key role in getting markets off the ground. Most important, Uber created a system to quickly identify, execute, and iterate on these concepts—it was supported by an entrepreneurial team culture, robust software tooling, and an understanding that each city would be its own Cold Start Problem.

Enterprise Hustle

These ideas apply to both networked products in the consumer category and new products that target business customers—with some slight variations. In a research study called "How today's fastest growing B2B businesses found their first ten customers," startup veteran Lenny Rachitsky interviewed early members of teams from Slack, Stripe, Figma, and Asana. In studying how these earliest companies found their first customers, it was concluded that a significant number came from the founders tapping their personal networks:

Only three sourcing strategies account for every B2B company's very early growth. [These are: Personal network, Seek out customers where they are, Get press.] Thus, your choices are easy, yet limited. Almost every B2B business both hits up their personal network and heads to the places their potential customers were spending time. The question isn't which of these two routes to pursue, but instead how far your own network will take you before you move on.

It's a huge advantage to have a strong personal network in B2B, which you can also build by bringing a connector investor or joining an incubator such as YC. Getting press is rarely the way to get started.[44]

Just as Uber's ops hustle worked for solving the city-by-city Cold Start Problem, B2B startups have an equivalent card to play: they can manually reach out and onboard teams from their friends' startups, building atomic networks quickly, as Slack did in their early launch. Or, many productivity products begin by launching within online communities—like Twitter, Hacker News, and Product Hunt—where dense pockets of early adopters are willing to try new products. In recent years, B2B products have started to emphasize memes, funny videos, invite-only mechanics, and other tactics traditionally associated with consumer startups. I expect that this will only continue, as the consumerization of enterprise products fully embraces meme-based go-to-market early on, instead of leading with direct sales.

But don't completely count out sales—it's an important lever. Paul Graham of YCombinator famously argued that entrepreneurs should "Do things that don't scale." Embedded within this maxim is the idea that manually finding and convincing users, one by one, is a good way to start:

One of the most common types of advice we give at Y Combinator is to do things that don't scale. . . . The most common unscalable thing founders have to do at the start is to recruit users manually. Nearly all startups have to. You can't wait for users to come to you. You have to go out and get them.

There are two reasons founders resist going out and recruiting users individually. One is a combination of shyness and laziness.

They'd rather sit at home writing code than go out and talk to a
bunch of strangers and probably be rejected by most of them. But
for a startup to succeed, at least one founder (usually the CEO) will
have to spend a lot of time on sales and marketing.[45]

Graham goes on to cite examples from Stripe and Meraki as well as consumer startups like Facebook and Airbnb, which employed this philosophy.

Importantly, he also advocates that B2B startups think about doing consulting to start, treating an initial set of customers as if they were consulting clients. By building the functionality they need on an ad hoc basis, and then generalizing, they have a better chance to hit product/ market fit—even though this approach won't scale. You can't build a high-margin, scalable startup by consulting for thousands of clients.

But hustle works, whether it's for consumer or B2B products, and learning to scale operational and sales-driven approaches can help tip an entire market.

The Gray Area

The core of the rideshare industry is sometimes called "peer to peer"— where regular people sign up as drivers to ferry other people around— and it wasn't legal when it was first launched. And in fact, as I write this, there are many places in the world where it still isn't. There have been high-stakes disputes with cities, outright bans, police raids on local Uber offices, and many other hair-raising episodes in Uber's history. Has this hustle gone too far?

One of the more intriguing dilemmas within the Cold Start Problem is what happens when your initial network pulls you into a gray area. Build a networked product for hosting and playing videos, as YouTube did, and inevitably someone will upload "Lazy Sunday"—the *Saturday Night Live* skit that drove millions of users to its website in the early days. Build a networked product that allows easy-to-use pay-ments between people, as PayPal did, and it will be used for all sorts of illicit transactions. Dropbox's folder sharing features were used early on for pirating movies and music—this was an unexpected result for a cloud-storage service built to share and sync files for productivity.

When this happens, do you try to fix the loopholes or add more controls, potentially impacting the usability of the product? Is it even a good idea to scan through the contents of your users' folders? Or do you embrace it but nudge usage in the right direction over time? These are hard questions. YouTube started with significant amounts of pirated music videos and TV clips, but would eventually implement audio fingerprinting, moderation tools, and partner with content pro-viders. Norms have changed, too—today when users upload video clips onto YouTube and other social media, that's considered social media engagement, not potential piracy. PayPal did the same, keeping its easy-to-use interface and responding to fraud by innovating—implementing one of the first CAPTCHAs, the squiggly letters proving you're a hu-man and not a computer—as well as creating data science teams to battle scammers.

Uber chose to embrace the gray area, transforming its original li-censed on-demand black car and limo service—operating fully in the clear—into the peer-to-peer (P2P) model that constitutes the majority of rideshare revenues today. The transition happened so fast and so completely that during my time at Uber, there were no product or en-gineering staff—in a company of thousands—dedicated to the original licensed car business. Everyone had been re-tasked to the new, explo-sive rideshare market. There are downsides of this strategy, of course—Uber X invited controversy around labor laws, safety requirements, and regulators.

Like many Cold Start examples, embracing the gray area created issues in the early days. But following the network and what the market wanted allowed Uber to reach Escape Velocity in nearly ever major city in the world. Like many strategies to tackle the Cold Start Problem, the approach evolved over time as the initial atomic networks formed. Years after the company hit the Tipping Point, the company has worked with the government to establish more of the regulatory framework, to move the gray area into the clear. These days, rideshare is an option at almost every major airport, and cities even recommended Uber as an option when public transit was paused because of COVID. The app's features have also been enhanced over time to help alleviate safety concerns and better follow regulatory guidelines, while the massive network has been used to launch new businesses like Uber Eats, as well as bikes and scooters.

Uber 1.0 Cultural Values

Hustle and creativity help tip over markets, because each atomic network is not the same. The first, second, and third will likely require slightly different tactics. This was true in rideshare, where the Operations team at Uber was really the secret weapon for how the team solved the Cold Start Problem, over and over again, within all the 800+ cities that company launched. There was an ethos within the team that—for better, and sometimes worse—prioritized action and creativity rather than overthinking it.

At the Vegas "X to the X" retreat in 2015, one of the primary evening events was rolling out the cultural values of the company. In a stadium in front of the entire Uber team, Travis talked about how he and Jeff Holden (then chief product officer) met for hours to decide fourteen values for the company:

Uber 1.0 Cultural Values

- Make Magic
- Superpumped
- Inside Out

- Be an Owner, Not a Renter
- Optimistic Leadership
- Be Yourself
- Big Bold Bets
- Customer Obsession
- Always Be Hustlin'
- Let Builders Build
- Winning: Champion's Mindset
- Principled Confrontation
- Meritocracy and Toe-Stepping
- Celebrate Cities

Many of these values spoke directly to the efforts of the Ops teams—particular Always Be Hustlin', but also Celebrate Cities, Be an Owner, and Meritocracy and Toe-Stepping—all of which applied to the global, decentralized nature of the organization.

The list spoke to the heart of Uber's culture: there was the raw hustle of the city teams, combined with an ownership mentality where GMs felt they were the CEOs of their cities. Most of the GMs and city teams were young, and promoted internally, so they were constantly in direct and indirect competition with other similar cities (and Uber's actual competitors) on all their key metrics. This was the magic that helped tip the market in rideshare.

PART IV

ESCAPE VELOCITY

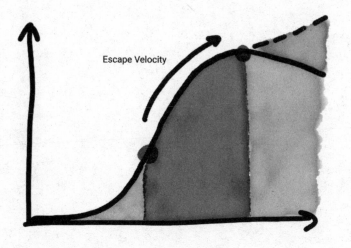

Escape Velocity

17

DROPBOX

When networked products start to work, they can really work. By the time of Dropbox's IPO in 2018, cofounders Drew Houston and Arash Ferdowsi had built a SaaS startup that was the fastest in the category to reach $1 billion in annual recurring revenue—faster than Salesforce, Workday, and Service Now at their IPOs. Across many of their key metrics, the growth curve looked like a classic hockey stick, compounding on a regular basis to over 500 million users in eight years.

I have been following Dropbox since its early years, and have gotten to know Drew Houston as a friend. I've served as an advisor to the team, working with them on new products and accelerating viral growth. I often met the team at the office, but Drew and I would grab lunch at Yank Sing, a busy, popular dim sum restaurant near the Ferry Building in San Francisco. Over siu mai and xiao long baos on unrushed Sundays, we would talk about business and life. I used one of these sessions to chat with Drew about the Cold Start Problem, and we covered one of the most fascinating periods for Dropbox—its teenage years.

Five years after Dropbox was founded at the Massachusetts Institute of Technology, the company had done the hardest part—solving the Cold Start Problem. The company did it with a classic "come for the tool" strategy, with file syncing across a person's computers as the initial tool, followed by a network of shared folders with colleagues, friends, and family. They innovated with a referral program where users could give and get storage by inviting friends. User growth was explosive.

By 2012, the company was on a fast trajectory but had even bigger ambitions. That year, Dropbox would see the product hit 100 million registered users.[46] High expectations had pushed up the value of the company to $4 billion by top venture capitalists, and now it needed to deliver. At nearly 200 employees (mostly engineers), the company was like an awkward teenager, neither a kid nor an adult. The product had massive usage, yet hadn't built out large teams for sales, marketing, and finance, as was typical of a more mature company.

The time had arrived for Dropbox to focus on making money. Drew told me:

We saw a lot of adoption early on but we didn't know anything about selling to big companies. There were a lot of cultural antibodies that kept us from going after the enterprise—after all, we were all in our 20s. We wanted to focus on consumers, and photos. But by a few years in we started hiring people to run marketing and sales, and let self-serve happen [on] its own.[47]

And the self-serve business worked—users would engage the product, decide to upgrade, and put in their credit card on the website. Just from having this upgrade page, the company was hitting tens of millions of dollars of recurring revenue without monetization being a top priority. Dropbox's metrics mirrored those of the top consumer products at the time—Monthly Active Users and Registered Users—and it was adding millions of new users every month. The bottom-up approach was working.

Perhaps because of the success of the self-serve approach, the sales team was small. To give you a sense of the company culture, in the early days when the sales team got overloaded, it was standard procedure to simply remove the sales team's email address from the website, so that users couldn't contact them. Eventually, the team realized it was better to hire more people in sales. But making money was still viewed as a "why would we care about that?" topic in the geeky, MIT engineering-oriented nature of the company. Revenue wasn't considered "Dropboxy."

However, the company was pushed to a crossroads by a mounting expense: cloud infrastructure bills.

Dropbox had initially been built on Amazon's cloud platform, and the product was growing so fast that the hosting bills had become very expensive. With hockey stick growth would come a second hockey stick, but this time, in file hosting costs. Building out in-house infra-structure[48] would save nearly $75 million in just the first two years, and hundreds of millions over time.

It was obvious it had to be done. But it would require a tremendous amount of up-front capital to lease and build out data centers, which in turn would push the company to unprofitability for the first time in years.

To kick off an effort to generate more revenue, a cross-functional Growth and Monetization team was convened. It had a core of quantitative, business-minded product leaders who also teamed up with engineers and designers, led by ChenLi Wang and Jean-Denis Greze. This team would be empowered and given the resources to directly drive growth and monetization opportunities. They would create new insights about Dropbox's business, identify and prioritize opportunities, and execute against them by shipping new features and updates to the product.

The concept of a "Growth Team" at Dropbox, while becoming more commonplace in the industry, was then a controversial move across the company. Strong product-driven cultures like Dropbox tended to believe that the only thing that mattered in attracting users was a great product—why waste the talent of skilled engineers working on landing pages or optimizing email notifications when they could be building the next generation of great features? A similar objection often comes from the marketing teams at technology companies who historically owned customer acquisition—why create a duplicate team that overlapped with their work? Yet the track record speaks for itself—growth teams have emerged across the industry as a focused way to scale products toward Escape Velocity.

Amid these questions, the newly minted team quickly kicked off their efforts. They started with a succession of quick wins on monetization, from optimizing the pricing page to nudges that reminded customers when they were likely to hit their storage limit. In the early days, a small design change might result in millions of dollars for the company. In parallel, the team began to explore the data, looking for critical insights that made one user more valuable than another. Not every user is the same, nor is every network the same.

Dropbox's insights on this were profound: some users joined Dropbox as part of the "come for the tool" strategy—but stayed with the tool without increasing their engagement by sharing folders and documents with others. In contrast, the ones who used Dropbox for collaboration and sharing—the network features—became significantly more valuable over time. Dropbox's users could be divided into High-Value Actives (HVAs) and Low-Value Actives (LVAs), which was useful as a quality indicator. It could be overlaid into the strategies for marketing channels and partnerships to make sure HVAs were being acquired, not LVAs. Drew described this change in thinking to me:

> *Originally, we thought our mission was trying to serve "everyone on the internet" but we realized that we shouldn't be fighting every war. Our most valuable users were probably using us for collaboration in businesses and storage, not sharing full-length movies in developing markets.*

Understanding the value of users impacted Dropbox's growth strategy. When they partnered with one of the largest mobile companies to provide photo backup services, the Dropbox team realized that the partnership generated a lot of new users but they were all LVAs. This created substantial costs in supporting the users but not necessarily future revenue as they were unlikely to upgrade. The HVA versus LVA concept helped the Dropbox team understand and prioritize its various efforts.

Just as there are high- and low-value users, there are also high- and low-value networks. In 2012, nearly 100 million people had signed up to use Dropbox. This vast network was made up of smaller, atomic networks—comprising hundreds of thousands of businesses, both big and small. The Dropbox sales team was able to "fish in their own pond," prioritizing outreach to companies that had many, many users already on the product—using their email domains as a clue. Just as years back, Facebook had used edu email domains to partition smaller, engaged networks and spread from Harvard to other universities, Dropbox could do the same with the dot-com corporate equivalent. An even more important signal was how many shared folders were being used at a company—the more collaboration via Dropbox, the stickier the product, and the easier upgrades would be to sell.

Data could be misleading sometimes, too. In the early days, Dropbox was growing so fast that it was often hard to do analyses on what types of content people were putting in their folders. One of the simplest analyses was to randomly sample snapshots of folders, and count the file extensions. Perhaps it is not surprising to some that the most popular files were photos—lots and lots of photos, especially on mobile. Combined with the natural virality of this media type, Dropbox embarked on a road map of photos-related features, culminating in the launch of Carousel, a separate app to let consumers manage and view their photos on Dropbox. It did okay, but underperformed relative to expectations and was eventually shut down so that the company could invest in what is now its core focus: businesses.

The company's focus on businesses came from multiple directions. First, the team surveyed users and realized that many High-Value Actives were upgrading their Dropbox accounts for use at work. It was much easier to sell to businesses—again, fishing in your own pond—especially once Dropbox built out features that companies expected: additional security and administrative controls, integrations into commonly used workplace products like Microsoft Office, and so on. Later on, the same analysis on popular files stored on Dropbox was performed, but led to a different conclusion once the focus was on which types of files were at the center of user engagement.

The right question was: Which files did people tend to go back and edit or move, again and again? What types of files did multiple users within a network tend to share, collaboratively edit, and interact with? The answer was clear—Documents. Spreadsheets. Presentations.

Dropbox, in the years before its IPO, came to orient itself in a new direction—to focus on highest-value users in the highest-value networks interacting with the highest-value files. At its IPO filing documents, it would describe its mission along these lines: "Unleash the world's creative energy by designing a more enlightened way of working." It would describe itself as "a global collaboration platform."

This was a long way from the founding of the company, which was really driven by consumer demand—not necessarily business use cases. The origin story is now part of startup lore: Drew Houston was a student frustrated by misplacing his USB drives, and to solve this problem for himself, he built and launched Dropbox. The product was launched with a self-narrated, four-minute video[49] showing a "magic folder" that automatically synced files across computers, obviating the need for fragile USB drives. The first version didn't have shared folders, though that would quickly come later. The video was released in April 2007, and it attracted a torrent of demand from users of social media sites Reddit, Hacker News, Digg, and others.

Drew recounted later:

It drove hundreds of thousands of people to the website. Our beta waiting list went from 5,000 people to 75,000 people literally overnight. It totally blew us away.

The origin story for Dropbox often ends with Drew and classmate Arash Ferdowsi moving to San Francisco to join the startup accelerator YCombinator, and quickly raising venture capital funding. A decade later, in 2018, the company IPO'd and was listed as NYSE:DBX, with an opening valuation north of $10 billion. Often startup stories skip the middle part of the story, going from origin story to IPO in a few short paragraphs.

The years before and after 2012 are critical middle chapters in Dropbox's startup journey. Over its decade-long journey from its founding to its IPO, the company had learned the networks and attributes of its most valuable users, introduced key features to appeal to businesses, and added new marketing channels. All of these efforts helped scale the network effects into Escape Velocity, leading it toward a successful IPO.

Introducing Escape Velocity

When new products see success and start to scale, it's often called hitting "Escape Velocity." The mythology is that the product begins to hockey stick, going up and to the right forever. But it's not so simple—in reality, the journey isn't over and instead the focus changes. In this phase, the challenge quickly becomes maintaining a fast growth rate and amplify a successful product's network effects.

In Dropbox's case, the product moved through multiple phases: The Cold Start phase began as a replacement for USB drives—as a tool—while upselling users to use shared folders. As consumer and business use cases multiplied, the product reached the Tipping Point, leading to hundreds of millions of active users. In the Escape Velocity phase, the company needed to continue scaling the use base, and ultimately build a real revenue-generating business. The key to unlocking this phase was to understand its high- and low-value users, eventually targeting the workplace:

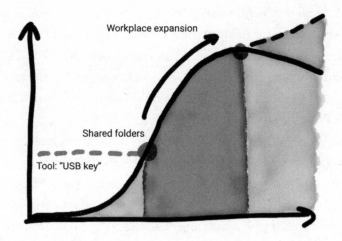

Figure 11: Dropbox curve—USB key, shared folders, workplace

Every new product eventually has to achieve, and then sustain, Escape Velocity. In the next few chapters, I talk about this middle phase, where the hard work is focused on scaling growth. This stage of the Cold Start framework, Escape Velocity, is the most relevant to teams working within established franchises—this is where growing an already successful product is so different than the startup zero-to-one efforts I've addressed earlier in the book.

I'll start by reinventing "network effects" into something much more concrete.

In the chapter "The Trio of Forces," I describe how the industry uses "network effects" as a broad term that is simply too vague to be useful. To make it concrete enough for product teams to act upon, I argue that there are a trio of network effects: Engagement, Acquisition, and Economics. The following chapters deep dive on each of these effects.

"The Engagement Effect" is what happens when a product gets stickier, and more engaging, as more users join. This is the closest to the classic definition of the network effect, as defined by Theodore Vail of AT&T. However, I'll describe it in modern terminology, using the language of retention curves and engagement metrics that we use in dissecting the performance of new apps. "The Acquisition Effect," on the other hand, is the network effect that powers the acquisition of new customers into your product—in other words, viral growth. Products are inherently viral when people bring their friends and colleagues into a network simply by using it—as Dropbox, messaging apps, and social networks do. I'll talk about how the Acquisition Effect works, and how to best amplify its impact. And finally, I'll introduce the third of the trio of network effects, "The Economic Effect." Network effects can help improve business models over time, in the form of improved feed algorithms, increased conversion rates, premium pricing, and more.

18

THE TRIO
OF FORCES

Escape velocity is often described as a kind of end state, the moment when a product becomes dominant in the market, where every-thing gets easier. These companies are supposed to have uncon-tested growth based on their strong network effects. Yet look inside any product team that's reached Escape Velocity and you see something different—what looks so easy on the outside is not so easy on the inside. Thousands of employees are working furiously to scale up the network. Dropbox, for example, employed 2,000+ full-time highly paid design-ers, engineers, and marketers, doubling or tripling the employee base each year leading up to the 2018 IPO.

While you may only need a small handful of employees to achieve product/market fit—famously, Instagram had thirteen employees and 30 million users when it was bought by Facebook—you need a significant coordinated effort to scale a product to its full potential. This is a big contrast to our everyday, overly simplistic explanations of hockey stick growth curves: "They've got lightning in a bottle!" Or, for many of the tech products I'm unpacking in this book—from multiplayer games to chat apps to workplace products—sometimes the offhand explanation is: "Of course, they're growing fast—they have network effects!" But this is superficial.

It takes a tremendous amount of energy to scale a network—both in playing defense to counteract market saturation and competition, and on the offense, to amplify network effects over time. It's not just Dropbox with this kind of story—Pinterest, Slack, Zoom, Uber, Airbnb, and others also have thousands (or tens of thousands) of full-time employees, many of them working within the confines of a single app or small family of apps. Ask any of these teams, and they'll tell you they feel understaffed, and there's so much more to do. This is what Escape Velocity actually looks like. It heralds a new stage, focused on building up network effects to amplify their strength. It is not a period where teams can coast on their momentum, because inevitably, momentum will slow as market saturation, spam, competition, and other forces appear.

Strengthening network effects is easier said than done. Everyone wants to improve their network effects, but what does that really mean? Product teams work in the concrete—in designing and picking product features, in deciding timelines for launching new products, and in trading off engineering complexity for functionality. Tell a team something abstract like "go improve your network effects!" and you'll get blank stares. In the coming chapters, I will discuss how to move from strategy to execution. To create a plan to strengthen a product's network effects, we need to connect the abstract with the concrete, so that the output can reflect the practical reality of picking and prioritizing projects.

Three Systems Underlying the Network Effect

Let's start with a surprising idea that goes against the grain of industry jargon: the network effect is not one effect. Instead, the network effect is a broader umbrella term that can be broken down into a trio of underlying forces: the Acquisition network effect, the Engagement network effect, and the Economic network effect. Each one of these can contribute to a business in a different way, and is stronger the more dense a network is.

The "Acquisition Effect" is the ability for a product to tap into its network to acquire new customers. Any product can buy Facebook or Google advertising, for instance, to attract new users, but only networked products can tap into viral growth—the ability for users in its network to tell others in their own personal networks. This keeps customer acquisition costs low over time, fighting against the natural rise that comes with market saturation and competition. The types of projects that amplify the Acquisition Effect are oriented around viral growth: referral features that reward users when they invite others, tapping into contacts to create suggestions for who to add to an app, and improving conversion along the key moments in the invitation experience. All of these help increase metrics like new user sign-ups, the so-called viral factor of a product, and bring down the cost of acquiring a customer (CAC).

The "Engagement Effect" describes how a denser network creates higher stickiness and usage from its users—it is a more specific form of the classic description of network effects that I covered at the beginning of the book, "the more users that join the network, the more useful it gets." However, the classic definition can be refined to include the underlying system that drives the value—use cases and "loops" that define how users derive value when engaging with a product—as well as the specific metrics that increase with a denser network. For example, Twitter is a lot more interesting to use, now with media outlets, celebrities, and politicians on it, than in the early days when you might just have a nerdy friend or two on the platform. Because there's more types of content creators in the network, what might have felt like an app to stay in touch with friends in the early days might eventually evolve into a diverse set of use cases: tracking political news, keeping abreast of what's happening in your industry, keeping up with your favorite celebrities, and so on. In turn, these elevated use cases drive key metrics, as more engagement directly maps to number of sessions per user, or the number of days per month that you're active in the product. Retention curves, often one of the most important visualizations of how long people are sticking around, can be improved as stickier use cases emerge.

The "Economic Effect" is the ability for a networked product to accelerate its monetization, reduce its costs, and otherwise improve its business model, as its network grows. Workplace products, for example, often convert to higher tiers of pricing as the number of knowledge workers using them grows within a company. The more workers that adopt a product, the more advanced features they might want to upgrade into, particularly when the features are collaborative in nature—like Slack charging for the ability to search messages from all users across the organizations. Similarly, app stores and other marketplaces will grow their average revenue per user as the number of listings increases. If customers have more choices, they often have a better chance of finding exactly what they're looking to buy. Then, conversion rates increase.

The Growth Accounting Equation

I use Engagement, Acquisition, and Economic network effects as the core taxonomy for the reason that they map to the key outputs that product teams care most about: active users and revenue, and the leading indicators to these metrics. Active users are made up of a combination of new users signing up, and how engaged and retained the existing users are. Revenue is a by-product of active users and the average revenue each user is generating, whether that's from purchases or advertising revenue. Growth rate, another important metric, is the ability to repeatably scale these network effects consistently over time.

The relationship between these inputs and outputs is just arithmetic. Here is what's often called the "Growth Accounting Equation," which shows how these key metrics relate for active users:

Gain or loss in active users = New + Reactivated − Churned

Then based on the delta of each time period, you can figure out if you'll gain or lose active users:

This month's actives = Last month's actives + gain or loss

This example uses "Active users"—relevant more for social networks and messaging apps—but it could be "Active subscribers," too, for a SaaS product like Dropbox or a consumer subscription service like YouTube Red. It's become a best practice to take this equation and build dashboards out of its inputs, so that in any given month you know how the underlying components are trending. If your goal is to grow 3x year over year, and sign-ups are way down, then it becomes clear how much churn has to be improved in order to still make the target—it's just some simple math. Overlaying revenue is easy, too. You just add two more variables, multiplying the active users number with the average revenue per active user (ARPU).

Every product can be thought of in this way, and it's the product team's goal to increase each of these metrics. However, networked products are special in how they can leverage their networks to drive up each of these variables—something that traditional products can't. As they grow and hit Escape Velocity, the density of the network makes the Engagement, Acquisition, and Economics effects more powerful, causing the input metrics to increase. More new users will appear, based on viral growth, and the product will get stickier, decreasing churn. More money will be made, as conversion rates increase. The central inputs into a networked product's growth equation will improve on their own, as a function of the network as opposed to the features of the product—creating an accumulating advantage over time. This is the magic of network effects.

And while I describe each of these network effects independently, in practice they all work together in concert. A more engaged and retained audience will have more opportunities to share the product with their friends, driving up viral growth. A stronger Acquisition Effect means there will be a steady stream of new people to engage the existing community, keeping them more engaged. Stronger monetization might mean that users make more money, which then stimulates more engagement. Amplifying one will often drive the others up as well.

19

THE ENGAGEMENT EFFECT

Scurvy

The modern techniques we use in studying the stickiness and engagement of technology products have their origins in the study of disease.

In 1753, Scottish doctor James Lind published a celebrated paper called "Treatise of Scurvy," one of the first reported clinical trials in history. In it, he described his studies and experiments on scurvy while he served as ship surgeon on the HMS *Salisbury*, a Royal Navy warship. At the time, scurvy was one of the most devastating diseases for sailors in the navy. It is said that more sailors would die of scurvy than of contact with the enemy, and it had become a major barrier in conducting warfare and trade over long distances.

In his paper, Lind described one of the first randomized controlled trials in history. He divided twelve men suffering from scurvy symptoms into six pairs, and gave the following mixture on a daily basis: cider, diluted sulfuric acid, sea water, and vinegar. One lucky pair, the experiment group, also got two oranges and a lemon. Then Lind would check on how the sailors were doing over time. The improvement in the two receiving vitamin C from the citrus was obvious, and by the end of the trial, when they had run out of fruit, this pair were almost fully recovered.

These techniques were so powerful that hundreds of years later, they are the basis for how tech companies measure and optimize for engagement and retention for their products.

In the modern usage, users are often divided into separate groups—called cohorts—which then allow them to be measured separately. Instead of tracking for scurvy, instead users are monitored on how active they are within a product—how many are still around a day after they sign up, versus seven days or thirty days? Are newer users having a better experience over the first few weeks, compared to an older cohort that was using a buggier version of the product?

These graphs—often called "cohort retention curves"—are the foundational method for understanding whether a product is working or not. And we have James Lind and his study of scurvy to thank for the technique.

The Sad Truth about the Stickiness of New Products

Retention is the most critical metric in understanding a product, but most of the time, the data is not pretty. When you look at the engagement data for the entire industry, the data has told the same story over and over—users don't stick to their apps. One study[50] published on tech blog TechCrunch told the story in its headline: "Nearly 1 in 4 people abandon mobile apps after only one use." The authors looked at data from 37,000 users to show that a large percentage of users would quit an app after just a single try. Unfortunately, I've found similar results. In collaboration with Ankit Jain, a former product manager at Google Play, I published an essay titled "Losing 80% of mobile users is normal," which illustrated the rapid decay that happens right after a new user signs up to a product.

Of the users who install an app, 70 percent of them aren't active the next day, and by the first three months, 96 percent of users are no longer active. The shape of the retention curve matters a lot—ideally, the curve levels out over time, indicating that some users consistently come back. But this is not true for the average app—its curve consistently falls over time, eventually whittling itself to zero.

The brutal conclusion is that the usual result for most apps is failure—but there are, of course, exceptions. This is why out of the 5+ million apps on iOS and Android, just a few hundred have large audiences, and only a few dozen dominate all of people's time and attention. Data from analytics company comScore, revealed that people spend 80 percent with just three apps[51]—and I'm sure you can guess which ones.

As a rough benchmark for evaluating startups at Andreessen Horowitz, I often look for a minimum baseline of 60 percent retention after day 1, 30 percent after day 7, and 15 percent at day 30, where the curve eventually levels out. It's usually only the networked products that can exceed these numbers. That's because networked products are unique in that they often become stickier over time, which cancels out the inevitable customer churn.

In rare but exceptional cases, the curve will "smile"—meaning that retention and engagement will actually go up over time, and churned users will reactivate. I've learned that when a startup shows a smile curve, you should probably try to invest. It's exceedingly rare.

Because of the Engagement network effect, the networked products used as case studies in *The Cold Start Problem* see some of the highest retention curves in the industry—it is a core part of their success. Their unique ability to tap into the Engagement network effect lets them drive up retention over time—first, by creating new use cases as the network develops; then by reinforcing the core "loop" of the product; and lastly, by reactivating churned users. I'll unpack how these levers work.

How New Use Cases Drive More Engagement

The first lever comes from the Engagement Effect's ability to raise retention curves by layering on use cases. As an example, when a small team first adopts a chat product like Slack—before the rest of the company does—they might just use a few channels to discuss items relevant to the team. But as more of the company also onboards employees onto the product, new use cases are unlocked. There might be a "Pool Party" channel, as we had at Uber, with thousands of employees chatting about random topics. Or channels for each office, to announce location-specific events for San Francisco versus New York versus other cities. At Andreessen Horowitz, we have channels like #2030 about cool technology trends that might affect our near future, or #books and #movies-tv to share our favorite reads and Netflix specials. Each of these new channels signifies a new use case—one might be around company announcements, or socializing, or working on projects together. The more people on the Slack network, the more likely these additional use cases will develop.

What starts as infrequent and noncommittal usage often deepens into daily usage. Luckily, nudging users into more frequent usage can be part of the product design. The key is to target relevant users with messaging or incentives, or otherwise to try out new use cases over time. This moves them from low engagement into high engagement.

But to do this, teams have to do what Dropbox did and find a way to segment higher versus lower value users. Monetary value might not be the right segmentation—it might be something else, like frequency, lifetime value, use cases, or some other defining characteristic.

For example, LinkedIn's user base was tiered based on frequent usage, as my good friend Aatif Awan—the former vice president of growth at LinkedIn—describes:

> At LinkedIn, we segmented our users as:
> - Active the last 7 days out of the last week

- *Active the last 6 days*
- *Active the last 5 days*

. . . and so on. This let us dig into each segment separately and understand their needs, motivations, and what it would take to move them up in engagement.[52]

Based on this segmentation, product teams can search for a "lever" that will move users from one level of engagement to the other. But it's often not all the same lever—depending on the type of users, and their motivations and intent, different approaches will work. Awan describes this in the context of LinkedIn's strategy to increase frequency:

The levers you use to increase the engagement of an infrequent user are different than deepening engagement for a power user. Early users might just need a few more connections to colleagues at their company. Power users might need to discover advanced features on search, recruiting, and creating groups, so that they have new and more powerful ways to connect with people. Segmenting our users gives us the granularity to connect the right features and user education to impact their usage.

These insights are often found by examining a power user segment—or HVAs, in Dropbox's parlance—and trying to understand what makes them unique. Perhaps they're using a particular feature, or engaging with the network in a certain way. It might be tempting to force every user to then use the product this way, but unfortunately correlation does not mean causation. You don't want to study fire departments and fires and conclude that the former cause the latter!

This is where the A/B test becomes so valuable. Just as James Lind did with her scurvy experiment, users can be randomly divided into separate cohorts and given different experiences. A correlation like "High-value LinkedIn users connect to other users at a higher rate than low-value users" can then be converted into a real lever. It's powerful to be able to state "When LinkedIn users connect with more people in their early days on the product, they are likely to become high value later on."

The question then becomes how to get these users to take the various actions that will make them higher value. This usually happens in the form of educating users—with content or otherwise—or simply introducing and promoting new features. In LinkedIn's case, a new feature might be a prominent suggestion to an early user to connect with people from their own company, to help them form their initial network. Content and communications might be a series of how-to videos teaching effective use of LinkedIn's connection features. And an incentive might look like a free subscription when the user completes certain actions. A product road map can be generated with hundreds of these ideas, large and small, and then prioritized.

In Dropbox's case, this segmentation revealed that a user who has installed the product across multiple devices—home and work computers, or on their mobile devices—is more valuable than someone who just has a single device and uses the service for backup. Better yet, high-value users often share folders and collaborate with other users, particularly for work purposes. As I described earlier, Dropbox segmented their users by value—High-Value Actives and Low-Value Actives, as opposed to LinkedIn's frequency-oriented segmentation. To encourage users to take these high-value actions, Dropbox could improve the functionality of syncing and sharing. It could send or show educational content, showing users the fastest way to get set up on multiple devices. Or it could use incentives—free storage, for instance—to compel users to properly set up their accounts.

Engagement Loops

As I've discussed, the Engagement network effect makes products stickier over time, but how? This process can be modeled as an "engagement loop" that describes how users derive value from others in a network in a step-by-step process.

For a social or communication product, the loop often starts with a content creator posting or sending content. The content is then sent to everyone they are connected to, and depending on the size of the network, they get a nice stream of likes and comments back. That's the payoff that keeps them going. Marketplace products have a similar loop, where sellers list their goods, which are then seen by buyers browsing the listings. The bigger the network of customers, the more likely an interested buyer will see it, which then increases the probability that a transaction happens. Collaboration products in the workplace function in a similar way—a member of the hard side of the network initiates by sharing a project or document, and their coworkers engage to close the loop. These engagement loops are often best visualized, step by step, as a series of actions that tie into each other. Improving any step in the loop benefits all downstream actions.

Conceptualizing network effects in this manner helps us understand why the Cold Start Problem exists, from a user's point of view. If the network is too sparse, the loop is broken—not enough users will see a photo to reply with likes, and not enough buyers will see a listing to purchase a product. If a loop is broken, then the user churns, which further cascades the network problem.

Users need to trust the loop to rely on it. If the network is too small or too inactive and the loop breaks, then users will be less likely to use it in the future. After all, if you text a friend on a new messaging app and they don't respond, or if you share a document at work but don't get a reply, then trust goes down. But in the positive case, if a network scales and the connections get denser, then the loop gets tighter—content creators get more social feedback, marketplace sellers get more purchases at higher prices, and users of workplace tools can effectively collaborate with their coworkers.

The Escape Velocity phase is about accelerating these loops, by making each stage of the loop perform better. For a marketplace listing, how might you make creating a listing easier? How might you make sure more potential buyers see the listing? Can the purchase process be one click, so that the conversion rates are higher, and the seller sees more purchases? For a workplace chat product, how do you make sure the right people are in the channel where you post your content? How do you create easy, positive feedback to encourage people to continue participating—whether that's emojis, likes, or something else? Do your users have enough connections to consistently close the loop, and if not, how do you quickly get a critical density of networks around them? Answering these questions generates a long stream of potential experiments and ideas to try. It's incredibly useful to lay out an engagement loop, one screen at a time, and brainstorm ways to increase each step— this method is at the heart of what I typically do when advising startups on creating higher stickiness.

Back from the Dead

The Engagement network effect has the superpower of being able to re-activate churned users, which in turn grows the active user count. Based on data I've seen from startups, a typical product might only have 25–50 percent of its registered users active in any given month, expressed as a ratio of actives divided by signups. In other words, up to 75 percent of users are inactive at any given point, most of whom will never come back. The ability to reactivate users provides a powerful counterweight to churn, keeping this ratio in check over time.

This is an important tool that is unique to networked products. Traditional products that lack networks often struggle with this, because they rely on spammy emails, discounts, and push notifications to entice users back. This usually doesn't work, and company-sent communications rank among the lowest clickthrough rate messages. Networked products, on the other hand, have the unique capability to reactivate these users by enlisting active users to bring them back. Even if you don't open the app on a given day, other users in the network may inter-act with you—commenting or liking your past content, or sending you a message. Getting an email notification that says your boss just shared a folder with you is a lot more compelling than a marketing message. A notification that a close friend just joined an app you tried a month ago is a lot more engaging than an announcement about new features. And the more dense the network is around a churned user, the more likely they are to receive this type of interaction.

These churned users are sometimes called "dark nodes." When they are surrounded by deeply engaged colleagues and friends, even if they've been inactive for months, they are often flipped back into an ac-tive user. These frequent network-driven interactions can drive further investment by the user over time, eventually tipping an inactive user into a very active one. Initially, a Dropbox user might engage infrequently because they are only on one important shared folder. But when their colleagues eventually share a dozen more important project folders, Dropbox might become a critical part of their workflow. The bigger the network, the more likely an infrequent user continues to get reengaged, and over time, that might make all the difference.

To amplify the Engagement Effect as it relates to reactivation, the key question to ask is, what is the experience of a churned user? If you're inactive, what kinds of notifications are you getting from other users, and are they compelling enough to bring you back? Almost always, churned users don't receive any communication at all. You can boost reactivation success rate significantly just by sending a weekly digest of the activity in a user's network, or "Your friend X just joined" notifica-tions. The other question to ask is, if a user wants to reactivate, how hard is it? At Uber, we had a staggering statistic where several million users were failing their password recovery per week—how do you make this much easier, and treat reactivation with the same seriousness as the sign-up process?

While reactivation is typically not a concern for new products—they should focus on new users, since their count of lapsed users won't be large—for products that have hit Escape Velocity, there will be a pool of many millions of users to draw upon. Reengaging them can become as big a growth lever as acquiring new users.

The Impact of the Engagement Effect

When teams are asked to improve their product's retention rate, they often think that the answer will lie in some magical product improvement. The Engagement network effect, and its underlying loops, provide a systematic way to tackle the problem.

The early work on scurvy gave us the foundational tools. But instead of providing citrus and measuring for malnutrition, tech companies can reason by analogy: create user cohorts by levels of engagement, and analyze what differentiates high value users from lower value ones. These start out as correlations, so use A/B testing to prove causality—once the best levers are found, test many variations of these ideas. Rinse and repeat, to systematically strengthen the Engagement network effect.

The good news is that the Engagement Effect will automatically kick in as colleagues, influencers, and other people join the network But getting these people onboard can be its own challenge.

20

THE ACQUISITION EFFECT

PayPal

The second force I'll outline is the Acquisition network effect—the ability for a network to attract new customers as it scales. This is one of the most magical, explosive forces in the technology world: viral growth.

The PayPal Mafia

When I first moved to the Bay Area more than a decade ago, it was one of my goals to understand the "secret sauce" that spawned so many top consumer companies. I was told that the PayPal Mafia held the answers. This small but highly influential alumni group founded tech giants LinkedIn, Eventbrite, YouTube, Yelp, and Affirm, among others. It was in conversations with members of the early PayPal founding team that I first learned of a unique approach to launching products. They didn't simply use traditional marketing techniques like branding and advertising but had developed a systematic and quantitative approach that emphasized viral growth.

They took the typical form of viral marketing—often emphasizing squishy notions like "buzz"—and made it a science. Many of the PayPal Mafia startups utilized some form of viral growth to reach millions of users. One example is the embeddable player for YouTube, that could be added to any blog or MySpace profile. Or LinkedIn's use of email contacts to connect with your work colleagues. Or Eventbrite's emailed invitations to an audience of potential attendees. Perhaps it shouldn't be a surprise that it was the PayPal alumni who mastered these dynamics, because payments are a naturally viral interaction—after all, there's no better value proposition than someone wanting to give you money!

Max Levchin, cofounder of PayPal, was one of the people I met during my first year in the Bay Area. By then, he had already started and sold PayPal to eBay, and was onto his next adventure. By the time I reconnected with him for this book, Max had gone on to start Affirm, a fintech startup—a portfolio company of a16z's—which would go on to an IPO and have a market capitalization in the tens of billions.

I asked him about the magic in the early days about payments and viral growth. Not surprisingly, there was a more complicated back-story. PayPal started with a product called FieldLink, which let people send and receive money on Palm Pilots and other PDAs (personal digital assistants). These were funny little devices. They were the predecessors to today's smartphones and had contacts, notes, calendars, and so on, but importantly, no internet access. Not a ton of people had these devices initially, which created an obstacle—you need the sender and receiver of payments to both have PDAs for this to make sense. Field-Link was not going to work, and in the search for a new idea, PayPal was born.

Max described the early days:

Our original idea related to letting people send payments over their PDAs, but eventually our idea evolved: Let people send money

across the internet, no handheld devices required. This became Pay-
Pal, and could grow much more virally, because you just had to click
on a link, sign up, and then you could send or receive money across
the internet. In fact, you had to sign up if you received money, and
once that happened, you might send money to others, who might
create even more signups.[53]

Offering peer-to-peer payments is great in theory, but in the early
days PayPal's growth was still slow. The value proposition was vague,
since the web was still in its infancy. Users didn't quite know why they
would pay each other—the product had not found its killer use case.
David Sacks, now a venture capitalist, was at the time leading product
at PayPal, and describes the situation in the early days of November
1999: "Without a clear picture of the ideal user, we didn't know who to
target, and adoption had been tepid."[54] That's right, in the early days of
the internet, people needed to be taught to send each other money—it
was not yet clear that this was a useful service.

Sacks described how an inbound email from an eBay PowerSeller
changed all of that. The seller had designed a "We accept PayPal"
button by themselves, and asked to use it on their auction listings. For
David and team, it was a surprising use case—they didn't quite know
the ins and outs of the auction site, and why people would use it. Upon
searching the eBay website for other mentions of "paypal" it was clear
that hundreds of listings mentioned the company as a means of payment.

There was natural virality emerging, and it was up to the team to
supercharge it. The team responded to the inbound email, saying yes to
the use of the PayPal logo, and furthermore, integrated this idea deeply
into the product. Sacks describes:

To reduce friction further, we allowed sellers to enter their eBay
credentials and we would automatically insert the button into all
their auctions. In other words, we productized the idea.

Soon enough, "We accept PayPal" badges began to appear on more and more eBay listings. Buyers (and other sellers) would find a listing, sign up for PayPal, and then embed the badge onto their own listings—and this repeated over and over. As this started to work, the team used every lever to amplify its traction, including money.

Max Levchin described to me how this worked:

Growth started to pick up after we gave $10 to every PayPal user who invited a friend, and also dropped $10 into the account of the person as soon as they signed up. The motivation to sign up was strong, but so was the motivation to continue inviting. People were already inviting each other, but this incentive supercharged viral growth. While it might have seemed like this would burn a lot of money, it increased engagement as well—we saw users send money back and forth within the network, and every time it happened, we recouped a little bit of the incentive. It was more cash efficient than you'd think.

The eBay community was a tight-knit network, and PayPal quickly spread. The initial product had fewer than 10,000 users. Within a few months, PayPal had 100,000 users. A few months after that, 1 million. Within a year, 5 million. PayPal used viral growth to take on one of the most important problems that any new product faces, and succeeded such that today, its valuation is over $300 billion—more than six times that of its former parent company eBay. PayPal's early days are a perfect example of the Acquisition network effect, which utilizes the participants of a network to acquire new users—and the bigger the network, the better it works.

Some of the most viral products ever created—like WhatsApp—have been able to generate over 1 million installs per day, without paid marketing. Contrast this to traditional products that often have to buy advertising, take on partnerships, and undertake other expensive marketing activities to scale their user acquisition. It's hard to hit hundreds of thousands of new users a day when you have to pay for each one.

These new users are important to fuel the overall growth of product. Early-stage companies, in particular, are on a kind of treadmill where they must bring in enough new users each week or month to offset the ones they are losing to churn. And on top of this, they need to add enough users to build top-line growth to hit aggressive targets. While it is tempting to throw money at the problem, without a scalable, repeatable source of new users, it is likely that budgets will get out of control and advertising channels will eventually tap out. Viral growth builds on the power of networks to acquire users, often free of charge.

Product-Driven Viral Growth

Viral growth is deeply misunderstood—you might read the phrase and think, is this the same thing that happens when a funny video "goes viral"? Or maybe it makes you think of an ad agency organizing a clever stunt to share on social media, like a flash mob where dozens of people simultaneously begin to dance.

No, what I'm referring to is completely different. What ad agencies have called "viral marketing" is usually taking consumer goods or services—with no network effects—and building an advertising campaign around them, anchored by a bit of shareable content. What I'm referring to—network-driven viral growth—is much more powerful.

Networked products are unique because they can embed their viral growth into the product experience itself. When a product like Dropbox has a built-in feature like folder sharing, it can spread on its own. PayPal's badges and core user-to-user payments accomplishes the same. This is the Product/Network Duo at work again, where the product has features to attract people to the network, while the network brings more value to the product. Workplace collaboration products like Slack ask you to invite your colleagues into your chat, and photo-sharing apps like Instagram make it easy to invite and connect to your Facebook friends. They can tap into your phone's contacts, integrate with your company's internal employee directory, or tap into the sharing widgets built into your phone. This is software, not just building a buzzy, shareable video.

Amplifying the Viral Factor, One Step at a Time

Just as the Engagement network effect can be thought of as a step-by-step loop, there is an equivalent framework for the Acquisition Effect as well. For example, consider this process: A new user hears about a service, signs up, finds value in it, and shares the product with their friends/colleagues, who also sign up. These new users then repeat the same steps—this is the viral loop. This loop is fundamentally created within the product experience by software engineers writing code, which makes it different from a fun, viral video—because it's software, it can be measured, tracked, and optimized to make it more effective. This makes the Acquisition Effect such a potent force.

To make these loops actionable for product teams, you can break them down into more granular steps, and A/B test them. For example, Uber's viral loop for drivers involved a referral program that was exposed during the onboarding process. There were a dozen or so screens on the app that a driver moved through during the sign-up process—entering their phone number creating a password, uploading their driver's license, etc. Each of these steps could be optimized so that more users would pass through. Then, drivers would be presented with an explanation on how to refer their friends, and what type of bonus they'd get for doing so. This could be improved as well—should the message offer $100 to sign up, or $300? If you invite five people should you get a bonus? Should an invite mention the name of the inviter, or just focus on Uber, as an app? On the sign-up page, should you ask for a driver's email or their phone number, or both?

A product team can brainstorm hundreds of these ideas and systematically try them, measuring for conversion rates and the number of invites sent. Optimizing each of these steps with A/B tests might only boost each step's conversion by 5 percent here or 10 percent there, but it's a compounding effect. Hundreds of A/B tests later, the millions of dollars you might be spending on acquiring customers is made substantially more efficient.

Measuring the Acquisition Network Effect

To increase the Acquisition Effect, you have to be able to directly measure it. The good news is that viral growth can be rolled up into one number. Here's how you calculate it: Let's say you've built a new productivity tool for sharing notes, and after it launches, 1,000 users download the new app. A percentage of these users invite their colleagues and friends, and over the next month, 500 users download and sign up—what happens next? Well, those 500 users then invite their friends, and get 250 to sign up, who create another 125 sign-ups, and so on.

Pay attention to the ratios between each set of users—1000 to 500 to 250. This ratio is often called the viral factor, and in this case can be calculated at 0.5, because each cohort of users generates 0.5 of the next cohort. In this example, things are looking good—starting with 1,000 users with a viral factor of 0.5 leads to a total of 2,000 users by the end of the amplification—meaning an amplification rate of 2x. A higher ratio is better, since it means each cohort is more efficiently bringing on the next batch of users.

Once you have calculated this metric, you can use A/B testing and implement new product features to try to improve it. This might involve easier sharing to social media, or multiple SMS reminders after an invite is sent. Perhaps the landing page is optimized to ask for less information upfront to get prospective users to sign up in just a few clicks. If you increase the viral factor of your product to 0.6, then the product will 2.5x the users you bring. At 0.7, then the product will 3.3x the users you bring. The real magic starts to happen as the viral factor starts to approach 1. After all, at a viral factor of 0.95, 1,000 users show up and then bring 950 of their friends, who will then bring 900, and so on—ultimately the amplification will be 20x. This is the mathematical expression of when a product "goes viral" and starts growing incredibly fast. The viral factor can also be above 1, in rare cases, but this typically can't last for long—eventually market saturation and changing user demographics start to drag down the metrics.

Once a metric like this has been defined, it becomes much easier to understand what changes in the product drive it higher. Retention is usually the strongest lever. In the example of PayPal, if a user continues to send money over weeks and months and years, each transaction might help bring in new users onto their platform. In other words, their viral factor grows over time, slowly inching toward a magical >1.0 metric. On the other hand, if users are always one-and-dones, then they have to invite a ton of users in one big spammy blast in order for the product to propagate—which isn't ideal. However, that's not to say that innovations that generate large blasts of users—like using email contacts to easily invite friends, or referral programs with big bonuses—don't help. They definitely do, but it's a combination of big virality projects, lots of little optimizations, and strong retention that ultimately drives big viral factor numbers.

Measuring and optimizing viral growth in this way may make it feel like a spreadsheet project, but I assure you it is much more copywriting, user psychology, and product design. The teams working on growth must be aware of what's worked in the past—there have been viral loops built on birthday alarm clocks, sending sheep emoji, comparing personality test results, building photo collages where you tag your friends, and much more. Some of these ideas are based on user psychology, which doesn't change, and can be tweaked and iterated upon for any new product.

In fact, it's the psychological elements, combined with the value proposition of a product, that make the best viral growth strategies difficult to copy. They are often unique to the product itself—making them proprietary and more defensible. Dropbox's folder-sharing viral loop is effective, but only those in a similar product category can utilize the same type of loop. Videoconference software like Zoom makes it easy to add meeting details that include links to the software itself—again, hard to copy unless your product has something to do with meetings. Contrast that to traditional marketing channels like online advertising, which can be bought by practically anyone, naturally driving up costs and lowering effectiveness over time.

Acquisition Can't Exist without Engagement

One important insight is that the Acquisition Effect can exist independently of the Engagement or Economic effect. In other words, you can acquire a lot of customers but still have a network that ultimately isn't sticky. I'll use a historical example to make this point.

Chain letters—yes, the type you still occasionally get via email, or see on social media—have their roots in snail mail, first popularized in the late 1800s. One of the most successful ones, "The Prosperity Club," originated in Denver in the post-Depression 1930s, and asked people to send a dime to a list of others who were part of the club. Of course, you would add yourself to the list as well. The next set of people would return the favor, sending dimes back, and so on and so forth—with the promise that it would eventually generate $1,562.50. This is about $29,000 in 2019 dollars—not bad! The last line says it all: "Is this worth a dime to you?"

It might surprise you that in a world before email, social media, and everything digital, the Prosperity Club chain letter spread incredibly well—so well, in fact, that it reached hundreds of thousands of people within months, within Denver and beyond. There are historical anecdotes of local mail offices being overwhelmed by the sheer volume of letters, and not surprisingly, eventually the US Post Office would make chain letters like Prosperity Club illegal, to stop their spread. It clearly tapped into a Depression zeitgeist of the time, promising "Faith! Hope! Charity!"

This is a clever, viral idea (for its time), and I will also argue that this is an analog version of a network effect from the 1800s, just as telephones and railways were, too. How so? First, chain letters are organized as a network, and can be represented by the list of names that are copied and recopied by each participant. These names are likely to be friends, family, and people in the community, furthering the Prosperity Club's credibility, thereby increasing the engagement level. It follows the classic definition of network effects: the more people who are participating in this chain letter, the better, since you are then more likely to receive dimes. And it even faces the Cold Start Problem: if enough people aren't already on the list and playing along, then it will fail to grow.

However, even if chain letters have network effects, they suffer from being heavily oriented around viral acquisition, and lacking strong retention mechanics. Ultimately the value of these networks is primarily driven by novelty and requires a constant inflow of new people into the chain. Yes, in this way, it's just like multilevel marketing campaigns, Ponzi schemes, and the like. And of course, what happens with both chain letters and Ponzi schemes is that they collapse when the supply of new, novelty-seeking recipients dries up. As a result, existing participants stop getting paid. This in turn causes churn, which then unravels the network entirely. A network needs retention to thrive; it can't just continually add new users.

The Impact of the Acquisition Effect

The cornerstone to amplifying the Acquisition network effect is to understand how one group of users taps into their respective networks to bring in the next group of users. Because these groups of users generally live inside of atomic networks, the other thing that happens is that networks tend to attract other atomic networks. And so on.

There's a reason why the term used for viral growth is to "land and expand"—to build new networks as well as increasing the density of existing networks. By "landing," viral growth can start new atomic networks, as a Dropbox invite from an ad agency to their client brings a new company into the collaboration network. Or, when a WhatsApp group chat invite brings onboard a new set of friends who hadn't previously used the service. But then the product "expands"—increasing the density of a network as all the coworkers in an office ultimately join Dropbox.

It's for this reason that networks built through viral growth are healthier and more engaged than those that are launched in the typical "Big Bang" fashion, as Google+ did years back. Big Bang Launches can be great at landing, but often fail at expanding—and as we discussed, many networks with low density and low engagement will fail. The result of increasing density and engagement isn't just easier new user acquisition, but also stronger Engagement and Economic network effects. That's because these network effects are ultimately derived by the density and size of the network, and as more users join, they naturally become stronger.

I've discussed how the Engagement and Acquisition network effects work, and next, I'll tackle monetization and business models.

21

THE ECONOMIC EFFECT

Credit Bureaus

The final force I'll discuss is the Economic network effect, which is how a business model—including profitability and unit economics—improves over time as a network grows. This is sometimes driven by what are called data network effects—the ability to better understand the value and costs of a customer as a network gets larger. This helps in driving higher efficiency when promotions, incentives, and subsidies into a network. The Economic Effect also can grow revenue by increasing conversion rates, by building features for the network as opposed to tools for the tool. By understanding these systems, product teams can strengthen this important force.

Interestingly enough, lending money is one of the earliest manifestations of this network effect—and to unpack this, let me start with a story from one of the world's earliest human civilizations.

The Network Effects of Lending

Ever since the ancient times, people have been lending each other money. Just look at the Code of Hammurabi, one of the oldest deciphered writings in the world—carved thousands of years ago in 1754 BC to govern commercial interactions via fines and punishments. Law 88 says:

> *If a merchant has given corn on loan, he may take 100 SILA of corn as interest on 1 GUR; if he has given silver on loan, he may take ¹/₆ shekel 6 grains as interest on 1 shekel of silver.*[55]

In other words, this is a law that dictates the maximum interest rate a lender could charge a borrower. And by the way, this is 33.3 percent annually on a loan of grain, and 20 percent on a loan of silver, for all of us who don't do interest calculations in the form of ancient Babylonian measurement units. Not much different from a credit card these days.

While we've been making loans for thousands of years, what's changed in the past few hundred is how we think about creditworthiness. After all, what the Babylonian text leaves unsaid is how to decide if someone should be lent money in the first place. In small communities, the answer often lies in local reputation. But when lending activity scales, we have to look at late 1700s London, where the activity became more formalized. The Industrial Revolution created rapid access to manufactured goods and unlocked consumer spending for clothing, furniture, machinery, and other goods. As many of us have experienced, a large purchase is more easily paid in installments, which in turn drove up the popular use of loans.

What does a merchant do when a potential customer walks into a store and wants to purchase a ton of goods on credit? A solution was offered by the "The Society of Guardians for the Protection of Trade against Swindlers and Sharpers," established in 1776. This society pooled data from 550 merchants to collect information on the reputation of customers. This would make it much harder for a bad customer to defraud multiple merchants. Its key principle: "Every member is bound to communicate to the Society without delay, the Name and Description of any Person who may be unfit to trust." In other words, this was the beginning of credit scores as a means to assess the trustworthiness of a customer for loans—no swindlers or sharpers allowed.

This Society of Guardians was not the only credit bureau—thousands of similar small organizations were formed over the years, collecting individual names and publishing books with various comments and gossip. Modern giants Experian and Equifax grew from these small, local bureaus. Experian started as the Manchester Guardian Society in the early 1800s, eventually acquiring other bureaus to become one of the world's largest. And Equifax grew from a Tennessee grocery store in the late 1800s, where the owners started compiling their own lists of creditworthy consumers. These bureaus tended to combine into larger bureaus over time because of what's often described as a "data network effect." When a bureau works with more merchants, it means more data, which means the risk predictions on loans will be more accurate. This makes it more attractive for additional merchants to join, who contribute even more data, and so on.

Being able to accurately assess lending risk allows the rest of the network to function—consumers can borrow to get the goods they want, merchants can sell their products profitably, and banks can help underwrite the loans. This network is held together by credit bureaus like Equifax and Experian, who centralize consumer data. But improvements in lending risk aren't the only way that the Economic Effect expresses itself—instead, I think of it as a broader idea. As a network grows and gets stronger, it also develops advantages in the form of premium pricing and higher conversion rates, as well as cost improvements, like incentives and risk-taking. I'll talk about some of these other network-based advantages next.

Efficiency over Subsidy

As I've discussed earlier, launching a new network often requires subsidies for the hard side, which are paid back over time. These might be structured as up-front payments to content creators and influencers, to get them to participate on the platform. For example, when Microsoft introduced a new livestreaming service to compete with Twitch, it guaranteed Ninja, a streamer with millions of followers, a deal worth tens of millions. Elsewhere, in the streaming content world, there is an ongoing multibillion-dollar battle between Netflix, Hulu, Amazon, and others to sign exclusive content for their subscription content services. As they build up a base of subscribers, aggregating niche audiences compelled by teen horrors, international documentaries, and more, they are able to more efficiently support the up-front funding of content. This can become a huge advantage that increases over time as the networks get bigger.

Uber made extensive use of this strategy, but in early 2017, it had reached a breaking point.

The company declared it was the year of "Efficiency over Subsidy." The prior year had been a tough, long year—the company got a "silver medal" in China, eventually combining with Didi after burning nearly $50 million a week in rider and driver incentives to launch the market. This effort totaled over a billion dollars of cash burn that year. The mood of the company had shifted from "growth at all costs" into creating a path to profitability. It was here, at the beginning of 2017, that Travis used the weekly forum to announce a series of dramatic new goals, focused first and foremost on "Efficiency over Subsidy"—improving Uber's unit economics.

One of the biggest sources of spend was driver incentives. Uber's driver incentives constituted much of its billion-dollar-a-year spend on marketplace subsidies—particularly hourly guarantees for drivers ("$30/hour for the next 4 weeks when you drive for Uber"), to provide enough availability for riders.

These incentives were used all the time: First, to subsidize the driver side of a market when it was first getting launched. Second, to supplement slow seasons, especially January right after the holidays, so that drivers would not sign up during the busy holiday season and then subsequently all churn the next month. And third, as a competitive tool to make drivers stickier to the Uber platform over rivals—offering higher guarantees when new entrants came into markets, or with structured incentives ("Do X trips and get $Y"—called DxGy at Uber). The math around Uber's marketplace subsidies looked like this, at a high level:

- Offer a $25/hour guarantee to drivers
- A small network might provide 1 trip per hour
- Let's say drivers earn, on average, $10/trip
- This means drivers can earn $10/hour, so to hit the guarantee, the company must subsidize an additional +$15/hour to make up the difference
- This means the "Burn per Trip" is $15. Ouch!

On the other hand, once the network was fully grown, the density of demand and supply means that Uber could provide far more trips to drivers:

- Same guarantee: $25/hour to drivers
- However, a larger network provides 2 trips per hour to drivers
- At $10/trip, the larger network generates $20/hour—much better!
- At $20/hour and a $25/hour guarantee, the subsidy is only $5/hour
- In other words, only $2.50 Burn per Trip

This is a clear example of the Economic Effect, where a larger network has much higher efficiency than a small one—the company burns significantly less per trip, because the network can deliver more demand on an hourly basis. It also means that a bigger network could give even larger incentives, allowing it to efficiently win over drivers who are the hard side of the network. These drivers in turn provide better, cheaper service to riders who are the easy side. Furthermore, a larger network can stimulate the rider side by cutting prices, as Uber did on a yearly basis every January during its early years. After the holidays, with all the parties and New Year's celebrations, usage in January is sluggish. Because consumers are sensitive to price, lower prices meant a lot more engagement, which increased trips per hour and in turn kept hourly earnings high. Drivers were placated with a temporary hourly guarantee while the market adjusted. A smaller network might be nervous to do this if they feel their burn per trip is already too high.

This is an important dynamic in rideshare, but it's also true if you think about getting content creators onto a video platform, or paying app developers to build new products against your new API platform. As a network grows over time, its ability to subsidize the ecosystem grows as well. Many networks have this type of dynamic that drives cash inflows and outflows. After all, subsidies are just another word for discounts, promotions, and other kinds of sales that companies give to customers—all of which provide incentives for users to buy a product or service. Almost every large marketplace company is built on an underutilized asset, whether that's unused real estate in the case of Airbnb, a car that's sitting idle for Uber, or unused time for many labor marketplaces. Marketplaces allow owners of these idle assets the ability to monetize them more efficiently as the network grows larger.

This form of Economic network effect can be strengthened as more participants join a network, because the additional data allows for personalization and targeting. In Uber's case, instead of a fixed $25/hour guarantee across the whole network, drivers can receive personalized offers based on sophisticated machine learning models. In YouTube's case, creators can be paid different amounts based on the quality of their viewer engagement. For a bottom-up SaaS product, data can be used to determine when and how to target customers for upsells. These can all move the needle, improving the business model of a networked product as it scales.

Higher Conversion Rates as the Network Grows

For many networked products, the heart of the business model is some kind of conversion—whether that's a collectibles marketplace trying to increase the number of transactions for sneakers or basketball cards, or a workplace product converting users from free to paid. But the Economic network effect states that for networked products, conversion can go up over time as the network grows.

Dropbox's High-Value Active Users is an example of this—users were found to upgrade into paid subscriptions when they had collaborative use cases with their coworkers, like shared folders and collaboration around documents. If sharing folders on Dropbox becomes the norm in a team, the more paid users emerge, and eventually the entire company might upgrade. Premium features can be designed in a way where they are more useful as the network gets larger, as opposed to being based on individual usage. Thus, the larger the network, the greater the incentive to convert to premium.

Similarly, Slack's pricing allows users to upgrade for a number of collaborative features: better voice calling, searchable message history for all your coworkers, and more. Each of these features becomes more useful as organizations adopt Slack as the standard way to communicate, which in turn drives more conversions from free accounts into paid. Fareed Mosavat, who headed up the growth teams at Slack in the company's early years, described why this happened:

> When there's a premium feature that is useful for everyone using Slack, it means that anyone on the team—not just the IT staff— has a reason to upgrade. The more people in the company that use

Slack, and the more engagement means it's more likely someone might pull out their credit card and decide to unlock key features for everyone.[56]

It's not just workplace collaboration tools that have higher conversion rates, it's also networked products like marketplaces and app stores—though for different reasons. When more sellers are part of a marketplace, there's more selection, availability, and comprehensive reviews/ratings—meaning people are more likely to find what they want, and each session is more likely to convert into a purchase.

Social platforms often monetize users by providing social status, but status has value when there's more people in a network. For example, on Tinder, users can send a "Super Like," which lets a potential match know that you really like them. A feature like this is most useful once there's a rich network of potential suitors and matches, giving users more of a reason to try to stand out. Same with virtual goods in multiplayer games like Fortnite, which has generated hundreds of millions in revenue on "emotes"—the virtual dances that differentiate a player. This only holds value if many of your friends play and appreciate the premium emotes you've purchased. As a result, a more developed network creates an incentive for people to invest in their standing within the game—this is the Economic Effect at work.

The Impact of the Economic Effect

The Economic network effect, alongside its siblings in acquisition and engagement, provide a strong defense against potential upstarts. By acquiring and engaging large networks of users, a new competitor has to be significantly better than the status quo. But furthermore, the Economic Effect means that the leading network often has a better business model. Products with a strong Economic Effect are able to maintain premium pricing as their networks grow, because switching costs become higher for participants who might be looking to join other networks. Google is able to use their auction mechanics in their advertising platform to charge very high fees—sometimes hundreds of dollars per click—because their network of advertisers, publishers, and consumers is unrivaled.

Widespread viral adoption of products also means that price shopping becomes less of a problem for a market leader versus its small competitors. If a product like Dropbox becomes very widely used throughout a company, it will be hard to force them to all use a different cloud-storage product, even if all of its features are similar. When a networked product becomes dominant, typically the alternatives—even when they have the same features—just won't be considered a substitute. As a result, Dropbox will feel less pressure to match the lower pricing of a new competitor. It may be easy to copy features, but it's nearly impossible to copy a network. The winners end up with pricing power, and generate enormous economic benefits.

It might seem that premium pricing is a bad thing, but for many networks like marketplace companies, cryptocurrencies, and payment networks, the users of the network actually win as well. If eBay becomes the trusted, primary place to trade collectibles, then higher conversion rates and higher prices will benefit the sellers. They will make more money, and build their own businesses. When startups like Patreon and Substack create the ability for creators to earn a living by creating content on YouTube or via premium email newsletters, all parties benefit.

The Economic network effect is a powerful force that strengthens a product's business model over time. It allows the leading network to more efficiently subsidize participation, increase conversion rates, and maintain premium pricing. Smaller networks compete at a huge disadvantage once these larger networks hit Escape Velocity. When combined with the Acquisition and Engagement network effects, this trio of forces creates a huge advantage in the market that's difficult to overcome.

However, this trio of network effects does not create permanent invincibility in the market. While a large network often enjoys years of uncontested dominance during the scaling phase, eventually it gets harder. So hard, in fact, that growth might slow to zero.

PART V

THE CEILING

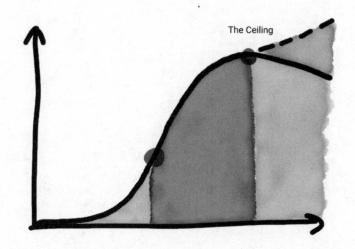

The Ceiling

22

TWITCH

Hitting the ceiling is painful, especially after years of endless growth. But as a product reaches scale, its growth curve eventually reaches a point where it teeters on the edge between expansion and contraction—bursting into expansion during some phases, and then contracting in other. An exponential growth curve turns into a squiggle. Why? Because there are negative forces that appear during the late stage of a network's life cycle. Market Saturation. Churn from early users. Bad behavior from trolls, spammers, and fraudsters. Lower-quality engagement from new users. Regulatory action. A degraded product experience, as too many users join. When users are leaving a network as fast as new users sign up, then top-line growth naturally slows.

This is why the growth curves of the best products are rarely smooth. Instead, the trajectories of even the top products—Facebook, Twitch, and others—grow in fits and starts. When a ceiling is hit, product teams scramble to address the underlying causes. Ship the right innovative features, and the ceiling is pushed off—only to return again awhile later in a different form. But when teams stumble at this stage, then the entire network weakens. Network effects can unravel just as fast as they gathered, pulling down acquisition, engagement, and monetization all at once. Hitting the ceiling hurts.

Twitch is the result of the efforts of a couple of friends to maneuver their startup, then called Justin.tv, past one such growth ceiling. In doing so, Emmett Shear and Kevin Lin, alongside their friends Justin Kan, Michael Seibel, and Kyle Vogt, built Twitch into one of the most iconic technology startups of the past decade. Their eventual exit to Amazon for $970 million would just be the beginning of the company's rise. Today Twitch reaches hundreds of millions of active users who watch millions of streamers play games, dance, talk, paint, and more. It is now worth many times its sale price.

But earlier on, in 2010, the future was not so clear. The predecessor to Twitch—called Justin.tv—had grown to millions of users but had hit a ceiling. The original idea concept for the product was to focus on streaming video of all types, not just gaming. It had grown well, but plateaued, and the team was getting restless. CEO and cofounder Justin Kan described the situation:

About the end of 2010, the company turned profitable. We did a ton of hard work to make it profitable, but we were at an impasse. We weren't growing very much. Actually, we weren't growing at all. When something's not growing on the Internet, it's basically on the brink of declining, precipitously.[57]

Up to that point, Justin.tv had been a general video streaming network. It had a colorful founding story, with its CEO Justin Kan, walking around with a camera mounted on a baseball hat, broadcasting his life on a laptop connected to multiple cellular networks inside a backpack. Justin was the first streaming video creator on the platform, and the viewers consisted of mostly tech insiders who'd watch his life—this was the service's first atomic network.

It was through watching Justin.tv that I got to know Justin, along with his cofounders Emmett Shear and Kevin Lin. I watched them work via a livestream, just as I was working on my own startup. It was impressive to see them build Justin.tv. The tools that allowed Justin to walk around and stream from the camera on his baseball cap were eventually repurposed to let anyone stream. This allowed the first atomic network—Justin and tech viewers—to jump into the next set of networks.

With this, the product evolved into a general streaming platform, with an eclectic mix of people producing content on everything from singing and dancing, sports broadcasts, and of course, video games. I remember watching a bootleg NFL game or two—a popular activity before the days every media company had a streaming app. Justin.tv was moderately successful in its early years, but retention wasn't strong enough and growth eventually stalled at a few million users.

Stalling at a few million users—particularly with a profitable business—may seem like a good problem to have, but for an ambitious, young team that was looking for new challenges, it was getting boring. If Justin.tv was going to stay flat, they might as well work on other startup ideas that might have more potential. They could have gone to work at one of the big, successful technology companies that were seeing more growth. Or they could try to evolve Justin.tv into something bigger—and luckily for the world, this was the option they picked. To break through the ceiling, it was time to scale the product and take a bigger bet. But how? The team decided to go after a few opportunities all at once.

First, part of the team would work on mobile video and streaming—eventually called Socialcam. The core Justin.tv product would still be maintained, so some team members continued to work on that. Second, there was a small team, led by Emmett Shear and Kevin Lin, that would focus on video games. Gaming content already existed on Justin.tv, but it was a tiny amount of the traffic—maybe only 2–3 percent of the overall mix. It existed as part of the main website, styled in retro gaming pixel art-themed style, with a highly engaged audience that clamored for more features and better support for their needs. After interviewing dozens of power users, Emmett and Kevin charted a path that would evolve both the product and the network forward.

Thus, Xarth.tv—yes, that's what Twitch was originally called—was born. Unfortunately for the team, the board of directors hated the plan. This new plan would turn a profitable startup into one losing millions of dollars, and it wasn't yet obvious it would work. And yet the team forged ahead, knowing that a spurt of energy and investment was needed to reignite growth.

As Emmett would recount to me at Twitch's purple-clad offices several years later, this new strategy had some key differences to Justin.tv's original one:

> *We did a lot different with Twitch than Justin.tv. The biggest thing was to focus on streamers, whereas originally it was more about the audience. This meant we worked on tools for streamers, which we improved over time. Making money was important to streamers, even small amounts, so we added tipping features. This was a big deal, because Justin.tv gave streamers some social status by having lots of viewers, but it was a big deal to even be able to make an extra $50/month. We also redesigned the whole website to allow streamers to be discovered based on which game they were playing, sorted in a way that rewarded the most popular streamers. By focusing on games, we could make all of these changes in a way that served our streamers and audience much better.*[58]

Many of these changes were just tweaks to Justin.tv's features, but there were also deep investments in the product that would specifically benefit streamers. For example, many of them wanted to push out high-definition streams of their gameplay, rather than the lower-resolution versions that were common during that time. Watching someone play video games can be complex, with dozens of characters on the screen at a given time, and the high-resolution helped viewers follow the action. Streamers could also be more easily found if content was organized by the game they were playing, so the team did that, adding categories for League of Legends, PUBG, Grand Theft Auto, and other popular games at the time. Twitch also decided to sort the list of streamers by the number of people watching, so that the most popular streamers—usually the most entertaining—would be shown to more users. All of these product changes made it easier for the best and most popular streamers to quickly gain a following.

But the changes weren't limited to the product—a new partnerships team was also started to provide white-glove service to top streamers and up-and-comers. Twitch began to participate in large esports tournaments—in particular, the popular League of Legends events that would come to draw a hundred million people. The company also eventually started their own annual conference, TwitchCon, which became a real-life venue for viewers to meet their favorite streamers.

Twitch streamers came from many places, but the team initially targeted YouTube. The early theory was that creators like Day9—who focused on popular real-time strategy game Starcraft—would switch from uploading videos to streaming in real time, and could bring their thousands of fans over to the new platform. The Twitch team asked popular YouTubers to refer others that would want to try the new platform, and built a small base of streamers in time for their launch at E3 in 2011. This theory turned out to be wrong—in the longer term, homegrown streamers on Twitch would come to dominate the network. The skills needed to be entertaining in real time are different than the skills needed to edit and upload videos. These Twitch-native streamers would ultimately turn into a defensive moat for the business, as this network prevented YouTube and other video platforms from coming into streaming as easily.

In the end, what mattered was that Twitch was a highly engaging experience for streamers, even if they had a small audience. The new features and functionality were built on the observation that the atomic network for Twitch could be as few as just one streamer and one viewer watching them. Kevin Lin, Twitch's cofounder and ex-COO, described this dynamic to me when we got together at his Corona Heights house in San Francisco:

Playing video games with even one Twitch viewer is way more fun than playing by yourself. If they're watching and chatting while you play, there's a human connection that you want to come back for.[59]

Of course, it's fun to have one viewer, but even more fun to have more. And the depth of the experience for a streamer gets even stronger with more viewers as the economic angle is added. Kevin added:

The real magic starts to happen once [you] have enough followers on Twitch, and you consistently have viewers every time you start streaming. Then every session on Twitch becomes fun, since there's always an audience. But it's even more fun to make money. Once there's enough viewers, then you'll eventually make your first dollar. This is a real aha *moment—our streamers talk about how making even $20 or $50 a month is an eye-opener. But then build enough of an audience, and eventually, it's possible to "go pro" and just work by streaming full-time.*

This life cycle of a streamer meant that it wasn't long after Twitch's launch that the top streamers began to make $300,000+ per year.

All of these efforts served to attract new streamers at a critical period when the original product had hit a ceiling. While the original name, Xarth, would eventually be replaced, the original strategy mostly lives on: It's all about the streamers. It's about helping streamers create content, find audiences, and monetize.

The results of Twitch's new efforts paid off within their first year. The combined strategy of new features, emphasizing games content, and addressing the needs of streamers worked. It unlocked a tremendous amount of growth above and beyond Justin.tv's initial success.

Within a month after launch, Twitch had 8 million unique viewers, and within a year after that, it had doubled to 20 million. And then doubled again, and so on, so that today it is one of the most highly trafficked websites in the world. Individual streamers can have over 5 million followers, and make millions in revenue per year. The early code name "Xarth" also lives on, as the name of the main boardroom at Twitch offices today.

It's impressive to read the story of a successful product like Justin.tv hitting a ceiling, and then transforming into a much larger success through the hard work of its team. But this is an inevitable challenge that every networked product must face, as it saturates its market, deals with spammers and trolls, and faces churn from its earliest users.

Even Facebook struggled with this challenge as it hit its ceiling. Steven Levy, a journalist for *Wired* and author of a book on Facebook, described the social network's predicament:

> *"Growth had plateaued around 90 million people," Zuckerberg recalls. "I remember people saying it's not clear if it was ever going to get past 100 million at that time. We basically hit a wall and we needed to focus on that."*[60]

Facebook eventually built its first Growth team, and shipped a series of projects to break through the plateau. This included getting user profiles better indexed by Google via SEO, creating recommendations for people you should add as friends, and hundreds of other projects both big and small.

It's not just consumer companies that face this—workplace products and bottom-up SaaS startups use their network effects to grow virally, but eventually saturate their initial market of startups and early adopters. Then they need to learn how to sell into the enterprise to build the next phase of their business. We see this all the time at Andreessen Horowitz, where my colleague David Ulevitch says:

> *In the early days, startups often see success as other startups and small businesses adopt their product—this is the "bottom-up" distribution model that has propelled Slack, Zoom, Dropbox, and*

many others. Problem is, smaller customers are always churning out because they're price sensitive, running out of money, and changing their business model—sometimes all three! Larger enterprise customers, on the other hand, are sometimes harder to break into but can grow revenue over time as more and more users adopt it within a company. Thus it's natural for B2B startups to begin with a bottom-up sales motion but eventually add expertise to sell into enterprises.[61]

When B2B bottom-up startups can't execute on layering on a sales team, then growth will inevitably slow. No wonder Slack and Dropbox, even with their early success with small businesses, eventually added enterprise sales teams as well.

This is a recurring pattern for new products, whether they are consumer services like Twitch or Facebook, or B2B workplace products. A product launches to torrid growth, but momentum eventually slows. The media declares the product over. People become jaded. But if the team can hold it together and keep shipping new features and countering the slowdown, they often pull through.

Introducing the Ceiling

Over the next few chapters, I'll cover what happens when products inevitably slow down. This phase, "The Ceiling," is what happens as products bump against an ongoing range of problems—when growth stalls, network effects weaken, and hard decisions must be made. It happens for a variety of reasons, including market saturation, degradation of marketing channels, overcrowding, spam, and so on. No wonder large, scaled networked apps end up employing large teams to fight these negative dynamics—products don't just hit one ceiling, they bump up against plateaus over time.

In "Rocketship Growth," I'll start by defining success—what it means to be on track, versus hitting the ceiling. It's a high bar, and I describe a framework for why the best companies need to grow several hundred percentage points per year to be on a rocketship trajectory—no easy feat! At the same time these aggressive goals are pursued, multiple anti-network effects arise to slow the growth rate down.

First among the causes of slowdown is "Saturation." I describe how many networked products launch within a niche market—like a college, city, or other market segment—and then spread out from there. But what happens when a product saturates the entirety of its market and can't grow into the next one? If new products and segments aren't layered on, growth inevitably slows. At the same time, the marketing channels that companies rely on to grow are degrading, which I deem "The Law of Shitty Clickthroughs." This law describes how marketing channels inevitably become less effective over time—banner ads and email marketing are two good examples. If your product's network effects depend on these channels—for example, people sending each other invites over email—growth will inevitably decline over time.

At the same time this is happening, the network itself is changing. As a network grows, often the hard side of the network gets even more concentrated and powerful, and begins to act accordingly. Uber's power drivers are its most important users, and the company faced a tough situation when they came together to demand higher pay, benefits, and other changes. As I describe in "When the Network Revolts," it becomes incredibly hard to keep everyone happy.

While the hard side evolves, the rest of the network is changing as well. Early communities are often special, curated and molded to share attractive norms and qualities. Slack launched to a market of leading startups for a reason, as did Tinder with their college-by-college strategy. As I describe in "Eternal September," there's an unfortunate downside in reaching a more mainstream audience: more and more people jump in, and what makes the early community special often gets diluted.

And finally, I describe how discovery of relevant people and content becomes hard—I call this the "Overcrowding" dynamic within networks. More users and more content mean that you need to bring in features like search, algorithmic feeds, curation tools, and a plethora of other tools to manage this. If you don't solve this problem, then users will start to leave, potentially preferring competitive products that are smaller but more curated.

In many ways, this phase—the ceiling—is a fancy problem to have. The good news is that if you're facing these challenges, you have an enormously successful product. However, the bad news is that these issues are open-ended. There aren't any silver bullets for handling spam, market saturation, and the other topics listed in this section—the largest networked products in the world are continually battling these issues. In the end, only new products and innovation will kick off the next big growth curve, which is what encourages startups to grow from single products into multi-product companies. But for teams tasked with scaling a singular product, dealing with the ceiling is a never-ending battle.

23

ROCKETSHIP GROWTH

T2D3

I n the United States, there are roughly 6 million new businesses started each year, of which only a small number are a strong fit for venture capital investments—estimated to be in the tens of thousands. These startups are then referred to about 1,000 active venture capital firms, and each firm might evaluate a few thousand investment opportunities per year. Of those, just a dozen or two are selected by a firm for investment after multiple meetings, pitches, and hours of time together. Across the entire industry, there are about 5,000 venture capital investments per year available to new and early-stage startups.

Given this intense level of filtering, you might think that these startups would be bound to perform well. Statistically, that's not the case. The team at Horsley Bridge—a high-profile investor in venture capital funds—has shown that industry-wide the failure rate of venture-backed startups is over 50 percent. Venture investors only have a coin flip's chance of making any money at all. While our newspaper headlines are filled with stories about Google or Apple, in fact, only 1 in 20 venture-backed startups end up with the >10x exits the industry is focused on.

There are hundreds of exits per year, but only a few dozen are large enough to define the industry.

In other words, even once a team has shown enough promise to be backed by investors, very few ever make it through to the other side in the form of an exit. There are many reasons why this happens, but generally, the outcome is the same: they stop growing, peter out, and never achieve success. Given the low probability of an exit, why invest in startups at all? Why do startup opportunities attract nearly $85 billion per year[62] from sophisticated investors, both institutional and angel?

It's because when a product really takes off—particularly networked products that have achieved over a billion global users—the returns are huge. The biggest companies each year eventually come to employ over a hundred thousand people, like Amazon, Oracle, Microsoft, Apple, Intel, Google, and others. They represent nearly 20 percent of the S&P 500 and several of them became worth more than a trillion dollars at the start of 2020. These outsized returns are why Stanford researchers have ascribed 57 percent of the value of the US stock market to companies initially backed by venture capital.[63] These companies employ over 4 million people, investing $454 billion on R&D. Incredible.

These are the world-changing products that many entrepreneurs dream of building.

The Rocketship Growth Rate

How fast do you have to grow to follow the trajectory of the biggest technology companies in recent years? It's become common to throw around terms like "it's a rocketship" or "it's working" or "it's hit Escape Velocity" in a casual way, without defining it formally. I think we can do better. Let's put some numbers to these trajectories.

This is the Rocketship Growth Rate—the precise pace at which a startup must grow to break out. How do you calculate this rate of growth? First, by setting a goal of exceeding a billion dollars of valuation—thus being in a position to achieve an IPO—and working backward.

Hitting a $1 billion valuation generally requires at least $100 million in top-line recurring revenue annually, based on the rough market multiple of 10x revenue. You'd want to hit that in 7–10 years, to sustain the engagement of the key employees and also reward investors who often work in decade-long time cycles. These two goals—revenue and time—work together to create an overall constraint.

Neeraj Agarwal, a venture capitalist and investor in B2B companies, first calculated this growth rate by arguing that SaaS companies in particular need to follow a precise path to reach these numbers:[64]

- Establish great product-market fit
- Get to $2 million in ARR (annual recurring revenue)
- Triple to $6 million in ARR
- Triple to $18 million
- Double to $36 million
- Double to $72 million
- Double to $144 million

SaaS companies like Marketo, Netsuite, Workday, Salesforce, Zendesk, and others have all roughly followed this curve. And the rough timing makes sense. The first phase, in which the team initially gets to product/market fit, takes 1–3 years. Add on the time to reach the rest of the growth milestones, and the entire process might take 6–9 years. Of course, after year 10, the company might still be growing quickly, though it's more common for it to be growing 50 percent annualized rather than doubling. The argument is that products with network effects both can see higher growth rates as they tap into the various network forces I've discussed, and can compound these growth rates for a longer period of time—and looking at the data, I think that's generally true.

You might say, well, I don't care about being a $1 billion company—I'm okay to shoot for $500 million. Or perhaps you want to build a

$10 billion company, but do it over fifteen years. Great—then do your own calculations and tweak the numbers to devise your own trajectory. These can become goals for the team. For those seeking venture capital, it is a pretty standard minimum bar to get to $1 billion in valuation over ten years, but there's no reason why it couldn't be dialed down if the plan is to bootstrap a business or to only use angel investment.

The Rocketship Growth Rate was originally developed for SaaS software companies where the business model is powered by a subscription, and so for companies like Dropbox, Zoom, Slack, and DocuSign it's directly applicable. Although this framework was initially devised for SaaS/B2B companies, revenue is revenue, and it also generalizes to consumer companies. The framework can be reverse engineered to get guidance for any type of company, with a few parameters needed to get there:

- Valuation goal
- Input metric
- Years to get to the valuation
- Empirical data on front-loaded growth

Rocketship Growth Rates for Marketplaces

Let's use a marketplace example. For instance, say you have the goal of a new marketplace product hitting $1 billion in valuation. You generally want a leading indicator—for marketplace companies, gross merchandise value (GMV) or net revenue is often used—that maps to that valuation. For other products, like social media, it might be the number of Daily Active Users, net revenue, or something else. Either way, the key is to select a metric and work backward. In the marketplace case, you could look at publicly traded marketplace companies and see them trading at roughly five times net revenue. This means to achieve $1 billion in valuation, a company must hit $200 million in net revenue. And you want it to happen in year 10.

Next, you want to set goals for the intermediate years. In year 1 and 2, you might argue there's probably zero revenue since the team will be focused on product development. Then year 3 becomes about solving the Cold Start Problem, and only in year 4 does it get to meaningful revenue. The company might hit $1 million/year in revenue that year. Then to extrapolate out, the marketplace product needs to grow from $1 million to $200 million over year 4 to 10—in other words, 266x over a year period.

This is where the Rocketship Growth Rate starts to look formidable. It turns out that doubling a product's revenue each year isn't enough. Doubling over six years is 64x, and it wouldn't hit the goal in time.

An equation to calculate the target growth rate is handy here. The equation looks like this:

Rocketship growth rate = ((target revenue-starting revenue) / starting revenue)^(1/years)

Or filling in our numbers:

Rocketship growth rate = (($200M – $1M) / $1M)^(1/6) = 2.4x

In other words, starting from $1 million a year, you'd need to grow at an average rate of 2.4x over 6 years to hit $200 million. This is an average growth rate, and typically products grow fastest in the early years when revenues are small. A trajectory like 5x 4x 3x 2x 1.5x 1.5x would work, as would 4x 3.5x 3x 2x 2x 1.2x. Usually by the time a company is doing this analysis, they already have a year or two of data, and they can use this equation to figure out what the rest must look like. Or they can take empirical data from companies that are further along to extrapolate the first few years. And this is exactly what I've seen—the fastest-growing marketplace companies are often able to hit very high growth rates, including 5x+ in the early years, and continue to compound over time.

This example is for marketplaces, but it's straightforward to figure out an equivalent trajectory for categories as diverse as workplace collaboration apps, massively multiplayer games, or messaging apps. You just need to set a target revenue, work backward on growth rate over a fixed amount of time, and weight the highest-growth years at the beginning. Whether your target revenue is based on an IPO, an M&A outcome, or just simply a scale for impact, the same analysis can apply. For all practical purposes, to build a new and impactful product from zero to scale requires very fast growth rates in the hundreds of percentage points a year.

Why the Rocketship Trajectory Is Tough

Do the math, and it's obvious the Rocketship Growth Rate is very hard. And even while each year's goal tends to triple or double, a company will simultaneously face countervailing forces—saturation of the market slows down growth, marketing channels degrade in performance, and product development never keeps up with user demands. The cardinal rule is that growth rates tend to drop over time, even as more investment is poured into adding employees, building the product, and servicing customers.

The psychology of a team that's working on a Rocketship product is disorienting, and at odds with a gradual slowdown in growth. When you grow fast one year, you start to expect that you'll need to grow as fast or faster in the next. Ambition grows, as the vision gets bigger. What was a social network for college students becomes a way to connect everyone on the planet. What once was a way to request a limo becomes a way to bring transportation globally, like running water.

High-octane teams want more resources and more people, and develop more ambition. For the two hundredth employee of this company, they want to know that there's still upside on their stock options. Investors start funding the company ahead of its valuation—perhaps a year ahead, to price in an extra doubling or tripling, but sometimes a lot more. What might have been a product targeted at a niche now has to go for the whole market. What must have seemed silly to ask before, becomes natural. "Will this be the next Facebook?" Or the next YouTube, or the next Slack? What might first have been answered with a laugh or a shrug, as not even a serious question, eventually becomes a real question. And it becomes natural to answer, "Yes, it is. And here's why."

To the cynical, this can seem like puffery. But as a high-growth product continues an up-and-to-the-right trajectory, people start making extrapolations against the growth. As the team recruits investors, advisors, and former employees from Facebook, Google, Twitter, Salesforce, and other companies who ended up fulfilling their incredible vision, they gain the expertise on what a rocketship looks like. The expectations get higher and higher.

This is why hitting the ceiling is so dangerous. The consequences for a product that can't reignite its growth are severe. In the ultra-efficient job market for star product designers, software engineers, and technology employees, everyone knows which products are on the rise and which ones are stuck. Defections to higher-growth, buzzier startups are common. Even venture capital investors, whose job it is to take risk are often paying ahead of progress—it's (relatively) easy to fundraise when growth is good. When it's not, then it becomes hard to attract more capital. Valuations might become flat, or even go down, exacerbating the impact on employees.

The Good News, and the Bad

Even a new product that successfully achieves a Rocketship Growth Rate in the early years will eventually begin to slow down. It's a natural pattern. After a growth spurt on early numbers, a product will grow more slowly in later years. When I peruse startup pitch decks, I'm more likely to see a 5x 4x 3x than a 3x 4x 5x, even if numerically the outcome is the same.

The reason is straightforward—teams tend to use all the obvious growth levers they can in the first few years, which quickly run out over time. If it's clear that adding new marketing channels is the best way to counteract a decline in customer acquisition economics, then all the obvious marketing initiatives are launched early. If there are too many steps needed to sign up for the service, the highest-friction parts are re-designed early. Eventually, the easy ideas are "taken," making the initial high growth rates difficult to sustain. That's what it means for a product to hit the ceiling.

The good news is that networked products often have more tools to counteract this plateau than products that lack network effects. For example, take a new consumer goods brand that sells clothing online— they will see declines in their marketing efficacy as it scales. However, this product category lacks network effects. As their social media advertising costs go up, the team will try to optimize creatives, media buying strategies, and product features—but it won't be enough. It's a tough problem to try to double revenues while trying to keep marketing costs the same, all without network effects. The outcome is an early plateau on growth, which is part of why consumer goods companies are often good businesses but not necessarily great ones that can be worth tens of billions.

Networked products, on the other hand, have a massive advantage— they can tap into their network effects to fight the slowdown. For example, while the steady decline of marketing channels is inevitable, teams can amplify viral growth by optimizing sign-up funnels, recommendations for friends to invite, and so on. Similarly, as discovery becomes more difficult over time due to user "overcrowding," teams can implement algorithmic recommendations and feeds to fight back. More users in the network actually helps accelerate many of these network effects. As the team works to further improve network effects over time, the life of the growth rate is extended even as traditional marketing channels falter.

Ultimately, this is why the most valuable products in the world—most of the apps and platforms with a billion users—are typically networked products. When they work, they usually continue to work for a long time.

Over the next few chapters, I'll talk about the concrete, underlying reasons that products inevitably stop growing. I'll start with a powerful force that emerges as a network becomes successful—too successful: market saturation.

24

SATURATION

eBay

Success comes with an inevitable problem: market saturation.

New products initially grow just by adding more customers—to grow a network, add more nodes. Eventually this stops working because nearly everyone in the target market has joined the network, and there are not enough potential customers left. From here, the focus has to shift from adding new customers to layering on more services and revenue opportunities with existing ones.

eBay had this problem in its early years, and had to figure its way out. My colleague at a16z, Jeff Jordan, experienced this himself, and would often write and speak about his first month as the general manager of eBay's US business. It was in 2000, and for the first time ever, eBay's US business failed to grow on a month-over-month basis. This was critical for eBay because nearly all the revenue and profit for the company came from the US unit—without growth in the United States, the entire business would stagnate. Something had to be done quickly.

It's tempting to just optimize the core business. After all, increasing a big revenue base even a little bit often looks more appealing than starting at zero. Bolder bets are risky. Yet because of the dynamics of market saturation, a product's growth tends to slow down and not speed up. There's no way around maintaining a high growth rate besides continuing to innovate.

Jeff shared what the team did to find the next phase of growth for the company:

> *eBay.com at the time enabled the community to buy and sell solely through online auctions. But auctions intimidated many prospective users who expressed preference for the ease and simplicity of fixed price formats. Interestingly, our research suggested that our online auction users were biased towards men, who relished the competitive aspect of the auction. So the first major innovation we pursued was to implement the (revolutionary!) concept of offering items for a fixed price on ebay.com, which we termed "buy-it-now."*
>
> *Buy-it-now was surprisingly controversial to many in both the eBay community and in eBay headquarters. But we swallowed hard, took the risk and launched the feature . . . and it paid off big. These days, the buy-it-now format represents over $40 billion of annual Gross Merchandise Volume for eBay, 62% of their total.[65]*

Launching "Buy It Now" was a large change that touched every transaction, but the eBay team also innovated across the experience for both sellers and buyers as well.

> *With an initial success, we doubled down on innovation to drive growth. We introduced stores on eBay, which dramatically increased the amount of product offered for sale on the platform. We expanded the menu of optional features that sellers could purchase to better highlight their listings on the site. We improved the post-transaction experience on ebay.com by significantly improving the "checkout" flow, including the eventual seamless integration of PayPal on the eBay site. Each of these innovations supported the growth of the business and helped to keep that gravity at bay.*

Years later, Jeff became a general partner at Andreessen Horowitz, where he would kick off the firm's success in startups with network effects, investing in Airbnb, Instacart, Pinterest, and others. I'm lucky to work with him! He recounted in an essay on the a16z blog that his strategy was to grow eBay by adding layers and layers of new revenue—like "adding layers to the cake." You can see it visually here:

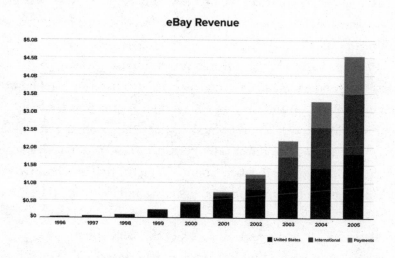

Figure 12: eBay's growth layer cake

As the core US business began to look more like a line than a hockey stick, international and payments were layered on top. Together, the aggregate business started to look like a hockey stick, but underneath it was actually many new lines of business.

This phase of eBay's story is not unique for fast-growing startups. What looks like an exponential growth curve is often, in reality, a series of lines layered quickly on top of each other. Uber's impressive growth trajectory was a combination of launching in more and more cities each year, while simultaneously layering on new products—like carpooling and food delivery. While each line inevitably tapers as each market saturates, adding them in layers can counteract the slowing growth.

Network Saturation versus Market Saturation

Although this entire phenomenon is often called market saturation, in a networked product there's actually something more subtle going on. I think of it as network saturation, not just market saturation. Here's how I define this term: the 100th connection for any given participant is likely less impactful than the first few, and as the network gets more dense over time, its associated network effects become less incrementally powerful.

In eBay's case, when you search something like "vintage rolex daytona," the product experience (and associated conversion rate) improve dramatically as you add the first few listings. It might even continue to improve with a few dozen. But you don't need the search to return 1,000 or 5,000 listings—the buyer's unlikely to browse through that many. This same idea applies to Uber, where adding the first one hundred cars on the road is important when you open the app to book a ride, but diminishing returns arise at larger numbers. And travel booking sites, app stores, and many other marketplaces face the same thing.

Social apps have a similar dynamic, where each additional friend connection is not as valuable as the previous one. In an internal memo to the Snapchat team, CEO Evan Spiegel reported on the diminishing returns of connections:

> *Your top friend in a given week contributes 25% of Snap send volume. By the time you get to 18 friends, each incremental friend contributes less than 1% of total Snap send volume each.*[66]

This provides another way to think of Facebook's famous "7 friends in 10 days" heuristic. Getting to 7 connections is great, but what about 14—is that better? Definitely. But is it 2x better? Probably not. And if you take it to its logical extreme, every person having 10,000 friends won't lead to 1,000x the engagement—in fact, it might start to lead to less engagement, as overcrowding effects take over.

Both network saturation and market saturation can slow down growth. Market saturation caps the total number of people on the network—you eventually run out of companies that can sign up to your collaboration tools, or gamers for your new massively multiplayer game. But network saturation also caps the effectiveness of your engagement over time as the interconnections slowly diminish in incremental value. These two dynamics together drive the saturation effects that slow a network's growth. The way to fight these inevitable forces is to constantly evolve your product, the target market, and the feature set—there's no way around it.

New, Adjacent Networks

In a network of networks, some will inevitably be more engaged than others. Usually the core networks that joined the earliest and are the most mature will work best. But go far enough away from these core networks, and you will find sets of users that are not as healthy. And beyond that, networks that aren't working at all. For eBay early on, the core market might have been the US collectibles community—the product might only be sort of working for users buying and selling big-ticket items like automobiles. Then there existed a vast swath of the network that might not be activated at all, like the international markets, where payments weren't yet working. Understanding these adjacent networks is key, so that they can be targeted one by one to expand and fight saturation.

My friend Bangaly Kaba, formerly head of growth at Instagram, called this idea the theory of "Adjacent Users." He describes his experience at Instagram, which several years post-launch was growing fast but not at rocketship speed:

When I joined Instagram in 2016, the product had over 400 million users, but the growth rate had slowed. We were growing linearly, not exponentially. For many products, that would be viewed as an amazing success, but for a viral social product like Instagram, linear growth doesn't cut it. Over the next 3 years, the growth team and I discovered why Instagram had slowed, developed a methodology to diagnose our issues, and solved a series of problems that reignited growth and helped us get to over a billion users by the time I left.

Our success was anchored on what I now call The Adjacent User Theory. The Adjacent Users are aware of a product and possibly tried using it, but are not able to successfully become an engaged user. This is typically because the current product positioning or experience has too many barriers to adoption for them. While Instagram had product-market fit for 400+ million people, we discovered new groups of billions of users who didn't quite understand Instagram and how it fit into their lives.[67]

In my conversations with Bangaly on this topic, he described his approach as a systematic evaluation of the network of networks that constituted Instagram. Rather than focusing on the core network of Power Users—the loud and vocal minority that often drive product decisions—instead the approach was to constantly figure out the adjacent set of users whose experience was subpar.

There might be multiple sets of nonfunctional adjacent networks at any given time, and it might require different approaches to fix each one. For some networks, it might be the features of the product, like Instagram not having great support for low-end Android apps. Or it might be because of the quality of their networks—if the right content creators or celebrities hadn't yet arrived. You fix the experience for these users, then ask yourself again, who are the adjacent users? Then repeat. Bangaly describes this approach:

When I started at Instagram, the Adjacent User was women 35–45 years old in the US who had a Facebook account but didn't see the value of Instagram. By the time I left Instagram, the Adjacent User was women in Jakarta, on an older 3G Android phone with a prepaid mobile plan. There were probably 8 different types of Adjacent Users that we solved for in-between those two points.

To solve for the needs of the Adjacent User, the Instagram team had to be nimble, focusing first on pulling the audience of US women from the Facebook network. This required the team to build algorithmic recommendations that utilized Facebook profiles and connections, so that Instagram could surface friends and family on the platform—not just influencers. Later on, targeting users in Jakarta and in other developing countries might involve completely different approaches—refining apps for low-end Android phones with low data connections. As the Adjacent User changes, the strategy has to change as well.

These adjacent networks are particularly interesting when examining the hard side of a marketplace, social network or otherwise. Marketplace products tend to become seller constrained over time, as Uber experienced with its drivers, or Airbnb with its hosts. Same with social networks and their creators, or app stores and their developers. In the framework of the Adjacent User, teams need to continually evolve their offering to attract the next set of sellers or creators to their platform. For example, when Uber ran out of full-time limo drivers for its service, the next set of Adjacent Users was people who had never driven as a form of income. But eventually this pool was exhausted as well, and the company started to think about signing up people who didn't own cars—the company would provide vehicles. And so on.

In the framework of adding layers to a cake, serving each adjacent network is like adding a new layer. Doing this requires a team to think about new markets, rather than listening to their vocal core markets—a hard feat when the core market generates most of the revenue. For the core market, there's a different way to grow: adding new formats for people to connect and engage with each other.

New Formats

The beauty of something like eBay's "Buy It Now" and "Stores" efforts is that they still fundamentally tap into the same network of buyers and sellers, but provide a new interaction that might better support new use cases.

I think of these as new formats, which allow people within a network to engage and connect with each other in new ways. Snapchat's Stories format—allowing people to broadcast a set of asynchronous photos and videos to their friends—can sit alongside their core photo messaging app, and increase usage. Some photos are better for 1:1 communication and others are better for a broadcast format—Stories allows Snapchat to collect both sets of photos instead of just one.

In eBay's case, "Buy It Now" makes the experience of buying certain kinds of products much easier. While you might want an auction format to help discover the right price for, say, a rare early edition of *The Lord of the Rings*, it's an inconvenient way to buy a brand-new hardcover book. Having a fixed price allows for the same buyers and sellers to engage around new types of products, increasing activity without needing to grow the network.

New Geographies

Layering on new geographies—as eBay did by adding international regions—is another way to build up the layer cake. This is particularly obvious for products that act on the hyperregional level, like OpenTable, Yelp, Uber, and others that grow city to city, and Tinder and Facebook, which went campus to campus. Other networked products can think more globally, adding new languages and payments as they cross from one continent to the other—primarily those that are purely digital in nature, like SaaS products and messaging apps. Each new region provides a fresh market to grow, but you also may need to solve the Cold Start Problem again in each region.

Regional expansion is easier when networks grow into directly adjacent networks. When a hyperlocal network that's primarily centered in San Francisco wants to expand into a nearby city, like Los Angeles, that often works well because both markets will share users. A product like Tinder might have users that have moved between cities. Similarly OpenTable might be able to leverage the fact that some restaurant chains are regional—the same owners may have locations in both San Francisco and LA, so it becomes easier to launch a new nearby market. For other kinds of products, an "adjacent" network won't be oriented around a city, but rather, a closely related network of companies. For example, success in proliferating collaboration tools within one company will make it more likely that a close partner will also adopt the tools, because those networks are so interconnected. If all of an accounting firm's clients use Dropbox, it's likely that they will eventually try it, too.

However, there are failure cases as well. A highly urban market like San Francisco possesses many unique factors: lots of early adopters, a high cost of living, a mostly urban environment, and a very educated consumer market. This is in turn very different from a market like Phoenix or Detroit, or many other markets that have their own special characteristics. Sometimes new startups will launch in a second or third market only to find out that, for instance, the market for dog walking mostly makes sense in wealthy urban environments and less so for a market that is mostly single-family housing with backyards.

Layering on growth from faraway geographies is far harder. This usually requires the team to start their network from zero once again, on top of all of the additional work: localizing content, finding local partners, implementing new payment methods, and potentially iterating on the product concept itself—because sometimes the idea doesn't fully translate. Unless your product is the rare type that possesses the global network effects of Airbnb, each new major geography is likely to take a big effort to kick-start—it's the Cold Start Problem all over again.

Laying on completely new international markets is hard because it generally requires a combined effort from many different team functions.

To give a sense for how different another market can be, just consider Uber, which succeeded in the United States initially as a private limo app for the iPhone, but ended up in Bangkok as a nearly unrecognizable product: consumers sign up with just their phone numbers (no credit card or emails!) on their low-end Android phones. They use their phone to book rides, but instead of a car, they request Uber Moto, where someone in a motorcycle comes to pick them up, and they have to hold on tight in the back! After getting to their destination, they pay cash, which the app supports, because credit card penetration is low in developing markets. Beyond this, innovations around vehicle types like motorcycles in Bangkok, tuk tuks in India, and ultimately scooter and bike rentals all require both operational and technical expertise to meld into a cohesive experience. It's a combination of operations with technology along with fintech, partnerships, and much more.

Why Fighting Market Saturation Is So Hard

The solutions to market saturation might sound straightforward—add new geographies, support more formats and business models, and other tips that sound like common sense. However, the challenge is in the execution, which can't be underestimated. Launching in every major country around the world while simultaneously staying on top of a hypergrowth startup in a core market is not easy. Yet that's exactly what eBay had to do, building one of the most valuable internet companies in the 1990s while simultaneously adding the international business, "Buy It Now," and new product verticals.

Once these obvious growth levers are mined, what's next?

Eventually new products have to be layered on. It's hard to ask teams to start and build new products from scratch. It's difficult enough as a startup, but trying to do this inside a larger company adds myriad of complexities—there's internal politics, distractions, lack of resources, adverse selection of talent, and dozens of other challenges. The types of teams that have been used to incrementally build large, multi-year franchises may never have encountered the Cold Start Problem, so they bring the wrong background and tools to the table.

Another way to think of the risk of new initiatives inside of a company: if a new product's success rate inside a company is similar to that of the venture capital industry as a whole, the success rate will be 50/50 at most. Exceptional outcomes might happen 1 in 20 times, if this pattern mirrors the startup world as well.

The cheat code for large companies is simply to buy startups that have hit Escape Velocity, and integrate them into a preexisting network. This is exactly what eBay did with PayPal, which must be one of the best acquisitions in the technology industry. It turned out to be a great idea, as PayPal would eventually be worth more than its parent. But these days, acquisitions are hard and expensive. It's easier said than done in a world where bad acquisitions are rampant, government antitrust concerns plague large networked products, and startups have become super expensive. Yet hitting the ceiling is an inevitable outcome of success, and companies need a response, lest they slow down to a crawl.

25

THE LAW OF SHITTY CLICKTHROUGHS

Banner Ads

The Law of Shitty Clickthroughs says every marketing channel degrades over time. This means lower clickthrough, engagement, and conversion rates, regardless of if you're talking about email, paid marketing, social media, or video. This is a core reason why products hit growth ceilings—when marketing channels stop performing, the growth curve starts to bend downward.

New products have a voracious appetite for adding new users. At the beginning, more and more sign-ups are the single most powerful growth lever. The math makes it obvious: if you have a small number of users for your workplace file-sharing product, it's hard to get those groups of users to share 100x more files or log in 100x more times per day—eventually you just run into the limits of natural usage and behavior. People just need to share files a few times per week, and it's hard to increase it much beyond that. On the other hand, it's possible to grow the network by adding more people—just add 100x or 1,000x the number of new users, and the aggregate engagement (and revenue) will go up.

The problem is, what might have worked before—whether that's conferences and events, or SEO and paid marketing—eventually stops scaling as fast as you need it to. When products need to hit 200 percent+ annual growth during the early periods of a Rocketship growth curve, the user acquisition channels need to scale that quickly as well.

But they don't, and I'll tell you a story about why.

Imagine the internet without advertising. As incredible as it sounds, between the years of 1989 and 1994, there was no such thing as ads on the internet—it had to get invented, alongside everything else on the web.

Consumers first experienced banner ads on Hotwired, the first commercial web magazine. As a part of Wired Ventures, it was a cousin to *Wired* magazine, the print magazine covering technology news and culture. Frank D'Angelo, part of ad agency Euro RSCG (now Havas), lined up an initial set of clients to become the first advertisers on the web:

> *Four of our then-clients placed ad banners as part of that first campaign, MCI, Volvo, Club Med and 1-800-Collect. (The other two advertisers were AT&T and Zima.) Keep in mind, this was 1994; the first graphical web browser, Mosaic, was less than a year old (soon to be replaced by Netscape Explorer). And Web access? Purely dial-up, 24.4kps if you were lucky, meaning these ads took a while to load. The online U.S. population? Two million, if that.*[68]

The advertisers launched the first campaign that included a banner ad that asked the viewer, "Have you ever clicked your mouse right HERE? You will." And with this one tiny banner, Hotwired kicked off an industry that now powers the businesses of Facebook, Google, and the world's technology giants.

Today, banner advertising clickthrough rates usually hover around 0.3–1 percent, but the first ads ever had incredible engagement: 78 percent at the start! This was a novel way to reach consumers, and people were curious, so they clicked. But more than two decades later, it's dropped to 1/100th of its initial levels.

It's not just online advertising that followed this trend—email did, too. At the start, it was novel to get an email invite to a social network, or an email alert about a colleague editing a doc. Years later, our inboxes are filled with emails we don't read. Gmail and other email clients have added easy ways to filter promotional emails, or "bacon"—notification emails from networked products that aren't quite spam, but aren't usually of interest—so that people can get more relevant messages. And consumers have moved to texting, Slack, WhatsApp, and other platforms to host their authentic communication.

No wonder email clickthrough rates have followed the same trend downward. ClickZ, an industry blog, published a graph showing that over a nearly decade time span, email marketing clickthrough rates dropped from 30 percent to under half that—13 percent.

The same can be found for nearly all growth channels over time. At the micro level, an individual marketing campaign will typically see declining clickthrough rates over time—so teams have to refresh the messaging, images, and channels. At a more macro level, channels like email or paid marketing degrade over years, though some channels fall even quicker—like the Zynga + Facebook platform era of the 2010s, which dropped off in months, not years. Why does this happen? Consumers acclimate to specific brands, marketing techniques, and messaging, and tune them out.

In studies where people are shown web pages and their eyes are tracked to see exactly where they are looking, they show incredible skill in ignoring ads and just focusing on the content. This was recognized as early as 1998 by usability researchers (Benway/Lane, Rice University) and termed "banner blindness." New advertising formats are constantly being introduced—right now video ads are in vogue, or ads with novelties like augmented reality—but it is inevitable that their performance also starts to sag.

This is happening at the macro level across marketing channels, but also for your specific product, too. This is the Law of Shitty Clickthroughs.

Degrading the Network

The degradation of marketing channels is an existential threat to a product's network effects. As I've discussed, the Acquisition network effect can be thought of as a series of steps where users encounter a product through an invite, then use the product and ultimately invite others. But what happens when one of these steps, like the invite email to bring a new user into the product, becomes less effective by half?

As an example, imagine a workplace collaboration app like Google Suite where teams collaborate by editing documents—the more people they invite and engage with, the stronger the loop. However, there's a dependency—people within a company have to check their emails, so that they get notifications when edits to a doc have been made. What happens if the Law of Shitty Clickthroughs strikes? If the product sends too many emails and notifications, then over time people will start to ignore them. If document creators feel like their edits and contributions aren't being seen by their colleagues, the network effects will start to slow.

This isn't just a qualitative outcome—it's a directly quantitative one, too. Imagine a new social app that's growing virally, and every 100 users who join a product eventually invite 75 others, then those in turn will invite 56, then 42, and so on. This is a nice, healthy viral factor of 0.75, as I've discussed in the chapter describing the Acquisition Effect. However, if those invites start to hit the spam folder and the conversion rate sinks by 50 percent, then the viral factor is reduced, too. Every 100 users can only invite 37, then they will invite 14, then 5—as you can see, this falls off much more quickly. When you do the math, the result is startling: for a 50 percent decrease in conversion of invites, there's an 80 percent decrease in total new users.

These negative impacts can cascade. New users are often the most engaged in connecting with others on the network. They often stimulate "welcome wagon" interactions with more tenured users, who engage to show them the ropes and introduce them to others. Remove the stream of new users, and engagement within the platform from more tenured users can decline, too.

Layering on New Growth Strategies

The solution to the Law of Shitty Clickthroughs is to embrace its inevitability. When new products launch, there are usually one or two acquisition channels that work—but they might not scale. In Dropbox's case, the initial wait list was formed by users who watched the announcement video about the product. They came in spikes, as early adopters from Hacker News and other social media products found it. Channels like these are great, but they often can't continue to drive growth over time. If you're getting a few hundred downloads per week through marketing channels, what do you need to do to 2x the number? Or 10x, or ultimately to 1,000x?

The usual response is simply to pour more money into marketing—but this often creates problems. Well-intentioned teams start with a highly efficient marketing spend, forecasting every dollar invested will pay back in six months. But the costs creep up over time. As more money is invested into marketing, it performs worse, so the team then shifts the payback period to allow for twelve months before recouping costs. Then eighteen, then onward, until the economics are severely upside down. Eventually the team puts a cap on marketing spend and can't invest more, which is when the growth curve hits the ceiling.

The best practice is for products—whether they have network effects or not—to constantly layer on new channels. A consumer-facing app should invest more in paid marketing on YouTube, Snapchat, Instagram, and other ad platforms. But it should also work on its viral growth loops, and engage content creators. It might also focus on content marketing—building SEO to rank more highly organically on Google. The key for a new product team is to understand which channels best fit its product, and to hire the relevant people who've already done it. Sometimes these exist as potential full-time employees, but there are also advisors/freelancers or firms that specialize in some of the more mature channels like SEO/SEM.

For workplace/B2B products, the focus will often turn toward adding a direct sales channel in combination with the other various "bottom-up" consumer-like acquisition channels, so that it all works in an integrated way. There is sometimes low-hanging fruit. Often, it's as easy as looking at all the users who are signing up or who are active, and checking out their email domains to figure out which companies to sell into. Or maybe just asking these users for their company name and team size—and then start emailing them to sell. Another quick fix is to add a "Contact us" tier of service on the pricing page. At the same time, run a parallel effort that emphasizes content marketing, events, and other programs that drive more top of funnel leads. Build a growth team that can score individual accounts and add life cycle triggers so that the sales team sees when the product reaches a certain footprint inside an organization. In doing all of this, multiple channels can be combined into a broader strategy.

Of course, if the Law of Shitty Clickthroughs says that marketing channels decline over time, the other strategy is to embrace new marketing ideas early. Every three to five years, there seems to be a rapid explosion of new media formats and platforms to experiment with. Most recently, with the rise of TikTok, Twitch, Instagram, and other forms of highly scaled visual media, there is a new crop of startups going to market with influencers and streamers. Similarly, new B2B startups have started to embrace referral programs, memes, emojis, video clips, and other tactics previously reserved for consumer products. The landscape is constantly changing, with new product and platforms emerging every few years, opening up opportunities for marketers to jump in before others do.

Tapping into the Acquisition Network Effect

Whereas a traditional product might lean more deeply into spending on sales and marketing, networked products can be more efficient by growing without spend, by optimizing their viral loops.

For example, in Twitch's journey, the team deeply focused on creators, giving them better tools and monetization, which in turn caused them to become more active. More satisfied creators meant they would broadcast live video streams more often, bringing in more viewers, which drove further engagement and monetization. It might have been easy to think they should just double down on their marketing spend, but instead the team looked toward amplifying the network effects that engaged its streamers.

Leveraging network effects for customer acquisition is the norm for the more successful products on the planet. Many of them have more than a billion active users, and as you might imagine, it's simply not tenable to buy this scale of users through paid marketing. A paid mobile install in a broad-based consumer category like Uber's might cost $10, at scale, and more high-value categories like personal finance or B2B might be several times that. Multiply this number by a few billion installs, which in turn translates to a billion active users, and you get to an important conclusion: you don't want to spend tens of billions of dollars on marketing.

The Law of Shitty Clickthroughs is best countered through improving network effects, not by spending more on marketing.

26

WHEN THE NETWORK REVOLTS

Uber

How do you get to the point where your most important customers end up protesting in front of your office?

During 2016, I lived in a loft apartment in the Hayes Valley neighborhood of San Francisco, close to the Uber offices on 1455 Market Street. My morning commute consisted of grabbing an americano from a tiny coffee shop located in the alley, then walking past the hip bars, restaurants, and boutiques that lined the streets—it was a short, pleasant walk to the office. A few times per year, this pleasant walk was interrupted with something not so pleasant: dozens of upset and highly vocal Uber drivers, holding signs outside the lobby. They shouted, banged drums, and were irate, and they often circled for hours. Security lined up at the front to make room for employees to get through, but it was a disturbing sight.

This became a regular occurrence. When things got serious, the facilities team would email everyone and tell them they needed to leave the office through the emergency back door because of what was happening outside. And sometimes, it was more personal—I once had an irate driver find out I worked at Uber via my social media profiles, and they waited in the lobby for hours to accost me when I arrived. I walked extra quickly to the elevators when he shouted my name.

This was a mind-bender because, as I got into the building and sat down for my morning meetings, my conversations trended toward a recurring theme: drivers are the most vitally important part of Uber's network. They are the hard side of the network, and even though they constitute about 5 percent of our users—Uber has something like 20–30 riders for every driver—the majority of the resources of the company need to be focused on them. We might pay $20–$50 for a new active rider, but more than ten times that for an active driver. In some very supply constrained markets like San Francisco, it became $1,000 or even $2,000 per driver sometimes.

This was exacerbated by the fact that a small minority of drivers had growing importance. Although most of the several million active Uber drivers were part-time, there was a contingent of so-called power drivers—the most active users who drove forty hours a week or more—who were very, very important.

And unfortunately, they were the ones outside holding the handwritten signs, asking for everything from higher pay to benefits and better treatment from the company and riders. I sympathized with the drivers, but the question was, how do you solve this problem in a way that made everyone in the network happy?

The Hard Thing about the Hard Side

Uber has faced many unique problems—surely an understatement—but it's not unique for the hard side of a network to grow in both importance and scarcity, while simultaneously becoming misaligned with the company over time.

It's standard fare across many categories of networked products: eBay's hard side is its sellers, who have revolted many times whenever listing fees have changed. Same with Airbnb hosts, Instacart workers, and Amazon sellers. These changes often benefit the easy side of their networks, the buyers, who appreciate lower fees, more buying guarantees, and so on. Yet the tyranny of the majority often overwhelms the scarcer part of the network. The same can be said for developer platforms like Microsoft Windows or iOS. These platforms depend on app developers on one side of the network to build products, often over many years and with millions of dollars invested upfront, that will cater to the desires of consumers, who are the easy side of the network. In Microsoft's case, fierce competition took place between the company and its developer partners including Netscape, Novell, Borland, Lotus, and a long list of other companies from the 1980s and '90s. Microsoft's hard side consisted of large, VC-backed public companies, not just individuals. Same with Facebook, which built a developer platform that attracted startups like Zynga and Pinterest. This was good news, until Facebook found themselves at odds with their developers over the overuse of notifications, social sharing of content, and other APIs. Reddit's moderators of its communities—their hard side, who organize, create, and curate the people and content—have protested policies by "going dark," substantially reducing the site's engagement and traffic.

A well-organized revolt by the major members of its hard side can kill a product entirely. Twitter once bought an app called Vine for a reported $30 million. It let users create and view six-second looping video clips—it was ahead of its time, and not dissimilar from the insights behind TikTok. Like many social apps, the most popular content creators became very successful, and they were important to attract an audience.

Unfortunately, a few years in, more than a dozen of the top content creators organized a revolt:

Led by creators Marcus Johns and Piques, the group pitched an idea:
If Vine paid each star $1.2 million and changed certain features

of the app, each creator would post 12 Vines per month. Other-wise, all 18 would leave the platform. "We were driving billions of views—billions—before we left," DeStorm Power explained of the monetary request.[69]

Vine turned down the plan, and a few years later, the service was shuttered. The hard side is worth the effort to cultivate. The most successful and prolific members of this side of the network also provide the highest level of service, are willing to make the investments to scale their impact, and ultimately become the defensible backbone of the network—assuming they can be retained. In Uber's case, the power drivers represented the top 15 percent of drivers but constituted over 40 percent of our trips. They were also among the safest and most highly rated drivers—after all, it was their primary source of income.

Other product categories are often even more concentrated. About half the top iOS apps are developed by a small group of elite developers: Google, Facebook, Microsoft, Amazon, and a few others. Just twenty apps drive 15 percent of all app downloads! Within SaaS collaboration tools, the concentration of paying customers gives a sense of their hard side—it's often IT and managers who authorize spending, fully roll out the tools, and help organize the broader employee engagement of the network. The numbers are similarly concentrated: Slack's S-1 filing showed less than 1 percent of Slack's total customers accounted for 40 percent of the revenue, and Zoom's indicated that 30 percent of revenue came from just 344 accounts, again less than 1 percent of their customer base.

We see this on social platforms as well. The most organized YouTube channels and Instagram influencers might start out as individuals, but eventually scale their production so that their millions of viewers see professionally created content. Reddit has these dynamics within moderators, who organize the largest communities with 20 million subscribers each! However, look further down the list and the numbers rapidly fall off in exponential fashion, such that a top 98th percentile community—ranked 20,000 out of over 2 million subreddits—has just a few thousand subscribers.

For the most part, this concentration is the result of healthy loops that drive a network toward higher quality. A good content creator gets likes, shares, and follows, and features like algorithmic feeds will distribute their content even more widely. A bad creator gets none of that boost, and will lower their engagement level into just being a passive viewer, or just churn. A good team organizer will create projects, post new content, and invite coworkers into workspaces that stay active. A bad one will create projects that don't pick up engagement, and they will eventually churn or their peers will pick up where they left off. A good restaurant on a food-delivery platform will get five-star reviews and eventually generate enough money to help them invest in a specialized kitchen for delivery, and expand into more markets. A bad restaurant will get bad reviews and eventually shut or churn. All of these feedback loops create more concentration within a small number of players, but to the benefit of the entire network.

A networked product generally wants to nudge its ecosystem toward professionalization, because it helps scale the hard side. The idea is to transform mom-and-pop sellers into power sellers, or solo app developers into software companies. This is a big and important transition since it improves the capacity of each member of the hard side, as the sheer numbers begin to slow down because of saturation. The company might offer training, documentation, and monetization. Often, enterprise features are added—like the ability for IT to manage a company's internal networks and tools, or analytics so that a social media agency can report metrics back to a content creator or brand. This "pro" or "enterprise" offering might turn into new tiers of the product, with dedicated teams improving these tiers over time. Customer success teams provide higher touch service to these customers, and in turn lock them in to contracts that offer favorable economics.

Up-front investment to try to professionalize the supply side early on in a network's development inevitably comes with risk. In a well-publicized misstep for Uber, the company sought to expand its supply side by financing vehicles to provide cars to potential drivers who didn't own vehicles, a program called XChange Leasing. The hypothesis was that this should push these drivers into power-driver territory quickly. Payments could be automatically deducted from their Uber earnings, and their driver ratings and trip data could be used to underwrite the loans.

XChange Leasing unfortunately lost $525 million and failed to professionalize the driver side of the market. The problem was, it attracted drivers highly motivated by money—usually a positive—but who didn't have high credit scores for good reason. They often failed to make payments, using their Uber-provided car to drive for competitors and avoid the automatic deductions. They would steal the cars and sell them for, say, half price. They would drive for Lyft instead of Uber, as a way to avoid the automatic payment deductions—they would try to have their cake and eat it, too. Uber needed to organize a massive repossession effort to get the cars back, but it was too late—many had been sold illegally, some finding themselves as far away as Iraq and Afghanistan, GPS devices still attached and running. This is a colorful example of how scaling the supply side, when a lot of capital is involved, can be tricky.

This example notwithstanding, there are tremendous positives to professionalization within a network. Encouraging successful players to get even bigger can inject huge amounts of growth. Because the most successful members of the hard side are the most likely to professionalize, they are also the most likely to have expertise on how to be successful. They can hire and train employees, and help the company expand into other services and categories. They can raise investment and spend on big projects where others won't, giving them an ability to scale quality and consistency on your network. Over time, these businesses often become a network's best partners, with a deep symbiotic relationship.

And thus the paradox—as a network scales, its hard side will professionalize. Quality and consistency will probably increase, and the most sophisticated players will be able to do it at scale. On the other side of the paradox, this dynamic eventually misaligns incentives—drivers, sellers, and creators might protest. App developers might complain, quit, or compete with you. Your SaaS partners might negotiate pricing, request custom features, or threaten to quit.

However, I argue that there's no choice but to embrace this.

How Professionalization Happens

Professionalization happens in two ways: homegrown professionals, and off-network professionals. For the homegrown, let's use eBay as an example. You might start out selling vintage clothing part-time on the site to make money, but find that you can do it full-time yourself. After some time, you might be able to start your own boutique and hire employees—becoming a "power seller," one of millions of businesses like this selling on eBay, Amazon, and other e-commerce platforms. Or similarly, the B2B version might start with a manager wanting to try out a new product, then having a specific team and set of experts own it, then having consultants and vendors professionally implement it for a broader ecosystem. That's what has happened for business software like CRM.

Sometimes these large professionalized outfits can get really big. The scale of the winners depends on the difficulty of aggregation—it's easier to become a larger video creator or app developer than a mega-Airbnb host. A big YouTube star can simply get there by consistently making videos, as some teenage stars do, whereas being a large-scale host requires millions of dollars of real estate as a requirement. A networked product like OpenTable has restaurants on their hard side, which are unlikely to grow to become giants within the platform, because food is inherently fragmented. It's unlikely to see a huge chain of restaurants representing a huge percentage of the business. On the other hand, the social platforms often get very large and concentrated, with just a few winners at the top.

When a network's biggest members become large, they can often become high-scale, investor-backed startups on their own. Developer platforms like iOS, the internet, and Windows have historically hit such scale and strong network effects that they attract investors and venture capital. The members of their network often become big enough to ultimately IPO and become large enterprises—many of the startups I've covered in this book fall into this category. Large-scale networked products in video, like YouTube, have homegrown their influencers into more professionalized production companies—Maker Studios is one such example, acquired by Disney for $500 million in 2014. Popular multiplayer games like Overwatch, League of Legends, and Fortnite have attracted professional e-sports teams that aspire to be the next New York Yankees, arguing that they could be worth billions as gaming goes mainstream. Even more recently, startups operating on the Zoom platform have emerged across sectors as diverse as kids' education, professional networking, events and conferences, and have also attracted investors from top-tier venture firms. These are all examples of professionalization.

The other way that the hard side professionalizes is through the largest off-network players joining over time. When the Apple App Store first launched, homegrown developers emerged to build the first apps, like Foursquare, Uber, and others. But tech-forward developers like Facebook, Yelp, and eBay launched as well, alongside homegrown early successes. It was only years later that Microsoft put its apps onto iOS—after new CEO Satya Nadella ascended, he signaled a strategy change to support Microsoft Office across all platforms, not just Microsoft ones. Nintendo held out for years, putting their first-party content like Super Mario and Zelda only on their own hardware devices, which they hoped would serve as anchors to their own network ecosystem. But, they eventually released an iOS app once mobile was too big to ignore.

When a network becomes large, rich, and diverse, it's often described as an "Economy"—you may have heard about the Gig Economy, the Attention Economy, the Creator Economy, and so on. Each of these respectively encompasses the worlds of Airbnb/Uber/Instacart, Facebook/Google, TikTok/YouTube/Substack, etc. And in turn, a rich ecosystem of players emerges. There are conferences, events, and journalists who exclusively cover companies in the space. Training programs emerge to onboard potential new employees into the ecosystem.

There are venture capital investors that specialize in funding companies in the sector, indicating that participants in the economy can themselves become large-scale companies. All of this is a sign that the various products in the ecosystem have reached enough dominance and stability that the network can now count on them to exist for a lengthy period of time. All of this is critical when the typical source for growing the hard side—acquiring new users—starts to slow down as the network hits scale and begins to saturate the market.

No Choice but to Scale

The hard side of the network is the most difficult and expensive to scale. As the market saturates, it eventually becomes more important to "scale up" than to continue to acquire new members of the hard side.

This was true for Uber, which started out by acquiring drivers through low-volume, unscalable methods—emphasizing hustle from the operations team, and tactics like Craigslist ads. But once tens of thousands of new drivers need to be recruited into a mature market, those tactics didn't work anymore. What might have been a $70 Craigslist ad to recruit a driver in the early days eventually became $1,000+ per active driver from every direction—paid marketing, referrals, even TV and radio ads.

Market saturation means that the new people joining the platform will begin to change. Eventually, Uber needed to convince people who'd never earned income by driving to try it—the market of professional drivers was saturated. It needed to grow the market, and onboard a larger and more mainstream segment of users. This segment of drivers required more education, more vetting, and more encouragement on how they should interact with riders. In Uber's early days, the limo license might be enough to indicate that a driver knew what they were doing, but this was a new group of people needing help on how to pick people up, dealing with airport rules, and so on.

A networked product is successful when people on a network know how to interact with each other. A content creator needs to learn the types of content that are successful on that particular platform—whether that's clever dances on TikTok or serialized fiction for podcasts. Marketplace sellers need time to understand how to best present their products and services—whether that's with Airbnb's professional photography for listings, or influencer-endorsed products on Instagram.

The penalty for acquiring new members of the hard side but not setting them up to be successful is steep: they churn. Unlike the innovators and early adopters, they might not stick around just because they think the product is cool or fun. They're doing it to solve a problem—often to earn a living—and if a networked product can't deliver, they'll leave.

The dilemma for networked products is stark. Embrace the professionalization of the hard side, and reap the benefits of increasing scale. Yet this leads to power concentration, and potential misalignments—though hopefully no protests outside your windows. Or reject the trend, and see the hard side struggle with scale. I distinctly believe that the former, done well, is the way to go. However, it's incredibly hard to finesse—no wonder nearly every marketplace company has to deal with labor issues, and every app development platform has ended up competing with or booting off its app developers. Yet the benefits strongly outweigh the costs—it's one of the key levers to break through the inevitable growth ceilings, and managing these dynamics well will extend the upside of the network.

27

ETERNAL SEPTEMBER

Usenet

Before Snapchat, Facebook, Friendster, or even Geocities or Yahoo Groups, there was the granddaddy of all internet communities: Usenet. Think of it as the very first social network. Created in the early days of the internet in 1980, Usenet was the first worldwide distributed discussion system, hosting newsgroups like talk.politics, rec.arts.movies, rec.crafts.winemaking, and a hundred other topics. During a period where the web and browser hadn't yet been invented, people from all over the world—generally from the universities and research institutions connected to the early internet—met online in Usenet message threads.

For the early internet, Usenet was a big deal—historic events happened on the network. Important announcements were made there, like the launch of the World Wide Web by Tim Berners-Lee and the Linux operating system by Linus Torvalds. So was the announcement of the modern graphical web browser by a16z cofounder Marc Andreessen. In the dozen years after its launch in the 1980s, Usenet built itself into the center for the global internet community, with clear network effects similar to the ones that drive Reddit or Twitter. Since Usenet had the most people, and the most comprehensive set of topics, why would you participate in discussions anywhere else?

But then something happened. By 2000, Usenet was practically dead, with its core participants fleeing elsewhere. Usenet hit the ceiling, and never recovered. What drove its collapse?

The problems that befell Usenet are the same ones that plague social networks today. But it was so early in the life of the internet that no one knew of the severe problems coming, much less the potential solutions. For example, everyone is familiar with "spam" now, but that originated on Usenet. Yes, during the early internet, there was a glorious period with zero spam and people just used Usenet and email authentically. But it didn't take long before spam was invented—and it was invented on the Usenet and early email. As the audiences grew large enough to attract commercial activity, people started to use the platform for selling products and services with unthoughtful, repetitive content sent to dozens of different Usenet newsgroups. Looking backward, we know that success on a communications network like Usenet will inherently attract spam. Same with flaming and trolling. Early internet users even made up a term, called "Godwin's Law"—the observation that every heated digital conversation devolves into comparisons with Nazis—to describe the vicious debates that happened on Usenet in the 1980s. These ideas are just as applicable today—and just as difficult to address—as they were decades ago. And Usenet was the first global internet community that had to deal with all of these bad behaviors, at scale.

Usenet grew uncontrollably, and that made it hard to manage. At the start, the first atomic network for Usenet was at Duke University, where creators Jim Ellis and Tom Truscott were based. Then nearby University of North Carolina was added, followed by institutions like Bell Labs, Reed College, and University of Oklahoma. Because many of the early organizations on the network were universities, every September a new cohort of students would join Usenet as they started school. Over the ensuing months, they would learn the social norms, jargon, and culture, and then integrate into the community, or otherwise quit as people flamed them for not practicing "netiquette." Many of the early Usenet participants knew each other from academic activities, creating a real-life bond that helped reinforce good behavior.

In September 1993, everything changed. AOL, the largest internet provider at the time, began a massive campaign to mail millions of CD-ROMs and floppy disks to consumers. Instead of a predictable, yearly spurt of users in September as students joined the Usenet network, millions of people began to join from all walks of life. This became a torrent that wouldn't end.

A few months later, early Usenet pioneer Dave Fischer noted:

September 1993 will go down in net history as the September that never ended.[70]

Today, this moment in internet history is known as the Eternal September, when a rush of inexperienced Usenet users flooded the network. The Usenet community and its netiquette was forever changed as the rapid growth of brand-new users meant its core culture was soon forced to evolve. The users brought with them new use cases, discussion topics, and demands for features. Some of this evolution was good, as the protocols were upgraded to be faster, scale with more volume, and notably, to support binary files like photos, music, and videos.

But with this also came pornography, pirated movies and music, and other salacious content. This flood of inappropriate content, spam, and newbies eventually made Usenet difficult to use. The breakdown of netiquette meant that it became harder to discover the pockets of high-quality conversation that defined Usenet's early years. People began to migrate to other technologies—online groups, mailing lists, and eventually social networks.

Eventually the core of the Usenet network collapsed. Duke University, where the protocol was invented, retired its servers after three decades, in 2010. AOL, Verizon, Microsoft, and other major ISPs cut off access around the same time, citing lack of usage combined with content piracy, pornography, and other issues. Articles like the one titled "Usenet has been dying for years" were published, citing September 1993 as the start of its collapse.

The entire life cycle of Usenet's rise and fall serves as a cautionary tale for when networked products hit scale—they suffer from the combined anti-network effects of spam, trolling and other bad behaviors, and most important, context collapse. These provide a strong natural counterbalance to the viral growth and engagement loops that make the network stronger, ultimately canceling these positive forces out. Given enough time, and left untreated, they can collapse the network entirely.

Context Collapse

Every network, if it starts with a focused atomic network, has a concept like "netiquette." There's a shared context in the early years of what you should and shouldn't do within a network—a culture. But eventually that becomes susceptible to a collapse in context, which is a subtle and unique problem to networked products. Let's use a story to describe how it happens—this one from Adam D'Angelo, CEO of Quora and ex-CTO of Facebook. He explains how it affects social and communication products:

> When you first join a social network with your close friends, it's easy to use it a lot. You might post photos and comments all the time—full of in-jokes and shared stories. You and your friends like it so much you invite your other friends, and then their siblings, too. And so on. But eventually, photos and content meant for your close friends might attract comments from people you don't know well. Your parents get invited, and maybe your teachers, or your boss. Those photos of a party you went to might get you in trouble.[70]

Adam's comment concerns consumers, but it's relevant for workplace products, too—replace close friends, parents, teachers with colleagues, managers, other teams, and executives, and it works. What you say in one context—like giving constructive feedback to a colleague 1:1, or venting about a project—might seem impolitic when everyone is watching. This includes what kinds of content you post, how you interact with people, and what constitutes an appropriate comment.

Context collapse is what happens when too many networks are simultaneously brought together, and they collapse into one. It's most problematic for social networks because it inhibits the behavior of content creators—the hard side—as they no longer are able to post photos that satisfy everyone in every context.

The term was first coined by researcher Michael Wesch in his analysis of YouTube, who asked:

> *What does one say to the world and the future? . . . The problem is not lack of context. It is context collapse: an infinite number of contexts collapsing upon one another into that single moment of recording. The images, actions, and words captured by the lens at any moment can be transported to anywhere on the planet and preserved (the performer must assume) for all time. The little glass lens becomes the gateway to a black hole sucking all of time and space—virtually all possible contexts—in on itself. The would-be vlogger, now frozen in front of this black hole of contexts, faces a crisis of self-presentation.[72]*

In other words, to restate Wesch, a video posted on YouTube might be watched anywhere in the world, and for all time. How can a creator ensure—whether their intention is serious or funny or otherwise—that they can properly convey their message? How will they know they won't offend, or be judged harshly, if the video floats into the wrong context? This "crisis of self-presentation" is exactly what drives anti-network effects on the creator side.

The negative consequences on users of a network are real. Parents, teachers, and bosses are some of the most powerful people in your life, and content you share may be quickly surfaced to them algorithmically. For real name networks like Slack, LinkedIn, or Facebook, the problem is particularly acute since your digital content directly affects your reputation. The bigger the network, the more people might see your content, rendering it unsafe to contribute. D'Angelo calls this the "unraveling" of networks—when a network loses its top creators, many of its consumers will leave as well. Lose enough consumers and it becomes less attractive to create. Continue this vicious cycle and an entire subcommunity within a network might leave entirely.

Context collapse doesn't just affect social networks. All atomic networks start with their own version of "netiquette" and isolated subsets of users. This could be Craigslist's culture of low prices and no frills, Airbnb's early focus for unique places to rent, or Slack's early use by the early-adopter tech community. These are three different categories—a classifieds site, a travel marketplace, and a SaaS workplace product—and yet they face the same thing. As the network grows, the hard side is often forced to participate less.

In the case of collaboration tools, the context collapse might be driven by going from the network made up of your immediate team to far more networks as the product lands and expands. When far-off remote offices, more managers, and many hundreds of other employees are added, your usage might become more muted, as a poorly phrased joke or overly casual remark that might be fun for your team might land poorly for others.

For a marketplace product, an early community of high-end sneaker enthusiasts might grow and eventually find itself inundated with casual buyers who care more about affordability. If they don't appreciate the products as much, or say the wrong things, this could turn off the initial sellers. On the other hand, new sellers might start to list more affordable but less cool products, making it harder for the early community of buyers to find what they want. What is an attractive product in one context might be less so to another, which is one of the reasons why context collapse can hurt the matchmaking at the core of marketplaces.

While the experience of these users is slowly degrading as the network grows, simultaneously the product teams building the network are pushing hard, continuing its growth. At its heart, this is the tension: network effects versus anti-network effects. And when the anti-network effects become strong enough to cancel out the efforts of the team, the network hits its ceiling.

Networks of Networks . . . of Networks

So how do you prevent context collapse? Products like iMessage or WhatsApp give us a clue. Messaging apps are resistant to context collapse. You talk to your dozen or so friends and family, and even if the network adds millions more people, it doesn't change your experience. Slack channels offer a different model—as more and more people within a company join, people set up smaller spaces to interact with their close teammates. This allows people to split the company-wide network into team-wide networks, or even project-based networks. If one of these channels get too big, then people can just reconstitute an even smaller one.

In other words, not all networked products experience context collapse as rapidly as others. When users are able to group themselves, they prove particularly resilient. Facebook Groups provide separate smaller and more disjointed spaces away from the main newsfeed, as do Snap Stories as a complement to the app's 1:1 photo messaging features— both provide a network within a network that can hold its own context. Instagram's usage patterns include "finstas"—secondary and tertiary accounts—where different content can be shared. Each has different sets of followers attached to them, so that photos can be posted away from the prying eyes of parents and bosses.

Product features can also make users aware when they are interacting across different contexts. When you type a message into a Slack channel and it warns you that your recipients are in another time zone, that helps you become aware that your context may be different from that of your recipient. Your totally appropriate work-related message may not be appropriate if it's being delivered on the weekend of your recipient. Similarly, permissions and privacy features like being able to share Google Docs with individuals, specific groups of people, or everyone within your corporate email domain provide the ability to create smaller spaces that then stem into larger ones.

There is a natural tension that comes with creating many smaller, private spaces. It's not a silver bullet. Split a network into pieces that are too small, and you'll soon have many one-off inactive channels or groups that aren't useful. Similarly, discoverability can become a problem as the number of channels and direct message conversations increases over time—even iMessage becomes unwieldy once you have dozens of active conversations or group texts happening simultaneously. Context collapse is meant to be managed carefully, so that there's enough discovery to hold the network together, but not in such a way that it alienates or overwhelms users.

The Power of the Downvote

Context collapse is also aligned with the other problems that plagued Usenet over time, spam and trolls. Perhaps unsurprisingly, this is not a new problem.

Imagine receiving an anonymous message:

> Sir, you will doubtlessly be astonished at receiving a letter from a person unknown to you, who is about to ask a favour from you . . .

The letter is from French royalty, and describes how through a series of accidents they have recently lost a great deal of money. However, they have a plan to recover it, if only you'd be willing to help. And of course upon completing the task it would only be fair to share a portion.

Sound familiar? The twist is, this was sent as a letter, not an email or LinkedIn message. The treasure is measured in gold francs, and it was lost in a French village, and the writer was a valet-de-chambre to a marquis. This type of letter was called a "Jerusalem Letter," and was described by Eugène François Vidocq, a French criminal turned detective, in his memoirs published in 1828.[73]

Although this scam is from nearly two hundred years ago, it exists in email form today. And these scams have since innovated—there are close cousins like romance scams, but also more far-flung examples of fraud—there's catfishing on dating apps, fake ICOs in the cryptocurrency ecosystem, and money laundering and fraud within on-demand marketplace apps. Networked products can hit a ceiling when they grow to be large and inevitably become attractive targets to fraudsters, spammers, and trolls. These bad actors use the openness of the network and its ability to connect users to each other—payments, messaging, following, and so on—for their own means, often swindling people with the same scams that have persisted for centuries. They flood the internal communication channels that connect nodes on a network, so that user-to-user messaging gets clogged up with spammy commercial content, automatically generated by bots. Multi-sided marketplaces like Craigslist and dating apps end up with dummy listings run by fake users who reply with scams. Corporate email networks are hit with fake messages in highly targeted phishing attacks that seek to steal credentials.

All of these harmful activities degrade networks and unwind the network advantages that products fight so hard to achieve. Retention falls if users become skeptical of notifications coming from an app—is it a real friend, or simply a spammer? Acquisition becomes harder if an experience degrades to the point where you don't want to invite or share with your friends. And the business is hurt when there's fraud and false transactions and highly valuable users begin to leave.

Leveraging the network itself to combat abuse is one of the most scalable methods of fighting bad actors. As the network gets larger over time, there are more users who can moderate, and will do so without cost. By giving users the ability to report spam, flag malicious accounts, block bad content, and so on, it not only creates ways for users to customize their own experience but also provides the data that can be used to moderate in other ways.

One of the simplest ways to do this is simply to allow users to upvote, downvote, and flag content. Reddit is one of the most complex and dynamic online networks, and has developed some of the most sophisticated policies over the years on this topic. Cofounder and CEO Steve Huffman wrote, in testimony submitted to the US House of Representatives, a description of Reddit's philosophy:

> *The way Reddit handles content moderation today is unique in the industry. We use a governance model akin to our own democracy— where everyone follows a set of rules, has the ability to vote and self-organize, and ultimately shares some responsibility for how the platform works.*
>
> *Users can accept or reject any piece of content. While most platforms have some version of the upvote function, an action to convey approval or agreement, we at Reddit see the additional downvote as equally important. The downvote is where community culture is made, through rejecting transgressive behavior or low-quality content.*[74]

In my chats with Steve, he often likens Reddit to a city, and to his team's role as city planners. The goal isn't to run all the activity in the city, but to set up spaces where communities big and small can flourish. To take the metaphor further, in order to administer the city it requires laws, culture, and best practices, all codified in software. This is why the ability to downvote, or to rate a rideshare driver one-star, or to write a scathing Yelp review for the Thai restaurant that recently made you sick are all related. Flagging and blocking content are important, too, if more serious actions need to be taken. They allow the network to self-govern, but within the framework set by the product team building the software. As Huffman notes, whereas in government we use laws to govern how we act toward each other, for networked products it is governed by code and the emergent culture shaped by that software.

In fact, I argue that software is the only way to govern large networks of people, and to keep bad actors out. Remember Dunbar's number? The theory by Robin Dunbar, a British evolutionary psychologist, argues that "the evolution of primate brains was driven by the need to coordinate and manage increasingly large social groups." He then describes a series of differently sized groups, starting in approximately multiples of three. You might expand from 3–5 people in your close friends and family, to your friend group, to a band, to about 150 in your clan, and a few steps later, to 1,000–2,000 people who together are in a tribe. But what happens to the "Dunbar number" when a technology product with network effects that's unconstrained by the rules of the physical world aggregates a digital network of 150,000 people? Or 150 million? Or a billion?

These are the scales of modern human networks, and it's Dunbar's number multiplied by millions. In these large-scale communities, standards and self-governance can't be maintained by people simply running around and talking to each other. Instead, the builders of these networked products must create features that nudge the interactions in the right direction. Reddit's upvotes and downvotes encourage funny, detailed comments. Google Calendar's "working hours" feature encourages people to be considerate of their colleagues in other time zones. The ability to report a Twitter user's account as hacked means it can be flagged for review.

Eventually, this is combined with machine learning and automation to further detect scammers and block them. Human upvotes, downvotes, and flagging are all inputs into automated systems that can be built. Software allows users to create and enforce standards on a network— this is "netiquette" embedded into the product, in software form.

As networks scale, functionality for people within the product to self-govern becomes both an inevitability and a necessity.

Usenet's Collapse, in Hindsight

With the benefit of hindsight—now decades of work in building communication tools and software—you might ask: could Usenet have been saved?

I think the answer is yes. After all, protocols like email and the web were invented in the same early internet era and are still thriving today. Email, by its nature, consists of a constant creation of smaller spaces (1:1 conversations, and group email threads). And as we all know, email has scaled to billions of users and is still usable, even as spam and trolls emerged over time. Email clients had to be upgraded and evolve—from Hotmail, to Outlook, to Gmail, and beyond—but it's still something that most of us still use every day. The web works the same, where there are a nearly infinite variety of private spaces to hang out powered by the combination of web domains, search engines, linking, and browsing.

Saving Usenet would have taken a significant amount of work. After all, it was built in an era where the internet was an open and trusted place, before spam, state-sponsored bots, and trolls. You could argue that had Usenet implemented algorithmic feeds, private messaging, the creation of smaller sub-networks, and so on, perhaps it would still be thriving. This is a tall order, though, and of course even our modern social products have not fully addressed these challenges.

Usenet was also blessed—and cursed—to be built as a decentralized, open-source protocol, as was common at that time. Networked products have to constantly tweak and iterate on their product to respond to the behavior and needs of their audience. In many ways, this is where centralized control—usually in the hands of a well-funded company—is in a better position to address the myriad of challenges that might crop up as the network expands. A startup can quickly make changes to their discovery algorithms, user interfaces, and hire moderators—as we've seen many social apps do.

In contrast, Usenet was never a company, never raised money, and didn't have hundreds of full-time staff. Any new product confronted with millions of users flooding in during an Eternal September will find it difficult to deal with, but the product will be particularly challenged if it's not backed with the resources and know-how to tackle it. Failure to evolve stalls growth, as the product hits the ceiling.

28

OVERCROWDING

YouTube

"When YouTube got to millions of videos, it got hard to find what you wanted to watch."

Yes, this is a fancy problem for a networked product but it's exactly the problem that YouTube faced as it grew. I interviewed Steve Chen, cofounder of YouTube, for *The Cold Start Problem* and asked him how they scaled the product so that the content would stay discoverable over time.

Too many videos on YouTube is a specific case of a broader phenomenon of overcrowding, which can hurt network effects and ultimately make a product unusable. It's what happens when there are too many comments, threads, and emails in your work inbox. It's when you've followed too many people on a social media app, and there's too much content to deal with. Or if too many players in a multiplayer game leads to server overload and difficulty finding the right match.

Steve cofounded YouTube in 2005, after a stint as a software engineer at PayPal. I'd gotten to know him as a frequent angel investor in new startups across games, social media, video, and more—he always had strong insights about the future of these industries. Although he had spent most of his twenties and thirties in the Bay Area, more recently he had moved his family to Taiwan, and so our conversations these days happen mostly through videoconference. He recounted the earliest days of the product, where their initial premise was quite different—you could only upload dating videos. That's right, YouTube started out as a dating site, where people could upload videos of themselves as part of a profile.

The Early Days of Organizing Videos

YouTube as a dating site didn't last long, and within a few weeks, the founders—Steve, Chad, and Jawed—realized it was a better idea to open it up to any type of content, not just people trying to find romance.

The ability to heart videos was quickly changed to a star icon. Soon any video could be uploaded, and the first video was a nineteen-second clip called "Me at the zoo," where YouTube cofounder Jawed Karim stood in front of some elephants, wearing a red and gray jacket. He remarks about their "really, really, really long, um, trunks," closing the video out with, "That's cool, and that's pretty much all there is to say."

As I've said throughout this book, networked products tend to start from humble beginnings—rather than big splashy launches—and YouTube was no different. Jawed's first video is a good example. Steve described the earliest days of content and how it grew:

In the earliest days, there was very little content to organize. Getting to the first 1,000 videos was the hardest part of YouTube's life, and we were just focused on that. Organizing the videos was an afterthought—we just had a list of recent videos that had been uploaded, and you could just browse through those. We had the idea that everyone who uploaded a video would share it with, say, 10 people, and then 5 of them would actually view it, and then at least one would upload another video. After we built some key

*features—video embedding and real-time transcoding—it started
to work.*[75]

In other words, the early days was just about solving the Cold Start
Problem, not designing the fancy recommendations algorithms that
YouTube is now known for. And even once there were more videos,
the attempt at discoverability focused on relatively basic curation—just
showing popular videos in different categories and countries. Steve described this to me:

> *Once we got a lot more videos, we had to redesign YouTube to
> make it easier to discover the best videos. At first, we had a page on
> YouTube to see just the top 100 videos overall, sorted by day, week,
> or month. Eventually it was broken out by country. The homepage
> was the only place where YouTube as a company would have con-
> trol of things, since we would choose the 10 videos. These were of-
> ten documentaries, or semi-professionally produced content so that
> people—particularly advertisers—who came to the YouTube front
> page would think we had great content.*

Eventually it made sense to create a categorization system for videos,
but in the early years everything was grouped in with each other. Even
while the numbers of videos was rapidly growing, so too were all the
other forms of content on the site. YouTube wasn't just the videos, it was
also the comments left by viewers:

> *Early in we saw that there were 100x more viewers than creators.
> Every social product at that time had comments, so we added them
> to YouTube, which was a way for the viewers to participate, too.
> It seems naive now, but we were just thinking about raw growth
> at that time—the raw number of videos, the raw number of
> comments—so we didn't think much about the quality. We weren't
> thinking about fake news or anything like that. The thought was,*

just get as many comments as possible out there, and the more con-troversial the better! Keep in mind that the vast majority of videos had zero comments, so getting feedback for our creators usually made the experience better for them. Of course now we know that once you get to a certain level of engagement, you need a different solution over time.

Within a year, it was clear that YouTube's growth in videos, comments, channels, and profiles rapidly exceeded the team's expectations. Its rise was rapid, and blew through every milestone that the team set in its first year. Initially, they tried to get to 1,000 views per day. Then 10,000 views/day, and when they hit that, 100,000 views/day. In less than a year, YouTube hit 1 million views per day—the start of a massive growth trajectory.

The YouTube team rolled out solution after solution to solve over-crowding, but focused on the simple ones first—displaying a list of recently uploaded videos, followed by a popularity-based sort, and eventually country segmentation. The evolution of YouTube's solution to overcrowding evolved from manual curation to popularity rankings to algorithmic methods. This is a necessary transition that every net-worked product has to make to solve the overcrowding problem.

Take the example of a marketplace startup—at the beginning, the relatively limited choices mean sellers don't compete with each other, avoiding overcrowding. Consumers have a more focused catalog from which to shop. Once it grows to millions of users, there might be hundreds of sellers for every product, and picking the best one may not be easy. Similarly, a workplace communications app needs to notify you of the most critical messages from important colleagues, which is easy when it's just your team. But eventually if everyone in your company is on a tool, then too many notifications can harm the experience. These are different variations of overcrowding effects that need to be solved over time.

Just as YouTube started with manual curation, most networked products can start with manual efforts. This means exercising editorial judgment, or allowing users to curate content themselves. The App Store has millions of apps, so when Apple releases a list of "Apps of the Year" in the App Store, it aids discovery for consumers but also inspires app developers to invest in the design and quality of their products. Or platforms can leverage user-generated content, where content is organized by the ever-popular hashtag—one example is Amazon's wish lists, which are driven primarily by users without editors. Similarly, using implicit data—whether that's attributes of the content or grouping the originator by their company or college email domain name—can bring people together with data from the network. Twitter uses a hybrid approach—the team analyzes activity on the network to identify trending events, which are then editorialized into stories.

The Rich Get Richer

So far I've just talked about the viewing experience on YouTube, but there's another constituent that can't be ignored: the creators. This is the hard side of the YouTube network and they play a critical role—uploading content, producing vlogs, shows, and other forms of entertainment. Early on, the video platform's most important content might have been uploads of *Saturday Night Live* clips of their "Lazy Sunday" sketch, but in later years, it's become the long tail of creators who post unique video content. It's this group that drives the platform's unique user-generated content library.

Overcrowding works in a different way for creators than for viewers. For creators, the problem becomes—how do you stand out? How do you get your videos watched? This is particularly acute for new creators, who face a "rich get richer" phenomenon. Across many categories of networked products, when early users join a network and start producing value, algorithms naturally reward them—and this is a good thing. When they do a good job, perhaps they earn five-star ratings, or they quickly gain lots of followers. Perhaps they get featured, or are ranked highly in popularity lists. This helps consumers find what they want, quickly, but the downside is that the already popular just get more popular.

Eventually, the problem becomes, how does a new member of the network break in? If everyone else has millions of followers, or thousands of five-star reviews, it can be hard. Eugene Wei, former CTO of Hulu and noted product thinker, writes about the "Old Money" in the context of social networks, arguing that established networks are harder for new users to break into:

> *Some networks reward those who gain a lot of followers early on with so much added exposure that they continue to gain more followers than other users, regardless of whether they've earned it through the quality of their posts. One hypothesis on why social networks tend to lose heat at scale is that this type of old money can't be cleared out, and new money loses the incentive to play the game.*
>
> *It's not that the existence of old money or old social capital dooms a social network to inevitable stagnation, but a social network should continue to prioritize distribution for the best content, whatever the definition of quality, regardless of the vintage of user producing it. Otherwise a form of social capital inequality sets in, and in the virtual world, where exit costs are much lower than in the real world, new users can easily leave for a new network where their work is more properly rewarded and where status mobility is higher.[75]*

This is true for social networks and also true for marketplaces, app stores, and other networked products as well. Ratings systems, reviews, followers, advertising systems all reinforce this, giving the most established members of a network dominance over everyone else.

High-quality users hogging all of the attention is the good version of the problem, but the bad version is much more problematic: What happens, particularly for social products, when the most controversial and opinionated users are rewarded with positive feedback loops? Or when purveyors of low-quality apps in a developer platform—like the Apple AppStore's initial proliferation of fart apps—are downloaded by users and ranked highly in charts? Ultimately, these loops need to be broken; otherwise your network may go in a direction you don't want.

The fancy term for this is preferential attachment, defined as: "the more connected a node is, the more likely it is to receive new links." Eventually this tamps down growth of the hard side of the network, because new users might start to seek another network where they can be successful. They want a more level playing field, and to get that, they will constantly try new products from competitors—not what a successful network wants.

The Power of Data and Algorithms

YouTube's solution to overcrowding—for both viewers and creators— has been shaped deeply by Google, which eventually acquired the company. In 2006, less than two years after it started, YouTube was purchased for $1.65 billion. It seemed like a huge sum at the time, yet the growth rate was so tremendous and the network effects so strong that years later, some analysts have estimated its value as a stand-alone company as north of $300 billion.

In the years following the acquisition, Steve described the company's focus very simply: "We were just trying to keep up with all the traffic." There weren't many huge feature releases, because the focus was on scaling the infrastructure as YouTube became the premier video platform for the internet.

What few feature updates existed focused on one thing: relevance, search, and algorithmic recommendations. In other words, the core levers to solve the overcrowding issues that might otherwise make

YouTube a confusing, fragmented place. This is where Google's expertise in dealing with massive amounts of data were crucial in developing two key features for YouTube in the ensuing years: Search and Related videos. Both helped users quickly navigate to videos they cared about, and because they were algorithmically driven, didn't require the company to manually edit or curate the content. The team also had early, furtive attempts at combining image recognition within the video content, but all too often a search term would match random text in the background—say, "cheerios" on a cereal box—as opposed to nailing key text.

Better matching between creators and their viewers alleviates the overcrowding issues that naturally emerge in a product that has more than a billion users. If new, niche creators are quickly connected to viewers that enjoy the work, in effect that is an algorithmically driven way of creating new networks within networks. It becomes a way to balance the supply and demand of content within the network, so that popular creators don't push out new ones, and viewers still see a stream of fresh and relevant content.

Today, years after cofounders Steve, Chad, and many of the early team have left YouTube, content discovery continues to improve even as the product scales to 2 billion monthly active users. YouTube's most popular videos hit 4 billion views in under a year. In recent years, the product has emphasized subscriptions and an algorithmically generated feed that surfaces highly engaging video. Autoplaying the next video— and better yet, picking the most relevant video to play next—stretches out session times. Applying Google's automated speech recognition on the audio within videos provides automatic closed captioning that is then searchable by users. Descriptions and other text content are automatically translated into multiple languages to make them more useful for international audiences. And even the much-maligned comments— often low-quality in the early years—have dramatically improved, as the ranking algorithms now elevate the best discussion points.

YouTube and its video recommendations aren't the only situation where machine learning can help alleviate overcrowding. These same ideas can also help build out a user's network.

One notable example of this is the ever present "People You May Know" or "Friend suggestions" feature. Every social platform at scale has some kind of implementation of it for a reason: it works incredibly well. My friend Aatif Awan, formerly vice president of growth at LinkedIn—who helped them scale to hundreds of millions of users and spearheaded their acquisition by Microsoft—explains how their algorithm works:

> *People You May Know was a key part of LinkedIn's success, generating billions of connections within the network. It started with "completing the triangle"—if a bunch of your friends have all connected with Alice but you haven't yet, then there's a good chance you might know Alice, too. Later, we incorporated implicit signals—maybe Alice just updated her profile to say she works at your same company. Maybe she's viewed your profile multiple times over several days. Putting all of these inputs into a machine learning model continued to give us mileage on this feature over many years.*[77]

This helped scale the density of the LinkedIn network so that even after you added hundreds of connections, the site could still help recommend relevant people to you. This is a direct example of alleviating the overcrowding dynamics of a social network, which is exactly why people recommendations, relevance-driven feeds, trending topics, and a slew of other algorithmic approaches have been layered onto social products over time.

The same rough approach can be applied to connecting people with their favorite dishes within food-delivery apps, or recommending a feed of relevant videos from a library of billions of pieces of content. Underlying all of these are both implicit and explicit signals from user interaction. Some products have gone so far as to base their primary value proposition on these algorithms—a good example is TikTok, whose "For You" feed is the primary way that users navigate content. The feed is driven by both explicit and implicit actions by users, and was described in a company blog post—an excerpt here:

> *On TikTok, the For You feed reflects preferences unique to each user. The system recommends content by ranking videos based on a combination of factors—starting from interests you express as a new user and adjusting for things you indicate you're not interested in, too—to form your personalized For You feed. Recommendations are based on a number of factors, including things like:*

- User interactions such as the videos you like or share, accounts you follow, comments you post, and content you create.
- Video information, which might include details like captions, sounds, and hashtags.
- Device and account settings like your language preference, country setting, and device type. These factors are included to make sure the system is optimized for performance, but they receive lower weight in the recommendation system relative to other data points we measure since users don't actively express these as preferences.[78]

TikTok's relevance algorithms make sure that even as hundreds of millions of videos are added over time, creators will still be matched with viewers who want to consume their content—and vice versa.

"Data network effects" are often invoked as a path for networks to solve relevance and overcrowding issues that emerge over time. The signals are a combination of individual actions but are also based on algorithmic models built on the combined behaviors of hundreds of millions of users. More users means more behavioral data, which in turn allows for more fine-grained content recommendations—a kind of data-driven network effect that belies the credit scoring examples I discussed earlier as well.

Algorithms Aren't a Silver Bullet

It's not just YouTube, LinkedIn, or TikTok that faces overcrowding issues. As networks grow, it becomes harder to connect users with what they're looking for. A marketplace with a carefully curated set of a few hundred sellers will look very different once there are hundreds of thousands or millions, with a multitude of offerings. Workplace collaboration tools are user friendly when there are only a few folders and people to keep track of, but once it spreads to the entire company, the UI needs to evolve to handle searching among the projects of hundreds of people. It even affects app stores, where Apple had to famously decree: "We have over 250,000 apps in the App Store. We don't need any more Fart apps." Methods might need to change, whether that's curation to browsing to search to algorithmically driven interfaces.

None of the approaches—algorithmic or otherwise—are a silver bullet, as the fight against overcrowding never ends. And in fact, the feedback loops can sometimes lead to unintended consequences. As we've seen in social media, you have to be careful about what you're optimizing for—if you pick pure engagement, then an algorithmic feed might just show a series of controversial click-bait content. Or if a marketplace purely optimizes based on revenue, you might get a series of low-relevance, high-price-tag items that have high expected value when someone does buy. But qualitatively, this doesn't feel fair.

In my conversations with Steve about his early days at YouTube, it was clear that organizing content in the product—the videos, users, and comments—was a major focus early on. But because of the breakneck speed at which the product grew—zero to millions of users, and a billion-dollar acquisition in less than two years—the techniques to aid content discovery had to rapidly shift. It didn't end after the first few years. More than a decade later, YouTube continues to grapple with the same overcrowding issues, but with more and more sophisticated tools. The most recent statistic is that YouTube adds nearly 600 hours of content every minute, as the product continues to grow its network into the many billions of users across web and mobile.

To me, the key learning from the YouTube story is the journey that every networked product has to take. When they started out, they needed very little organization, but as the network grew, more and more structure was applied—first by editors, moderators, and users—and then by data and algorithms. The earliest iterations weren't sophisticated, just whatever got the job done. Algorithms came later, and even years later, keeping the network healthy is still an everyday battle.

PART VI

THE MOAT

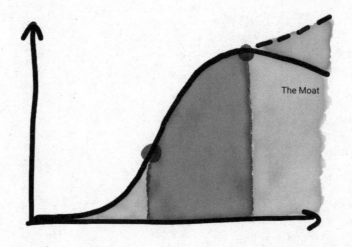

The Moat

29

WIMDU VERSUS AIRBNB

If your product has network effects, your competitors likely have them, too—which can create a dangerous situation. This is exactly what Airbnb took on, in 2011, when they encountered their first direct competitor—a fearsome new startup emerging out of Berlin called Wimdu.

When Wimdu launched, it had an eerily similar look to Airbnb—and this was by design. Wimdu set its web page title to "Apartments & Bed and breakfast" and included a big title of "Find Your Favorite Places to Stay," inspired by Airbnb's tag line "Find a place to stay." The bottom of Wimdu's homepage said the concept had been featured in the *New York Times*—but of course the article had been about Airbnb, not Wimdu.

Wimdu was a direct copy of Airbnb focused initially on the European market, and from day one, it was a scary competitor—it launched with $90 million in funding, the largest investment in a European startup ever, and within less than one hundred days, the company already hired over 400 people and had thousands of properties on its marketplace. Wimdu was spun up by the Samwer brothers and their startup studio Rocket Internet, which had an explicit strategy of cloning US businesses. They had done this before, with great success, starting with Alando, eventually sold to eBay for $50 million, and CityDeals, inspired and acquired by Groupon for $170 million after just five months. Rocket Internet would often unabashedly clone down to color schemes, text on pages, features, and so on. They executed this playbook with eBay, to great success, and were now ready to go after Airbnb.

Wimdu was not good news for Airbnb. Brian Chesky, Airbnb's co-founder and CEO, described the Samwer brothers and their approach in an interview for "Blitzscaling":

> So basically these two brothers not only, I was told, would kill any-one they cloned, they're like the attack of the clones, but they also had built what was, at least positioned at the time, to be the fastest growing, most successful startup of all time.
>
> Suddenly this giant dragon appears and you're like this is not possible to beat him. And now at this point, we had raised 7 mil-lion dollars.[79]

At that point, Airbnb was only two and a half years old, had 40 em-ployees, and had raised a small venture capital round. It only supported payments in USD, no European currencies, and hadn't been translated to any languages beyond English. Within a few months, Wimdu had hired 400 employees and had $90 million in funding—literally ten times bigger on paper than Airbnb, in a tenth of the time.

It was not just the European market that was at stake. There was precedent in the travel industry for this kind of competition becoming a much larger problem. Booking.com also originated in Europe and even-tually came to challenge Expedia, TripAdvisor, and other American startups as a global player. If Wimdu was able to build strong atomic networks originating in Europe, it might then become a direct global competitor that would challenge Airbnb across many markets around the world.

This was an important moment because for Airbnb, up to this point, the competition had been indirect or unimpressive. This was the first head-to-head challenger. When Airbnb first launched, there were already several adjacent competitors. First, VRBO—the acronym for "Vacation Rental by Owner"—was founded in 1995 to rent the founder's ski resort condo. It had effectively the same idea as Airbnb in matching homeowners and guests, but the product UI was less polished, with more friction to list and transact. VRBO was later merged with HomeAway, and more important, the network focused on vacation rentals located in out-of-the-way destinations rather than Airbnb's early focus on shared spaces within dense urban cities. Another product, Couchsurfing, already existed as well, and was an indirect competitor, albeit a peculiar one. Founded in 2003 as a nonprofit, Couchsurfing allowed for people to crash on each other's sofa while traveling but did not require payment. Instead the focus was on community and letting members guide each other around a new town. (The result was occasional romantic advances, both wanted and unwanted, in the absence of economic clarity and motivations.) And of course Craigslist existed as well, with a section for renting spare rooms and short-term stays, but lacked consistency in having descriptions, inventory, photos, and safety, as I've discussed.

By mid-2011, Wimdu was aggressive in taking on the European market. To quickly build supply, Wimdu focused on replicating Airbnb's listings through multiple coordinated efforts, both automated and manual. On the automated side, Wimdu built bots that would scrape listings—mirroring descriptions, photos, and availability so that if hosts wanted to maintain listings on both platforms, it would be easy. However, there were reports from the community that sometimes the listings were just fake—if you tried to book them and they didn't actually exist on Wimdu, guests would simply be rerouted to other listings that were available. On the ground, Wimdu would pose as guests and rent from Airbnb hosts, and during the process try to convince them to also list on Wimdu. Combine this with a big launch and PR blitz across Europe, and the company built over 50,000 listings and was on its way to $130 million in gross revenue in its first year of operations.

An article in 2012 described Wimdu's progress:

After one year, Wimdu's website boasts 50,000 properties listed, in over 100 countries, making it by far the largest social accommodation search website coming from Europe. . . .

The fledgling company is currently booking revenues of 5 million euros ($6.6 million) per month. Again, after just a year. It even expects revenue to exceed 100 million euros ($132 million) for the whole of 2012.

It's showing rapid growth, too: in fact, Wimdu says its monthly revenue has quadrupled in the past three months.[78]

After this fast start, an unbelievable thing happened: Wimdu went to zero.

It took just two years for Wimdu to unravel. Incredibly by 2014, it was laying off employees and accepting that it had lost leadership in the European market. Eventually, through several rounds of M&A, all the employees were laid off in 2018.

All the shortcuts that Wimdu took in the early years helped it gain supply on paper, but it ignored an important lesson about adding hosts to the hard side of the network. Michael Schaecher, an early employee at Airbnb (#17) who headed up some of the international efforts in the competitive response, said of Wimdu's strategy:

All supply isn't created equal. Wimdu's top 10% of inventory was at the bottom 10% of Airbnb's. They went for numbers, but recruited large property owners that managed hundreds of units in the form of low-end hostels. They went the easy route and would get 1000 listings via 10 property owners, but the experience for customers was disappointing.

In the early days at Airbnb, we would always talk about creating a positive "Expectations Gap." In the early days, when we were new, guests go in with low expectations, but then would be blown away by the experience. You need this high NPS to get people to tell their friends, and it makes hosts more likely to join too. Our competitors who took shortcuts couldn't deliver here.[81]

While Wimdu was able to quickly announce impressive numbers, the hard side of the network wasn't fully formed or curated to reflect quality. And to satisfy this rapid influx of inventory, Wimdu would be forced to simultaneously grow demand explosively as well. Thus as a result, the demand side of Wimdu—attracting travelers—also relied on trading off speed for quality. The rapid acquisition of travelers was driven primarily by paid marketing, as the site was too new to rely on word of mouth, viral marketing, SEO, or other low-cost user acquisition channels. Catalyzing both sides of the network can work if atomic networks quickly form and network effects kick in, but Wimdu's network had quality problems. It would take time to click. Plus, Airbnb's competitive response would be fierce.

Airbnb's small team rallied on the notion that it had been a "peacetime company, but now we've entered wartime." It had a lot to catch up on: much of the supply side of Airbnb's network had been organically built—it hadn't been deliberate. As long as a property had an address on Google Maps, a listing could be made, and as an open platform, hosts started to appear in Europe even given the lack of internationalized payment options and language localization. Brian Chesky and the early team would occasionally make their way through Europe, speaking at conferences and hosting parties and events, but there were no full-time employees on the ground to counter Wimdu's swift rise. This was about to change in a big way.

On the plus side, Airbnb's organic supply meant that it already had several years of unique high-quality inventory. The network in Europe had already formed into atomic networks, albeit at a smaller scale than in the United States. Travelers from the States could use Airbnb, pay in US dollars, and stay at listings in Europe where the hosts accepted PayPal. It was working, and Airbnb could leverage its success in the States to succeed in Europe—what many call a "global network effect." Airbnb's problem was more about scaling the network further than solving the dreaded Cold Start Problem.

When Wimdu launched, the Samwers reached out to Airbnb to discuss combining forces, as they had done with Groupon and eBay to facilitate a speedy exit. Discussions ensued between Airbnb and Wimdu cofounders and investors—meeting multiple times, touring the Wimdu offices, and checking with other founders like Andrew Mason from Groupon to best understand the potential outcome. In the end, Airbnb chose to fight. Brian Chesky described his thought process:

> *My view was, my biggest punishment, my biggest revenge on you is, I'm gonna make you run this company long term. So you had the baby, now you gotta raise the child. And you're stuck with it for 18 years. Because I knew he wanted to sell the company.*
>
> *I knew he could move faster than me for a year, but he wasn't gonna keep doing it. And so that was our strategy. And we built the company long term. And the ultimate way we won is, we had a better community. He couldn't understand community. And I think we had a better product.[82]*

To do this, the company would mobilize their product teams to rapidly improve their support for international regions. Jonathan Golden, the first product manager at Airbnb, described their efforts:

> *Early on, Airbnb's listing experience was basic. You filled out forms, uploaded 1 photo—usually not professional—and editing the listing after the fact was hard. The mobile app in the early days was lightweight, where you could only browse but not book. There were a lot of markets in those days with just 1 or 2 listings. Booking only supported US dollars, so it catered towards American travelers only, and for hosts, they could get money out via a bank transfer to an American bank via ACH, or PayPal.*

We needed to get from this skeleton of a product into something that could work internationally if we wanted to fend off Wimdu.

We internationalized the product, translating it into all the major languages. We went from supporting 1 currency to adding 32. We bought all the local domains, like airbnb.co.uk for the UK website and airbnb.es for Spain. It was important to move quickly to close off the opportunity in Europe.[83]

Alongside the product, the fastest way to fight on Wimdu's turf was to quickly scale up paid marketing in Europe using Facebook, Google, and other channels to augment the company's organic channels, built over years. Most important, Airbnb finally pulled the trigger on putting boots on the ground—hiring Martin Reiter, the company's first head of international, and also partnering with Springstar, a German incubator and peer of Rocket Internet's, to accelerate their international expansion.

In 2012, at a rental in Spain, the future international managers got together to start writing the playbook for the "Invasion of Europe." They would launch each region with a PR blitz, with an integrated marketing campaign featuring press, Facebook ads, email, and other touchpoints. They would launch seven offices over four months. All the new localized websites would launch in coordinated fashion.

And that's how Europe was won.

The story of Wimdu and Airbnb is a fascinating one because it encompasses many of the counterintuitive aspects of network-based competition. We see Airbnb, with its smaller European network, defeat a larger and laser-focused competitor. It's a battle of a global network trying to get enough density in a regional network. We see the importance of quality over quantity, and different approaches for the easy and hard sides of a network. These nuances apply to other network-by-network competitive situations like Uber versus DoorDash, or Slack versus Microsoft Teams. This case study also hints at some foundational underpinnings that dictate competition between two players who both have network effects.

Introducing the Moat

In this stage of the framework, the moat, I will describe what happens when networks compete with other networks, and why this form of competition is so unique. The chapters in this part cover both theory and case studies from Craigslist, Uber, Google+, eBay, and Microsoft.

To introduce the nature of network-based competition, I describe why it's high-stakes, where the loser can go to zero while the victor taps into its network effects to win the market—this is the "Vicious Cycle, Virtuous Cycle." But the dynamics of competition are counterintuitive. Networked products exist in a market where all their competitors have network efforts, too, and what you do differs based on if you are David or Goliath. If you're Goliath, what do you do when a high-momentum new startup is emerging? Or if you're David, what happens when a giant fast-follows you?

One of the core strategies in network-based competition is "Cherry Picking." An incumbent may look invincible, but its empire is usually made up of many, many smaller networks, some of which are more vulnerable than others—just look at Craigslist and its long line of cherry pickers, including Airbnb. From the standpoint of the biggest player in the market, it's tempting to take on a fast-growing startup with a Big Bang Launch—maybe a big, glitzy, media-driven announcement like the type that Steve Jobs made famous. Google+ is the quintessential case study, as they pursued Facebook. Yet these end in "Big Bang Failures" when the networks end up diffuse, weak, and prone to collapse.

I'll close this section by unpacking a theme that appears again and again in network-based competition: it's asymmetric. The smaller player and bigger player use different strategies. And the most intense competition tends to happen as networks compete over the most valuable users of one network to another—this is "Competing over the Hard Side." The drivers, creators, and organizers that do the hard work in the network are incredibly valuable, and by shifting them over, a new network can rise while an incumbent crumbles. Of course, the bigger player has its own moves, and none more powerful than "Bundling." By establishing a dominant position in the market, they can take over adjacent ones simply by combining products. I'll describe the dynamics of the Browser Wars of the 1990s, where Microsoft famously bundled Internet Explorer in its fight against Netscape. Sometimes this move works very well, and sometimes it doesn't.

The Moat is the final phase of the Cold Start Theory. The earliest chapters of the book focus on starting from zero, then on scaling, and eventually the incumbent establishes its monopoly on its industry. The moat is about a successful network that defends its turf, using network effects in a perpetual battle against smaller networks trying to enter the market.

30

VICIOUS CYCLE, VIRTUOUS CYCLE

The legendary investor Warren Buffett popularized the concept of the competitive moat, as he described his investing strategy:

> The key to investing is not assessing how much an industry is going to affect society, or how much it will grow, but rather determining the competitive advantage of any given company and, above all, the durability of that advantage. The products or services that have wide, sustainable moats around them are the ones that deliver rewards to investors.[84]

Because Buffett generally invests in low-tech companies like See's Candies or Coca-Cola, the moat he refers to is often a strong brand or a unique business model. For software products with network effects, a strong moat means something different: how much effort, time, and capital does it take to replicate a product's features and its network? In the modern era, cloning software features is usually not the hard part—replicating the complete functionality of a Slack or Airbnb might take time, but it is tractable. It's the difficulty of cloning their network that makes these types of products highly defensible.

I'll use an example to think through the competitive moat. Let's start from first principles, with an example of Airbnb trying to launch in a new city with no competitors in sight. As the early Airbnb team described, the Cold Start Problem lies in the difficulty of launching a new city to a Tipping Point of over 300 listings with 100 reviews. This requires real effort, because the minimum network size is quite large—contrasted to many other network types like communication apps, which might only require two or three people to get started. But once Airbnb has reached Escape Velocity in a market, the Cold Start Problem creates the defense against new entrants.

After all, every new competitor entering the city will need to solve the Cold Start Problem and build up the same density—as hard as it was for your product to go from zero to a Tipping Point, it will be even harder for competitors starting from a disadvantage.

This is why something more interesting happens once there is already a preexisting player. It is often not enough for a new competitor to simply re-create what Airbnb's already done and get the 300 listings. Once the network has scale and is growing organically, then they have taken many of the best and most easily acquirable supply and demand. A new competitor is competing with a network that's growing to 400 and to 500 and more, quickly. Furthermore, once Airbnb gets to a fully baked atomic network, a new entrant generally has to provide a better, more differentiated experience for guests and hosts. Otherwise, why not use what already works?

This is literally the moat, and reframes the Cold Start Problem for Airbnb's competitors. The anti-network effects that plague any new network are multiplied when Airbnb is already in the market. The wider and deeper the curve is, the harder it is for new companies to get started.

Yet a competitive moat might be limited in its effectiveness outside of a given city, in Uber's case, or a company, in Slack's. For Uber, being dominant in New York did not help the company succeed in San Diego, as its network effects were localized primarily to each individual city. This was always the critique of Uber's business, and the root cause of the vicious trench warfare that needed to be fought city by city. That's not to say that the moats within a particular city aren't formidable—it would certainly take billions of dollars to create a new network from scratch in, say, San Francisco or New York, which is why new rideshare competitors are no longer being formed in these mature markets. Fragmentation of the market was always inevitable based on the city-by-city structure of its network.

In contrast, Airbnb's moat is much stronger than Uber's due to the nature of travel. Having Airbnb hosts in Miami, Austin, and San Diego creates a stronger network for the demand side of travelers, and vice versa. As a result, it's hard to pick off an individual city, as you'd have to replace all the travelers that might visit from anywhere in the world. Thus Airbnb has a wide, deep global moat, in contrast to Uber's. And it would take an order of magnitude more capital to try to pick off a core city piecemeal. The same can be said for a networked product like Slack, Dropbox, or Google Suite, which are mostly used internally within company—the moat generally just applies there—whereas Zoom's network has a deep, overall moat, as it's used by participants connecting across companies.

The final part of the Cold Start framework, "The Moat," is about the unique challenges of companies facing network-based competition—how it's different, where new startups have advantages, and how incumbents can respond.

To start, let's zoom out for a moment and describe why these dynamics are so important.

The Battle of Networks

In a battle of networks, the stakes are high, especially when the success of one product means the potential annihilation of another. Just look at Airbnb and Wimdu, but also Slack and Hipchat, or Uber and Sidecar. Of each pair, one is a deca-billion-dollar company, and the other is ancient history.

This happens because networked products can lean toward "winner take all." When one product emerges as the winner in an atomic network, that's just the group choosing their favorite app. But repeat that enough times, and that becomes the playbook for a product to win across the entire market—and that's a monopoly. This happens because within an atomic network of users, whether they are friends or colleagues, it's common to standardize on a single product for convenience. For example, within the workplace, a team and sometimes an entire company will converge on the same set of products. They will use the same collaboration tools to store important documents, message coworkers, or edit spreadsheets. A single app in each category tends to receive the lion's share of engagement, so that the team that uses Slack will not spend an equal amount of time in Microsoft Teams as well—it's usually one or the other. One product eventually dominates, at least within that particular network.

If a networked product can begin to win over a series of networks faster than its competition, then it develops an accumulating advantage. These advantages, naturally, manifest as increasing network effects across customer acquisition, engagement, and monetization. Smaller networks might unravel and lose their users, who might switch over. Naturally, it becomes important for every player to figure out how to compete in this type of high-stakes environment. But how does the competitive playbook work in a world with network effects?

First, I'll tell you what it's not: it's certainly not a contest to see who can ship more features. In fact, sometimes the products seem roughly the same—just think about food-delivery or messaging apps—and if not, they often become undifferentiated since the features are relatively easy to copy. Instead, it's often the dynamics of the underlying network that make all the difference. Although the apps for DoorDash and Uber Eats look similar, the former's focus on high-value, low-competition areas like suburbs and college towns made all the difference—today, DoorDash's market share is 2x that of Uber Eats. Facebook built highly dense and engaged networks starting with college campuses versus

Google+'s scattered launch that built weak, disconnected networks. Rarely in network-effects-driven categories does a product win based on features—instead, it's a combination of harnessing network effects and building a product experience that reinforces those advantages.

It's also not about whose network is bigger, a counterpoint to jargon like "first mover advantage." In reality, you see examples of startups disrupting the big guys all the time. There's been a slew of players who have "unbundled" parts of Craigslist, cherry-picking the best subcategories and making them apps unto themselves. Airbnb, Zillow, Thumbtack, Indeed, and many others fall into this category. Facebook won in a world where MySpace was already huge. And more recently, collaboration tools like Notion and Zoom are succeeding in a world where Google Suite, WebEx, and Skype already have significant traction. Instead, the quality of the networks matters a lot—which makes it important for new entrants to figure out which networks to cherry-pick to get started, which I'll discuss in its own chapter.

Given that big companies and startups are susceptible to competition, what happens when you're at the receiving end of these competitive moves? Network-based competition is unique, and has its own dynamics. You might find yourself at the startup, facing impossible odds competing with a larger player that is copying your every move. Or you might be at an established company, finding that one of your ankle-biting startups has suddenly found a series of atomic networks gelling in a particular niche, and quickly growing to surpass you in a strategic market. Knowing that the conclusion to this battle might be existential, how do you respond?

Your Competition Has Network Effects, Too

To figure out a response, it's important to acknowledge a common myth about defensibility and moats: that somehow, network effects will magically help you fend off competition. This is a myth repeated again and again in startup pitch presentations to investors and entrepreneurs. It's a lie that entrepreneurs tell to themselves.

It isn't true—simply having network effects is not enough, because if your product has them, it's likely that your competitors have them, too. Whether you are a marketplace, social network, workplace collaboration tool, or app store, you are in a "networked category." It's intrinsic in these categories that every player is a multi-sided network that connects people, and is governed under the dynamics of Cold Start Theory. Effective competitive strategy is about who scales and leverages their network effects in the best way possible.

No wonder we often see smaller players upend larger ones, in an apparent violation of Metcalfe's Law. If every product in a category can rely on their network, then it's not about who's initially the largest. Instead, the question is, who is doing the best job amplifying and scaling their Acquisition, Engagement, and Economic effects. It's what we see repeatedly over time: MySpace was the biggest social network in the mid-2000s and lost to Facebook, then a smaller, newer entrant with a focus on college networks with stronger product execution. HipChat was ahead in workplace communication, but was upended by Slack. Grubhub created a successful, profitable multibillion-dollar food-ordering company, but has rapidly lost ground to Uber Eats and DoorDash.

In other words, for those working in the categories of marketplaces, messaging apps, social networks, collaboration tools, or otherwise—the good news is, your product has network effects. But the bad news is, so does your competition. It's how you grow and scale your network that matters.

Network Collapse

The maturity of the market also dictates the nature of competition. When a product category is early, and every networked product is gaining traction, life is good. In the earliest days of the social network category, multiple players—MySpace, Bebo, Hi5, Tagged, and a dozen others—all looked to be growing like weeds. But as the market matured, competition turned zero sum.

Cold Start Theory predicts that competition creates a vicious cycle alongside the virtuous one, where network effects provide a boost to the winner and simultaneously generate strong negative effects to the losing networks. If the value of a network exponentially grows as users join, the opposite must also be true. As people leave, the value of a network exponentially disintegrates, and it will impact Acquisition, Engagement, and Economics—meaning viral growth stalls, engagement is reduced, and monetization falls.

If pushed hard enough, a network suffers a complete collapse, reversing its way through the Cold Start Problem.

Sometimes the network goes to zero (or nearly so), and sometimes it ends up as a much smaller atomic network—a niche that it can hold on to, but as a shell of its former self. In Facebook's ascendance, LinkedIn and Twitter eventually thrived—their use cases were different and complementary—but its direct competitors, including MySpace and a litany of others, were eventually abandoned by users.

The vicious cycle is more dangerous than the gravitational pull I discussed in earlier chapters on the Cold Start Problem, because competition can force your network to fully unravel and collapse. This is what happened to Wimdu. When one atomic network collapses, the adjacent networks that are intertwined might also be pulled down—sort of a domino effect. If Wimdu loses supply in Berlin, it pulls down the aggregate usefulness of the service across Germany but also all of Europe, which then leads to even less engagement. This is the vicious cycle in action.

David versus Goliath

Asymmetry lies at the heart of network-based competition. The larger or smaller network will be at different stages of the Cold Start framework and, as such, will gravitate toward a different set of levers. The giant is often fighting gravitational pull as its network grows and saturates the market. To combat these negative forces, it must add new use cases, introduce the product to new audiences, all while making sure it's generating a profit. The upstart, on the other hand, is trying to solve the Cold Start Problem, and often starts with a niche. A new startup has the luxury of placing less emphasis on profitability and might instead focus on top-line growth, subsidizing the market to grow its network. When they encounter each other in the market, it becomes natural that their competitive moves reflect their different goals and resources.

Startups have fewer resources—capital, employees, distribution—but have important advantages in the context of building new networks: speed and a lack of sacred cows. A new startup looking to compete against Zoom might try a more specific use case, like events, and if that doesn't work, they can quickly pivot and try something else, like corporate education classes. Startups like YouTube, Twitch, Twitter, and many other products have similar stories, and went through an incubation phase as the product was refined and an initial network was built. Trying and failing many times is part of the startup journey—it only takes the discovery of one atomic network to get into the market. With that, a startup is often able to start the next leg of the journey, often with more investment and resources to support them.

Contrast that to a larger company, which has obvious advantages in resources, manpower, and existing product lines. But there are real disadvantages, too: it's much harder to solve the Cold Start Problem with a slower pace of execution, risk aversion, and a "strategy tax" that requires new products to align to the existing business. Something seems to happen when companies grow to tens of thousands of employees—they inevitably create rigorous processes for everything, including planning cycles, performance reviews, and so on. This helps teams focus, but it also creates a harder environment for entrepreneurial risk-taking. I saw this firsthand at Uber, whose entrepreneurial culture shifted in its later years toward profitability and coordinating the efforts of tens of thousands. This made it much harder to start new initiatives—for better and worse.

When David and Goliath meet in the market—and often it's one Goliath and many investor-funded Davids at once—the resulting moves and countermoves are fascinating.

Now that I have laid down some of the theoretical foundation for how competition fits into Cold Start Theory, let me describe and unpack some of the most powerful moves in the network-versus-network playbook.

31

CHERRY PICKING

Craigslist

Before Airbnb and Wimdu, there was Airbnb and Craigslist.

Craigslist is a classifieds listing site that is an embodiment of a paradox. On one hand, it has stayed the same—Craigslist has a 1990s-era web design with blue links and gray boxes—lacking a steady flow of new features or redesigns or additional new products. Yet it is also a behemoth. Today it serves 570 cities across the world and is estimated to generate $1 billion in revenue per year. Remarkably, it is wholly owned by Craig Newmark and Jim Buckmaster, who are two of the most understated billionaires in tech. Craigslist has an interesting founding story of its own, starting out as an email newsletter in 1995 focused on local events—literally, "Craig's List"—before it evolved into a website with categories for jobs, housing, services, sales, and more. Today it is a massive, horizontal network for many local categories—with 80 million classifieds listings per month and 20 billion page views. It is a top 100 website on the internet, and amazingly, it operates with a staff of only a few dozen people.

Yet for all of its success, a long line of startups have cherry-picked some of its most valuable audiences—famously referred to as the "unbundling of Craigslist." This was coined by Andrew Parker, then a New

York–based startup investor, who made the observation in 2010[85] that Craigslist was getting "unbundled" by an emerging crop of startups— from Indeed for the Jobs section, StubHub for tickets, Etsy for selling arts and crafts, and so on. Years later, this ragtag collection of upstarts has consolidated around a few billion-dollar players—including Airbnb, Tinder, Zillow, Reddit, and a number of other companies.

Craigslist could have retained control of all of these incredibly valuable categories, and yet it didn't. Why?

Craigslist should not be thought of as a single, monolithic network built on a unified classifieds product, but rather as a network of networks—the people who use the Seattle Craigslist are not the same as users in Miami. And within a geography, the Seattle Jobs section has a network around it that's distinct from the Seattle Community network. Jobs is a network that connects companies and consumers looking for work, whereas Community is about consumers meeting each other— yes, there will be overlap from folks looking for both at the same time, but that will be in the minority of cases. When these subnetworks splinter off, lured by a new networked product that potentially serves their need, it provides the opportunity to hit a Tipping Point in one fell swoop.

Every dominant network might seem invincible, but the networks-of-networks framing argues that some parts of the network are weaker than others. Some are serving their customers well, and others are ready for a better product to emerge. There is an upstart's advantage—they can cherry-pick the one really attractive use case that's the most valuable and poorly defended by an incumbent. Only one entry point is needed for an upstart to build their initial atomic network, whereas the incumbent has to protect all its entry points. When the incumbent network does a bad job of this, a new entrant can waltz right into the market. This is the core asymmetry of network-based competition.

When large networked products reach immense scale—like eBay, Craigslist, LinkedIn, and YouTube have done—they come to represent a network of networks that include an endless number of diverse needs. The needs of buyers and sellers of high-end collectible sneakers end up being different from those selling used cars. In a network representing thousands of such diverse communities, there are always a few that get underserved. This is especially true when larger networks hit a ceiling because they aren't able to keep the network discoverable, or maintain quality, or because of the other negative effects I explored in the past chapter. The parts of the network that are most affected by these negative factors are the ones most vulnerable to new, emerging competition.

The opportunity to unbundle these larger networks requires both building the necessary product features to support these splinter communities and also taking the direct action to message, advertise, or otherwise convince members of the larger horizontal community to shift over. Airbnb provides one of the most famous examples of this tango. Amid Craigslist's dozens of categories of local products and services, there was a smaller category for renting out rooms. However, the experience was terrible—sometimes there was accurate pricing and photos, but often not. Importantly, there was no way to easily check if certain dates were available, nor were there standard features like ratings and reviews. It just didn't work well. Airbnb started with a significantly better experience aiming to solve all of that. Just like Craigslist, Airbnb had listings with maps, descriptions, and pricing, but also extended the functionality with galleries of photos, reviews and ratings, integrated payments, reservations, profiles of the hosts, and much more.

At launch in 2008, a simple website was hosted at Airbedandbreak fast.com. It had a series of listings, with prices, and ways to contact the host. In retrospect, Airbnb's features might seem obvious. And hypothetically, Craigslist could have incorporated all of these ideas as well, but it would have been hard for Craigslist's small team to respond to this particular subnetwork when many other parts of its network were being unbundled. At the same time Airbnb was emerging, there were similar networked products going after dating, real estate, gig work, and so on. It would have been more natural for Craigslist to focus on features that might help horizontally across the entire site, rather than to follow one particular company into a vertical.

Finding the Soft Spot

In a way, this is a form of the Innovator's Dilemma. Clayton Christensen's influential book on business strategy describes how new players in a market start with seemingly undesirable niche segments, which are ignored by incumbents while they are focusing on the most profitable segments and use cases. He uses steel mills, disk drives, and mechanical excavators in his examples, arguing that eventually the incumbents start overserving their customers since there are diminishing returns to additional new features. The upstarts are often armed with a technology innovation that lets them dominate a niche and eventually go after the main market. Much of this is true, in the abstract, for networked products—but there are important additions worth discussing to make disruption theory even more powerful in the context of network effects.

First, the concept of atomic networks provides the clearest goalposts for an upstart network—it's all about splitting off, or creating from scratch, a distinct and higher-density atomic network. Initially, Craigslist seemed huge, both in audience size and the maturity of the features, relative to the smaller niche of renting rooms. However, as Airbnb built a dense community, city by city, it wasn't long before a given city had more comprehensive inventory than Craigslist, even if the aggregate number of listings was lower. Network density beats total size, a theme we've seen throughout the examples of this book. Once a niche player forms their atomic networks and begins to branch out, they enjoy network effects that become very hard to stop, particularly in their initial market.

The question is, which atomic network do you pick? If one were to try to unbundle Craigslist, should the focus be used goods? Gigs? Dating? Something else? Why was room rental such a strong starting point? The initial starting point matters because some are more easily able to access network effects. In Airbnb's case, the high value of every transaction and user stemmed from shared rooms ultimately being adjacent to travel, an industry where stays are often measured in the thousands of dollars in a single trip. This high economic value meant that Airbnb could quickly scale with the Economic network effect that translated each new successive listing into increased conversion rates, improved unit economics, and higher gross revenues for the network. The high average order value for Airbnb meant that it could then use this revenue to power the rest of its business.

As another example, let's examine Snapchat. The product's photo messaging features could be seen as just a feature of a larger social network product since, at the time, photos were one of many media types shared on Facebook, Twitter, MySpace, and other platforms. However, constraining the product to photo communication meant that Snapchat could cherry-pick the one highest-frequency and stickiest use case—driven by ensuing back-and-forth communication—that would quickly amplify stickiness as new users were added. In the early days as many as 10–20 photo messages per day were sent per active user, an order of magnitude of what's shared on many social networks. Dropbox's initial features gave it a boost in acquiring new users, thanks to its viral folder sharing. Of course, shared folders had been part of many products before—including the core Windows operating system—but Dropbox was able to carve off a key use case that was sticky, ultimately monetized well, and was inherently shareable.

Each of these examples, naturally, was able to leverage multiple network effects on its upward trajectory. Each of these companies did this in crowded markets in the face of successful incumbents—who also possessed various forms of network effects—and still established themselves. By picking the right entry points, these new startups were springloaded to quickly reach an atomic network quickly, and then scale up with multiple network effects.

Switching over Entire Networks

Part of why cherry picking can be dangerous for the incumbent is that the upstart networks can reach over and directly acquire an entire set of users who have been conveniently aggregated on your network. It's just software, after all, and users can spread competitors within an incumbent's network by using all the convenient communication and social tools. Airbnb is again an example of this. The company not only unbundled Craigslist and turned the shared rooms idea into an entire product, but they actually used Craiglist users to advertise Airbnb to other users.

How? Early on, Airbnb added functionality so that when a host was done setting up their listing, they could publish it to Craigslist, with photos, details, and an "Interested? Got a question? Contact me here" link that drove Craigslist users back to Airbnb. These features were accomplished not by using APIs provided by Craigslist, but by reverse-engineering the platform and creating a bot to do it automatically—clever! I first wrote about this in 2012 on my blog, in a post titled "Growth Hacker is the new VP Marketing" with this example in mind. By the time Craigslist decided it didn't like this functionality and disabled it, months had passed and Airbnb had formed its atomic network.

The same thing happened in the early days of social networks, when Facebook, LinkedIn, Skype, and others grew on the back of email contacts importing from Hotmail, Yahoo Mail, and other mail clients. They used libraries like Octazen—later acquired by Facebook—to scrape contacts, helping the social networks grow and connect their users. At the time, these new social networks didn't look like direct threats to email. They were operating within niche parts of messaging overall, focused on college and professional networks. It took several years for the email providers to shut down access after recognizing their importance.

When an incumbent has its network cherry-picked, it's extra painful along two dimensions: First, any network that is lost is unlikely to be regained, as anti-network effects kick back in. And second, the decline in market share hits doubly hard, which has implications for being able to raise money.

Let me explain. When one network wins at the expense of the other, the reemergence of the Cold Start Problem makes it difficult to ever recover that network. As a hypothetical, let's say that in the Seattle market all the short-term listings move from Craigslist to Airbnb—once this movement crosses a certain threshold, it's likely that the anti-network effects on Craigslist will cause the market there to become illiquid and go to zero. For Craigslist to get this market back, they'll have to solve the Cold Start Problem again—except this time with a competitor also in the market who might react with incentives and product features to counter.

The second way in which a head-to-head loss of a network matters is how it manifests in market share. This was a metric that the Uber team focused on, since investors would often focus on it. If Uber could show that it was winning increasing share in key markets while competitors fell, then it would attract more money while making other players less attractive. And it was head-to-head wins that moved this metric the most. If a market is split 50/50 among two players and one pulls ahead by 20 percent—by introducing new features, let's say, then the market will rebalance to 55/45. But if the 20 percent comes at the expense of the other—a 20 percent increase combined with a 20 percent decrease in the other network—then the market share would increase to 60/40. In Uber's case, these wins were circular, since more investment meant more spending on subsidizing the market, followed by more market share gains.

The Danger of Platform Dependence

Of course, cherry picking is not without its risks. Although the Airbnb versus Craigslist became a successful example of cherry picking, it became so because the outcome was that Airbnb became its own destination. Any new product that starts to cherry-pick must eventually be able to build its own stand-alone destination and scale it.

Sharing listings to Craigslist was an initial distribution tactic for Airbnb, but after a few years, the connection between the two networks no longer mattered—users were more likely to go directly to the mobile app or website of Airbnb. This in turn allowed it to develop its own Acquisition, Engagement, and Economic network effects separate from whatever dynamics existed on Craigslist.

Platform dependence can be disastrous if not managed well. If you integrate too closely with a preexisting network, allowing them to control your distribution, engagement, and business model, you become just a feature of their network. Had Airbnb been conceived as a tool to manage Craigslist listings and nothing else, it would have served at the leisure of its parent platform—grow too large, or make a wrong move, and it might be existential. Frequently the larger network will simply reach up and duplicate functionality if it gets too popular—a playbook that Microsoft executed in the 1990s with Office and Internet Explorer, among others. Or if the underlying network decides that it no longer wants to provide the same level of API access, as both Twitter and Facebook eventually did, any products dependent on this became worthless overnight.

In the end, cherry picking is an enormously powerful move because it exposes the fundamental asymmetry between the David and Goliath dynamic of networks. A new product can decide where to compete, focus on a single point, and build an atomic network—whereas a larger one finds it tough to defend every inch of its product experience. It's one of the reasons why, particularly in consumer markets, it's been so hard for "winner take all" to really happen in a literal way. The largest networks can take a lot, in many networks, but they remain vulnerable to any new upstart that uses cherry picking as a core strategy.

32

BIG BANG
FAILURES

Google+

The Big Bang Launch is often the strategy of the larger player in a market, which uses its advantages in size and scale to quickly overwhelm an opponent. It's particularly tempting when large companies compete with startups because it feels like an asymmetric advantage. And yet, counterintuitively, it often fails in the context of networked products.

How it happens is almost a cliché. The Big Bang Launch looks something like this: In January 2007, a black-turtlenecked Steve Jobs stood in front of a crowd of thousands at the Moscone Center in San Francisco, and announced a new device—the iPhone—to the world. It targeted a wide market of millions of mobile phone users, had break-through features addressing a wide degree of use cases—from email, texting, web browsing, and more. It was incredibly well received, covered by adoring media publications.

Startups and teams working on new networked products often look at this kind of launch—whether they think of it as classic or cliché—and work backward to emulate it. If there isn't a debut at a conference, perhaps it's more of a wide launch across press, social media, and paid marketing. Maybe it's accompanied by a big push from a company's main product—or perhaps a key partner—sending over a ton of users all at once. A big email marketing campaign will go out, and links to the new product will appear in prominent places, like the main app's home page. The intent is the same: launch big with the best product, get in front of as many people as possible, and draw a lot of new users and customers. Get the press, influencers, partners, and key users excited, and the network will be built from these most important nodes down into the individual users.

The Big Bang Launch is convenient for larger, more established companies as a method to launch new products because they often have distribution channels, huge engineering teams, and sales and marketing support. But counterintuitively, for networked products, this is often a trap. It's exactly the wrong way to build a network, because a wide launch creates many, many weak networks that aren't stable on their own.

When companies don't understand these nuances, it leads to disaster.

Anti-Network Effects Hit the Google+ Launch

A charismatic executive from one of the most powerful technology companies in the world introduces a new product at a conference.

This time, it's June 2011 at the Web 2.0 Summit, where Google vice president Vic Gundotra describes the future of social networking and launches Google+. This was Google's ambitious strategy to counteract Facebook, which was nearing their IPO. To give their new networked product a leg up, as many companies do, it led with aggressive upsells from their core product. The Google.com homepage linked to Google+, and they also integrated it widely within YouTube, Photos, and the rest of the product ecosystem. This generated huge initial numbers—within months, the company announced it had signed up more than 90 million users.

While this might superficially look like a large user base, it actually consisted of many weak networks that weren't engaged, because most new users showed up and tried out the product as they read about it in the press, rather than hearing from their friends. The high churn in the product was covered up by the incredible fire hose of traffic that the rest of Google's network generated. Even though it wasn't working, the numbers kept going up.

When unengaged users interact with a networked product that hasn't yet gelled into a stable, atomic network, then they don't end up pulling other users into the product. In a *Wall Street Journal* article by Amir Efrati, Google+ was described as a ghost town even while the executives touted large top-line numbers:

> To hear Google Inc. Chief Executive Larry Page tell it, Google+ has become a robust competitor in the social networking space, with 90 million users registering since its June launch.
>
> But those numbers mask what's really going on at Google+.
>
> It turns out Google+ is a virtual ghost town compared with the site of rival Facebook Inc., which is preparing for a massive initial public offering. New data from research firm comScore Inc. shows that Google+ users are signing up—but then not doing much there.
>
> Visitors using personal computers spent an average of about three minutes a month on Google+ between September and January, versus six to seven hours on Facebook each month over the same period, according to comScore, which didn't have data on mobile usage.[86]

The fate of Google+ was sealed in their go-to-market strategy. By launching big rather than focusing on small, atomic networks that could grow on their own, the teams fell victim to big vanity metrics. At its peak, Google+ claimed to have 300 million active users—by the top-line metrics, it was on its way to success. But network effects rely on the quality of the growth and not just its quantity. Eventually the collection of weak networks and high churn caught up, and in 2019, Google+ finally shut down after years of meandering irrelevance.

Of course, it's not just the launch that affected Google+'s outcome—the choices they made in their product inhibited the success as well. The hard side of any content platform like Google+ lays in attracting the content creators who are the reason why viewers come to the network in the first place. However, the product choices were questionable. The ability to create private, shareable groups of friends sounded good in theory, but it resulted in more work in configuring lists of friends, and also diminished the amount of comments/likes from a smaller audience of friends. The sharing features were the same as Facebook and Twitter, focused on photos and links, which presented a status quo experience as opposed to a 10x improvement for content creators. Without a breakthrough for the hard side of the network, Google+ wouldn't get the unique content to differentiate from other platforms.

Contrast this with the teams that eventually succeeded in competing with Facebook where Google+ failed. Snap famously grew within the high school segment before breaking out into the mainstream, and the ephemeral photos captured a whole unique set of content that had never been published—casual, unposed photos that were meant for communication. Early on, with fewer than 10,000 daily active users, Snapchat was already hitting 10 photos/day/user, several orders of magnitude more than equivalent services—showing it had mastered the hard side of the network. Twitch, Instagram, and TikTok innovated in a similar vector, giving creators new tools and media types to express themselves.

The Problem with the Big Bang

The problem with the Big Bang approach to building networks is twofold: First, it is built on broadcast channels. The weakness of media coverage, conferences, or advertising is that while it might generate a large spike of users when successful, it is necessarily untargeted. Instead you are likely to get a smattering of users from across many networks, which might then churn out if the network around them isn't built.

The second issue is that it takes time for a product to have the right features, but also to have enough built out to drive viral growth—such as sharing, invites, and collaboration. The bottom-up motion has the advantage that once the viral growth features start to work, they are likely to continue across many different networks. Contrast that to the Big Bang Launch, which can present distracting, confusing aggregate information on an increasing total number of users that might go up without viral growth also improving. Unless you're specifically tracking and looking for this data, it's hard to assess if the network is growing properly.

When examined through the lens of Meerkat's Law and the central framework of this book, it is obvious why the resulting networks generated by big launches are weak. You'd rather have a smaller set of atomic networks that are denser and more engaged than a large number of networks that aren't there. When a networked product depends on having other people in order to be useful, it's better to ignore the topline aggregate numbers. Instead, the quality of the traction can only be seen when you zoom all the way into the perspective of an individual user within the network. Does a new person who joins the product see value based on how many other users are already on it? You might as well ignore the aggregate numbers, and in particular the spike of users that a new product might see in its first days. As Eric Ries describes in his book *The Lean Startup*, these are "vanity metrics." The numbers might make you feel good, especially when they are going up, but it doesn't matter if you have a hundred million users if they are churning out at a high rate, due to a lack of other users engaging.

When networks are built bottom-up, they are more likely to be densely interconnected, and thus healthier and more engaged. There are multiple reasons for this: A new product is often incubated within a subcommunity, whether that's a college campus, San Francisco techies, gamers, or freelancers—as recent tech successes have shown. It will grow within this group before spreading into other verticals, allowing time for its developers to tune features like inviting or sharing, while honing the core value proposition. Once a new networked product is spreading via word of mouth, then each user is likely to know at least one other user already on the network. By the time it reaches the broader consciousness, it will be seen as a phenomenon, and top-down efforts can always be added on to scale a network that's already big and engaged.

If Big Bang Launches work so poorly in general, why do they work for Apple? This type of launch works for Apple because their core offerings can stand alone as premium, high-utility products that generally don't need to construct new networks to function. At most, they tap into existing networks like email and SMS. Famously, Apple has not succeeded with social offerings like the now-defunct Game Center and Ping. The closest new networked product they've launched is arguably the App Store, but even that was initially not in Steve Jobs's vision for the phone.[87] Most important, though, you aren't Apple. So don't try to copy them without having their kinds of products.

The Paradox of Small Markets

Large, established companies naturally want to only win in huge markets. As a result, the core framework of this book—starting with smaller, atomic networks and tapping into its network forces to grow into a larger one—sounds counterintuitive. The objection is that, by itself, the first network often looks like a tiny market that doesn't deserve the attention.

Startups, on the other hand, have the advantage that they can start small, and grow, which is why some of the largest networked products in the industry—eBay, Facebook, Uber, Airbnb, and TikTok—started with small, atomic networks. Respectively, these initial networks began in collectibles, college students, limos for rich people, airbeds and breakfasts, and lip-syncing music videos. All of these sound like small, niche markets, and when a traditional "total addressable market" analysis is applied, it may look like it'll never be big.

But here's the paradox: To build a massive successful network effect, I argue that you must start with a smaller, atomic network. And use the success in the first set of networks to tip over the next set of small networks. I'm not convinced this step can be avoided.

eBay started out in the collectibles verticals, and built an atomic network focused there. This was a popular, early reaction to the business, by venture capital firm Bessemer Ventures:

> *"Stamps? Coins? Comic books? You've GOT to be kidding,"* thought David Cowan. "No-brainer pass."[88]

Fred Wilson at Union Square Ventures, one of the greatest venture capitalists of all time, didn't understand Airbnb's potential because at the time, it was focused on the lowest-end accommodations—literally, airbeds and breakfasts—and had not made much progress on breaking out:

> *At that time, Airbnb was a marketplace for air mattresses on the floors of people's apartments. Thus the name. They had ideas for taking on other listings but they had not yet made much progress on them.*
>
> *We couldn't wrap our heads around air mattresses on the living room floors as the next hotel room and did not chase the deal. Others saw the amazing team that we saw, funded them, and the rest is history. Airbnb is well on its way to building the "eBay of spaces." I'm pretty sure it will be a billion dollar business in time.[89]*

This is an easy mistake to make, and possibly the most common pitfall of trying to predict the features of startups that are trying to build new products with network effects. A product's first network is unlikely to be its last, when the team is working furiously to refine its network forces to conquer adjacent markets and networks. What might look like an airbed company eventually comes to disrupt the entire hotel industry. A chat product for small teams and startups eventually takes over the entire market as the de facto way for teams to communicate.

The Allure of the Big Bang Launch

The dynamics of larger, established companies make the big launch particularly attractive. They try to jump from zero to the Tipping Point in one bang, because of the internal pressures of starting and building a new product internally. "Why should we care about this new idea when we have XYZ generating millions (or billions) in revenue?" "What's our unique take on this idea? Why us?" "Why are you aiming for 5 schools/customers/cities when you could be aiming for 500?" All of these seem like great questions, but they lead down the path of a Big Bang Launch.

Having an app succeed in, say, a single high school or a single B2B customer seems trivial. If you have a core business that's generating millions or billions in revenue, any new product has to move the needle very quickly or it won't get resources. The individual leaders within a company will set very ambitious goals, because the fastest way to get more engineers or funding is to launch big. Even the CEO might get involved, but in many ways, a top-down directive creates even more pressure. To make it worth their while, a hyper-involved CEO will make sure that it's a "big bet" for the company, just as Google+ was.

In contrast, for a startup, the goals start small. When Tinder figured out how to get its first few hundred users at USC to use the app, it felt like a huge success—anything is better than zero! Then once it launched a second school, it felt like an even bigger win, prompting them to invest more effort, eventually growing school by school. The initial efforts for a network often focus on the ad hoc, with mechanics driven by operational hustle, burning cash to subsidize the early network, invite-only features, or just throwing humans at the problem. While these techniques might seem nonstrategic and unscalable—making them unattractive within a larger company—for startups they offer an asymmetric advantage to getting started.

33

COMPETING OVER THE HARD SIDE

Uber

In a simplistic retelling of network effects, the market is said to be winner-take-all, and the larger network is destined to win. After all, if you believe Metcalfe's Law, as a network gets larger, its value exponentially increases—which in turn should allow the leader to invest more, grow even larger, and eventually win.

Yet that's not what we see in the real world, whether we are examining the pitched battle between Wimdu and Airbnb for Europe, the global competition between Uber and Didi, Lyft, Ola, Careem, or Microsoft's successive battles over decades in browsers, operating systems, the Office suite, etc. Instead, the larger networked product often needs to execute an all-out effort to compete against a smaller player, and in the end, it still often loses! Just look at MySpace in social networking, Hipchat in workplace chat, or Billpoint, eBay's competitor to PayPal—at one point each of these was the largest network, and yet they lost. The eventual winners in these product categories were not the first to market, nor did they invent most of the underlying mechanics, but they still upended the big guys.

If network effects are so powerful, why are the larger networks so vulnerable? And what does an effort to take on an upstart look like?

North American Championship Series

Uber's competitive battles around the world offer a clue. In this book's opening chapter, I described the multi-hour, late-night strategy sessions hosted in Uber's War Room, where the competitive strategy was set for the company's various regional business units. A senior, cross-functional team of executives from operations, product, and finance joined the "North American Championship Series," often scheduled at odd hours, and which would run as long as it took to get everyone's questions answered. A meeting might be at 10 p.m., or on the weekend, to drive the competitive moves in the United States.

In China, India, Latin America, and other key regions, there was a parallel effort called "Black Gold China," "Black Gold India," and so on. In prior years, this effort had other secretive names, sometimes referred to as "SLOG"—as in, let's make it a hard slog to compete with Uber, though later it evolved into a backronym for "Supplying Long-Term Operations Growth." All of these efforts played a key role in successfully outcompeting large, venture capital–backed competitors like Sidecar, Hailo, and Flywheel. These meetings were focused on the premise that it wasn't enough for Uber to win; others had to lose.

Uber's competitive tactics were fierce and interdisciplinary. It combined shipping new product features built by a team of thousands of engineers with spending billions on incentives targeted at both riders and drivers to increase their engagement. If the rivals didn't counter these tactics with their own, then the network would fall apart. Sometimes it only took weeks. When I asked Sidecar cofounder Jahan Khanna to describe what it was like to compete with Uber, he said:

It was brutal. Near the end, Uber had us in a corner. Sidecar got to the point where we had expanded to too many markets and couldn't hold on to our riders and drivers in the way we had been before. We made the hard choice to stop giving out the kind of rider and driver bonuses that Uber was doing. The markets would need to stand on their own. Once we stopped the bonuses, within 6 weeks, the markets had all gone to zero. Incentives drove the whole thing, and it was a given if you wanted to compete.[90]

It wasn't only Sidecar that saw this level of brutal competition—Lyft, the eventual number two in the space, also received intense, focused efforts. It often happened at a hyperlocal and personal level. In the early years of the San Francisco market, the Uber team was specifically trying to "flip" Lyft drivers to drive for them. Thinking about where Lyft drivers might be found, the San Francisco Uber operations team realized many would be going to Lyft's headquarters for customer support. They arranged for trucks carrying mobile billboards to circle the block, telling drivers to "Shave the Stache"—referring to Lyft's pink mustache logo early on—and to drive Uber instead. Lyft in turn responded with their own campaign, driving billboards around telling drivers to "Be more than a number."

While NACS and the Black Gold meetings had slightly different names, at their core were a series of dashboards showing each city and Uber's market share. These metrics then helped drive the company's decision making. The dashboards pointed out something intriguing: while Uber might have, say, an aggregate 75 percent market share within a mega-region like the United States or Latin America, in reality that might be made up of several cities with nearly 100 percent control, followed by many at 50 percent or lower! A well-established network is actually a network of networks, and some are held more tightly than others.

While an upstart can pick and choose where it wants to compete, the larger network has more surface area to defend against multiple smaller players. In the case of Uber's US business, Lyft was particularly strong in San Francisco, Los Angeles, San Diego, Austin, and a smattering of other cities. While Uber looked like a Goliath in cities like New York, it had far fewer tools at its disposal in some of the West Coast cities. Airbnb, PayPal, and other products with global network effects connect people from all over the world into a single network—or at least big, regional networks. In contrast, Uber's networks stood segmented from each other in a city-by-city fashion. Its success in New York couldn't easily be parlayed into dominance in San Francisco. Thus, many of these battles started to look like trench warfare in cities where multiple players were nearly the same size, which the Uber team enthusiastically embraced.

Finding the Competitive Levers

When there's a battle between two networks, there are competitive levers that shift users from one into the other—what are they? The best place to focus in the rideshare market was the hard side of the network: drivers. More drivers meant that prices would be lower, attracting valuable high-frequency riders that often comparison shop for fares. Attract more riders, and it more efficiently fills the time of drivers, and vice versa. There was a double benefit to moving drivers from a competitor's network to yours—it would push their network into surging prices while yours would lower in price.

Uber's competitive levers would combine financial incentives— paying up for more sign-ups, more hours—with product improvements to improve Acquisition, Engagement, and Economic forces. Drawing in more drivers through product improvements is straightforward—the better the experience of picking up riders and routing the car to their destination, the more the app would be used.

Building a better product is one of the classic levers in the tech industry, but Uber focused much of its effort on targeted bonuses for drivers. Why bonuses? Because for drivers, that was their primary motivation for using the app, and improving their earnings would make them sticky. But these bonuses weren't just any bonuses—they were targeted at quickly flipping over the most valuable drivers in the networks of Uber's rivals, targeting so-called dual apping drivers that were active on multiple networks. They were given large, special bonuses that compelled them to stick to Uber, and every hour they drove was an hour that the other networks couldn't utilize.

There was a sophisticated effort to tag drivers as dual appers. Some of these efforts were just manual—Uber employees who took trips would just ask if the drivers drove for other services, and they could mark them manually in a special UI within the app. There were also behavioral signals when drivers were running two apps—they would often pause their Uber session for a few minutes while they drove for another company, then unpause it. On Android, there were direct APIs that could tell if someone was running Uber and Lyft at the same time. Eventually a large number of these signals were fed into a machine learning model where each driver would receive a score based on how likely they were to be a dual apper. It didn't have to be perfect, just good enough to aid the targeting.

Once tagged, the dual-apping drivers in the city could be sent a myriad of offers to compel them to change their behavior. To reinforce stickiness, one set of offers would ask them to drive as many hours in a week as possible for Uber rather than for rivals. Sometimes these were simple bonuses, called "Do X Get Y" (DxGy) offers, where a $100 bonus would be added once the driver hit 50 trips in a week. This could be extended into a tiered incentive, with a $25, $50, $100, and $200 bonus upon hitting 10, 25, 50, and 100 trips. Another would be "guaranteed surge," where after the 20th trip, let's say, every trip afterward would be multiplied by 1.5.

There were many different driver incentive structures, and new ones were constantly being tested by city teams—but the underlying goal was always the same. A driver who did 50 or 100 trips on Uber would be driving so many hours that it would be difficult to drive for another network. They had to pick an app at the start of the week, based on the offer, and then stick to one network to hit the top goals. During the peak of the incentive strategy, more than $50 million/week of driver incentives would be sent in a single region—it went over that rate in China, at one point, and also in the United States while I was part of NACS. The international competitive dynamics helped Uber get smarter in the States—it was clear that China's competitive market was leading to deeper personalization for drivers, combined with week-to-week incentives, and even sometimes daily bonuses. All of those systems and knowledge were brought into the US competition.

While the details of Uber's competitive tactics—tagging, targeting, incentives, and better product experiences—are specific to rideshare, the general approach still applies across a wide spectrum of products.

Focusing on the hard sides of the network, which are usually smaller in number, provides leverage in competitive moves. For a social network or video platform, it might make sense to pursue this side by giving content creators special economic incentives, or distribution for their content. For B2B products, it might be special features and pricing for enterprises. The core goal is the same regardless of the category—move the best and most important nodes from one network to another, and it will be a competitive win.

Competitive Intelligence

When a networked product takes competition seriously, it has to collect metrics to figure out the comparative position of all the players in the market. This in turn allows product teams to experiment and execute, while keeping an eye on results—it allows them to set goals, not only against their product's success, but also their competitors' declines.

Uber's NACS team invested substantially in understanding and tracking market share in every city. If they saw that they were behind rivals in a market, the team would quickly react. Not in a month, not next week, but rather, the goal was to flip the dynamics in the market as quickly as possible. This became a core part of the NACS and Black Gold meetings, where there was always a quantitative review of the various networks—broken down by city and region. There was an estimate of Uber's trips that week, and the trips of the largest competitors, providing a network-by-network market share report. There was a set of ratios, like the percentage of times users' trips ended up being "surge priced," an indicator there weren't enough drivers on the road. If a competitor had grown significantly in a city week-over-week while Uber had stayed flat or was negative, that would provoke a round of intense questioning from the attendees. There'd always be a regional general manager on the call to present a few slides on what happened.

Because some of the most important decisions in the company were made using these metrics, the NACS dashboards were expensively assembled from data across the company as well as external sources. One important source was large panels of anonymous credit card analytics resold and repackaged by the major card companies. Another source came from email analytics companies that had access to the emails— and thus receipts—of millions of consumers, and could offer market share metrics down to specific geographies and trip types. Think of these as "Nielsen ratings" for consumer credit card spend, where a small panel of a few million users could give you a sample for a much broader market. Even more important, you could slice and dice the data to get metrics for an individual city or even a particular destination in the city.

For a while, there was even a team called Counterintelligence (COIN), which reverse-engineered and scraped the APIs of rivals, initially focused on China. You could collect, say, the average ETA of drivers across the city by requesting that API and feeding it various addresses across the city. That would give you a sense for whether or not riders were facing longer wait times on Uber versus a competitor's app. There was another team, Global Intelligence, staffed with dozens of data scientists that took all the various data sources and augmented them with machine learning models and our own "ground truth" data, to create the best set of predictions.

While these specific methods aren't applicable to every networked product, there is an important idea at the core: any product that's in a head-to-head race with competitors should track the outcomes—market share, active users, engagement, or otherwise—while they execute in the market, to put together cause and effect. A marketplace startup might monitor which sellers are active on which apps, across different regions. A social network might try to make sure that creators are posting as much content on their apps as others—and figure out over time how to convince participants to post more. A videoconferencing tool might want to track the percentage of time people use their software versus another, by looking at work calendars. All of these efforts can help product teams connect their efforts to their results, to develop best practices over time.

Competing over the Hard Side

There are many lessons to be drawn from Uber's NACS efforts, on both its success as well as its limitations. The core of the strategy worked—it was effective to focus on the hard side of a network, combining financial incentives with product, with teams supported by sophisticated dashboards.

Uber's competitive efforts worked for a long time—but stalled in later years. The company's systematic approach vanquished Sidecar, Hailo, Flywheel, and a slew of smaller players. By understanding each competitor's spending on incentives, combined with referencing funding announcements, Uber could estimate what was remaining of a competitor's financial runway. As the runway got short, if pressure was applied at the right moments—using incentives and product improvements—Uber's competitors would find it hard to show consistent growth. Funding might dry up as their drivers migrated, in turn ruining the balance of supply and demand, causing prices to spike. This was effective when Uber was the biggest player in a particular city, because "the big guy is more efficient," as executives at the company would often state.

Yet for all of the time and effort that was put into the competitive efforts, it didn't always work. Although there was a string of early victories, it's also true that in the United States, both Lyft and DoorDash would go on to achieve successful IPOs and market valuations in the tens of billions. Elsewhere in the world, Uber fought hard but eventually exited China and Southeast Asia, ceding the regions to its regional competitors Didi and Grab.

What can be learned about the weaknesses of Uber's approach, in each of these losses? At its core, the Uber playbook for competition worked by relying on the Economic network effect—when it was the larger player in a city, it could subsidize the driver side of its network more efficiently. If Uber provides an hourly guarantee for its drivers of $30/hour but Uber's network ran at 2 trips per hour to its drivers whereas its competitor could only provide 1 per hour, then Uber was much closer to breaking even on each trip. Scale that up to millions of trips and the smaller player is bound to get driven out of a market.

But consider what happens when Uber and a competitor in a market are closer to 50/50, or when Uber is the smaller player, as was the case when two local players merged in China to form "Didi Kuadi." In both of these cases, the Economic effect doesn't aid Uber at all, and the company is no more efficient than its peers in the same market. In these cases, Uber has to differentiate through other means, which is hard in a utilitarian market with the expressed goal of "transportation like running water." When Uber and Lyft both share a large overlap of drivers that are active on both services, it's difficult for consumers to perceive a difference between the two products.

DoorDash found success through a variation of the Economic network effect. While Uber pulled its drivers from cities into food delivery, DoorDash started in suburbs and markets where there was less competition. As it solidified these markets and found strong economics, it entered adjacent urban markets to compete directly with a slew of players from Postmates, Uber Eats, Caviar, and others. Its suburban networks, combined with innovations in pricing and restaurant selection, gave it an early head start that allowed it to hit Escape Velocity against the competition.

However, the rideshare competition also shows the fallacy in believing in winner-take-all markets—instead, products compete as networks of networks, so that even when Uber's network was bigger in aggregate, it was only 50/50 in cities like San Francisco and Los Angeles against Lyft. It had similar, not superior, network effects, and it became hard to make competitive headway. This model of thinking about network effects explains why bigger networks find it hard to fully defeat competitors, whether you are looking at Facebook versus Snapchat, Zoom versus the litany of videoconferencing competitors, or another battle.

34

BUNDLING

Microsoft

Bigger networks are fearsome not just because of the inherent network effects that come with scale, but also because of their ability to expand into new categories and markets. Using their preexisting network as a launching pad, they can—at least theoretically—quickly solve the Cold Start Problem and establish traction for a new product. This is often called bundling—multiple products for one price—but in today's world of freemium workplace apps and ad-supported consumer social networks, it's referred to as building a "super app" or simply, upselling and cross-selling users into new products. At Uber, getting riders to start ordering food from Uber Eats was called R2E—"Rider to Eater."

Bundling has been at the center of many of the biggest battles in the technology industry, particularly the ones involving Microsoft. Perhaps most infamously, bundling was at the heart of the Browser Wars in the late 1990s, when Internet Explorer was shipped with Windows, to ultimately defeat Netscape. For many decades, Microsoft was seen in Silicon Valley as one of the most intense and fearsome competitors on the planet. Critics often accused the company of prevailing over competitors—including well-established companies with thousands of employees like WordPerfect, Lotus, Ashton-Tate, Stac, Novell, Netscape, AOL, and Sun—by leveraging its network effects.

To learn why bundling sometimes works, and other times doesn't, I went to the source. I asked Brad Silverberg, who in his decade at Microsoft headed up some of the company's most important product efforts—including the much-celebrated release of Windows 95, accelerating the franchise from $50 million to $3.5 billion, as well as all the early releases of Internet Explorer. He's been a mentor of mine for years, having served on the board of a startup I founded years back.

I interviewed Brad for *The Cold Start Problem* over videoconference; he was mostly retired and spending time with family in Jackson Hole, Wyoming. But his experience from the 1980s and '90s has made him the definitive authority on this topic, and perhaps surprisingly, he's skeptical of the power of bundling:

> *Bundling a product is not the silver bullet everyone thinks. If it were that easy, the version 1.0 for Internet Explorer would have won, by simply bundling it with Windows. It didn't—IE 1.0 only got to 3% or 4% market share, because it just wasn't good enough yet. Bing is another example, when Microsoft wanted to get into search. It was the default search engine across the operating system, not just in Internet Explorer but also MSN and everywhere Microsoft could jam it. But it went nowhere. The distribution advantages don't win when the product is inferior.[91]*

Even if bundling gets you a lot of new users trying out a product, they won't stick around if there's a huge gap in features.

As I've described with Google+, bundling is easy to describe but hard to execute. Can a larger network simply bundle in a new product and quickly lead to success? How do you reconcile this with all the examples where a larger company doesn't work—there is a litany of new projects launched each year by large technology companies, and most don't go anywhere. When does bundling work, and when does it not?

The Importance of a Killer Product

Microsoft Office is another famous example of bundling within the technology industry. I also spoke with Steven Sinofsky, now a colleague at Andreessen Horowitz, who previously spent decades at Microsoft shipping six major releases of Office. The early versions of Microsoft's word processing and spreadsheet applications—Word and Excel—were originally built for DOS and were keyboard-only and text based, without the menus, mouse pointers, and windows we're used to today. When asked why these applications weren't an instant success, Steven gave a blunt assessment:

> *When it came to word processing and spreadsheets, Microsoft was losing. Early on, it was a distant #2 or #3 in word processing and spreadsheets—following companies like Ashton-Tate, Lotus, Word-Perfect, and a slew of much better products. The earliest versions of Microsoft's applications were built for DOS—they were text-based, not graphical—and they just sucked. To create a successful bundle for Office, you needed Word, Excel, and PowerPoint to be great, and then they could be combined with established distribution.*[92]

For Microsoft's productivity applications, the break came when the world transitioned from text-based DOS applications to graphical user interfaces, in the mid-1980s. But as the industry shifted from text to graphical interfaces, it created an opening, as every application needed to be rewritten to support the new paradigm of dropdown menus, icons, toolbars, and the mouse.

While Microsoft redesigned and rethought their applications, their competitors were too stuck in the old world, and so Word and Excel leapfrogged their competitors. Then in an ensuing stroke of product marketing genius, it was combined into the Microsoft Office suite, which promptly became a colossus. Much effort was put toward making each application within the suite work with each other. For example, an

Excel chart would be embedded within a Microsoft Word document—this was called Object Linking and Embedding (OLE)—which made the combination of the products more powerful.

In other words, the product really matters, and bundling can provide a huge distribution advantage, but it can only go so far. It's an echo of what we now see in the internet age, where Twitter might drive users to its now-defunct livestreaming platform Periscope, or Google might push everyone to use Google Meet. It can work, but only when the product is great.

This is part of why the concept of bundling as been around forever—the McDonald's Happy Meal was launched in the 1970s, and cable companies have been bundling TV channels since their start. But at the heart of these bundling stories are important, iconic products that reinvent the market.

Competing with a Network, Not Just Features

The tactics to bundle a new product into an existing one can look similar—during the Browser Wars, Microsoft added Internet Explorer to the desktop and made it the default browser whenever you clicked on a link. In the modern era of mobile apps, video streaming, fintech, and workplace tools, bundling works differently than it did in the early Microsoft era—it's more about driving clicks from one product into another, and integrating into APIs, as opposed to bundling the diskettes for installing Word alongside the ones for Excel and PowerPoint. Take your successful product and find all the places you might cross-promote it to users. Create a big announcement on your home screen to grab your users' attention, and add links, buttons, and tabs on the bottom of your mobile app. Email your users and send push notifications. These tactics are immediately familiar because we see them from established products trying to promote their latest effort, whether that's Uber introducing its riders to Uber Eats, Dropbox launching Paper, or Google promoting their videoconferencing products.

While this helps generate a nice bump of new users, it doesn't solve the Cold Start Problem unless atomic networks are quickly formed. An incumbent's ability to prop up a set of network effects is surprisingly limited. Just consider each of the Engagement, Acquisition, and Economic network effects—while new user acquisition can be propped up by cross-selling users from one product to the other, the engagement and monetization effects will only kick in when there's a real critical mass. Google+ shows the danger of a stream of disconnected users that don't form engaged, atomic networks.

The move is to leverage a larger network across multiple touch-points, to accelerate all of its network effects—not just acquisition. Over the years, Facebook has executed an effective playbook that does exactly this, at scale. Take Instagram as an example—in the early days, the core product tapped into Facebook's network by making it easy to share photos from one product to the other. This creates a viral loop that drives new users, but engagement, too, when likes and comments appear on both services. Being able to sign up to Instagram using your Facebook account also increases conversion rate, which creates a frictionless experience while simultaneously setting up integrations later in the experience. A direct approach to tying together the networks relies on using the very established social graph of Facebook to create more engagement.

Bangaly Kaba, formerly head of growth at Instagram, describes how Instagram built off the network of its larger parent:

Tapping into Facebook's social graph became very powerful when we realized that following your real friends and having an audience of real friends was the most important factor for long-term retention. Facebook has a very rich social graph with not only address books but also years of friend interaction data. Using that info supercharged our ability to recommend the most relevant, real-life friends within the Instagram app in a way we couldn't before, which boosted retention in a big way. The previous theory had been that getting users to follow celebrities and influencers was the most impactful action, but this was much better—the influencers rarely followed back and engaged with a new user's content. Your friends would do that, bringing you back to the app, and we wouldn't have been able to create this feature without Facebook's network.

Rather than using Facebook only as a source of new users, Instagram was able to use its larger parent to build stronger, denser networks. This is the foundation for stronger network effects. Instagram is a great example of bundling done well, and why a networked product that launches another networked product is at a huge advantage. The goal is to compete not just on features or product, but to always be the "big guy" in a competitive situation—to bring your bigger network as a competitive weapon, which in turn unlocks benefits for acquisition, engagement, and monetization.

Going back to Microsoft, part of their competitive magic came when they could bring their entire ecosystem—developers, customers, PC makers, and others—to compete at multiple levels, not just on building more features. And the most important part of this ecosystem was the developers.

Locking In the Hard Side

When Microsoft competed in this era, it didn't just compete on features—it brought its network into the mix as well, particularly its developers, who are the hard side of the network. It took a huge effort to attract and retain developers to the Windows platforms: tooling to help build applications, stability in the platform, where possible, and finally, prioritizing developer needs—sometimes to the detriment of other sides of the network.

Microsoft's developer tooling launched on its earliest operating systems. It started with GW-BASIC and QBASIC to build applications that were mostly text for DOS, then Visual Basic and Visual Studio to build graphical applications on Windows. Having these tools was important because of the use cases they ultimately supported. Brad described the importance of Visual Basic (VB) in particular, to the Windows strategy:

> *Visual Basic was a key part of the flywheel for Windows. Every business, and especially small businesses, had all these programs that are part of their daily workflow. They weren't super complicated programs, but necessary. VB made it simple. Companies could write them themselves without much prior programming experience. Or there were legions of resellers and small consultancy groups who wrote VB programs for clients. It was a whole ecosystem that really drove Windows forward. And it was only for Windows. There was never VB for OS/2 or Mac. You had to be part of the Windows ecosystem. It empowered people with little prior experience to be developers.*

With Visual Basic, an infinite number of niche use cases, particularly within companies, could be automated. Thus the quote from early Microsoft execs, "For every copy of VB we sell, there are ten copies of Windows that go along with it."

Once the applications were coded up, the philosophy was that they would always run—called reverse compatibility. To make this point, let's look at what Apple did with their first generation of personal computers, like the Apple II and IBM PC, which primarily operated with arrow keys and a row of function keys at the top. When Apple transitioned to the Macintosh, which had a mouse and a graphical user interface, they explicitly broke compatibility—removing arrow keys from the keyboard and not running Apple II programs—in order to force developers to build graphical applications the "right way." Microsoft did the opposite, taking great pains to ensure reverse compatibility so new releases of DOS and Windows wouldn't break the code developers wrote. Even to this day, application code that is twenty or thirty years old can still be run on the latest version of Windows. This meant each new version of an OS would only increase the total number of applications available to run on it, and never decrease it—a key move that powers the core of the company's network effects. Microsoft took on the cost of supporting old, legacy applications, instead of asking its developers to take on the cost of constantly updating.

With its hard side locked in, Microsoft was able to approach competition creatively by using its ecosystem of developers.

Microsoft Takes on the Web

When Netscape launched its first browser in 1994, Brad Silverberg and his team were seriously impressed. He describes it in the most glowing terms: "It was clear the web was going to be the next evolution of computing. Just the way that graphical user interfaces changed the world with the Macintosh and Windows, the web would do the same." Netscape Navigator soon updated to include JavaScript, cookies, and Java, building the foundation for the kind of rich web applications we use today. It would inevitably become a full-fledged competitor to the desktop, which was a problem for Microsoft. The problem was, the company didn't yet have a browser. It quickly cobbled one together and released Internet Explorer 1.0, just to start learning. The problem was, the product was bad, even though it was free and bundled in various ways with Windows. The joke was, people would only use IE once, as a way to download Netscape, before abandoning it. These early versions of IE would only hit a few percentage points in market share.

As Microsoft began investing in getting its browser to parity, it also began a strategy to engage its developer ecosystem. Microsoft would make it easy to embed the web within any application, so that any product could incorporate browser-like functionality. For example, if a developer were building an email client, they could drop in some libraries to make it easy to view an HTML-based message with images from the web. Or a game developer might want to have an area in their application that showed internet-hosted discussion boards and help systems. Rather than having the internet run through the browser, instead, Microsoft would try to bring the internet to every Windows application. Brad spoke of this strategy and how counterintuitive it was:

> *AOL was in fierce competition with us at the time, and they didn't want to partner. We didn't want to either, because Microsoft had MSN, which was competing directly by offering a combination of content, community, and Internet access. But we put that all aside [and] tried as hard as we could to get them to integrate Internet Explorer into their products. It was a success, and AOL would offer a white-labeled browser—branded as AOL but with IE's code under the hood—to their customers, included in the blizzard of CDs they were mailing to every household in America.*

Each of these sessions from within AOL and Windows applications would officially be recorded as contributing to Internet Explorer market share. The goal at the time wasn't yet to win the market, but starting with a <5 percent share, to grow large enough that every web developer would need to start testing their websites with Internet Explorer. If web developers started to target toward the common standards between IE and Netscape Navigator, then it would be much harder for Netscape to build their own developer-driven network effects.

We know how this story ends. Microsoft brought their huge ecosystem and resources to bear in the competition, finally built to reach parity in product functionality, and yes, also bundled IE into Windows. A decade later, it would dominate nearly 90 percent of the browser market. While Microsoft didn't invent the browser, spreadsheet, or word processor, years later it would come to control each of these markets.

The Drawbacks of Bundling

Bundling, of course, works—at the minimum, it can drive users into a new product or feature that might otherwise struggle to get its first users. Yet it's perceived as an invincible strategy, when it has clear drawbacks. Bundling has both helped and hurt companies implementing it over the years. Many of Microsoft's security issues, instability, and less elegant interfaces can be traced directly back to the decision to focus on the needs of developers, particularly enterprise customers who made big investments in custom software that required reverse compatibility.

For consumer mobile apps, bundling new features to compete with Snapchat Stories, TikTok, or other popular apps has generally come with the downside of adding clutter to the design. New tabs, pop-ups, push notifications, and other tactics have to be used to let users know about the new bundled feature—it can work to drive some early traffic, but it can result in a worse product.

Bundling eventually stopped working for Microsoft. After the antitrust investigation, the company maintained its dominance on the PC operating systems market, but it lost control of many other markets. Eventually the industry jumped from PC to mobile. Microsoft tried to exactly replicate the network effects it had before—an ecosystem of hardware manufacturers who paid a licensing fee to run Windows Mobile, and app developers and consumers to match—but this time it didn't work. Instead, Google gave away its Android mobile OS for free, driving adoption for phone makers. The massive reach of Android attracted app developers, and a new network effect was built, derived from a business model where the OS was free but the ecosystem was monetized using search and advertising revenue.

Microsoft has also lost the browser market to Google Chrome, and is being challenged in its Office Suite by a litany of startup competitors large and small. It continued to use bundling as a strategy, adding workplace chat via Teams to its suite—but it hasn't achieved a clear victory against Slack.

If bundling hasn't been a sure thing for Microsoft, it's an even weaker strategy for others. The outcome seems even less assured when examining how Google bundled Google+ into many corners of its product, including Maps and Gmail, achieving hundreds of millions of active users without real retention. Uber bundled Uber Eats across many touchpoints within its rideshare app, but still fell behind in food delivery versus DoorDash. Bundling hasn't been a silver bullet, as much as the giants in the industry hope it is.

THE FUTURE OF NETWORK EFFECTS

I n late 2018, Uber had a new CEO and executive team, a new set of cultural values, and a new emphasis on profitability. It was telling that the War Room had been renamed the Peace Room, to reflect the "Uber 2.0" priorities. A lot had changed, and the aggressive, entrepreneurial startup that sought to revolutionize the transportation industry found itself with over 25,000 employees and slowing revenue growth across many of its core markets. Several hundred of the early employees that had fought in its fiercest battles had left the company and dispersed to start new companies, become investors, or take a couple of years off. Notably, there was a contingent in Miami, where there was plenty of sun, sailboats, and favorable taxes.

I had been out of the company about a year, but kept up with a broad constellation of Uber alumni via messaging apps, meetups, Facebook groups—many of us stayed close friends after our incredible ride together. It was fun to trade war stories about the earlier days, and to hear about how things were going, particularly in the year leading up to the IPO. (By that point, Uber had not gone public yet—it would later, in 2019.) In October, I got an email that would make me smile: Sent to a broad group of thousands of alumni, there would be a series of meet-ups to give everyone a chance to catch up. In true Uber fashion, they would be hosted globally, first, in Sydney, then Singapore, New Delhi, Dubai, Amsterdam, London, New York, Mexico City, and of course, San Francisco. William Barnes and Joshua Mohrer, two early Uber operations executives who helped run the company's LA and New York offices—among other roles—drove these gatherings, as part of their post-Uber activities.

The San Francisco alumni meetup was held at Monroe, described as a "1920s Old Hollywood–inspired Art Deco Lounge" in the North Beach district. It was a blast. I attended and caught up with old friends who trickled in throughout the night, and we reminisced about Uber's spectacular rise and the past few tumultuous years. About an hour in, the bar cut the music and there was a brief announcement—Travis Kalanick, cofounder and former CEO, was in the house. The room hushed as Travis grabbed the microphone:

> *The thing that this crew does—it makes me proud to come here and just spend time with you guys and see you. It's frickin overwhelming.*
>
> *I love hearing about the new things you guys are working on. I love the passion you're bringing to new places. We should do this every so often—just come back together. It's a community I don't know if we're going to be able to replicate again. I'm certainly in my new company trying to. I know a lot of you are doing the same. Follow your dreams. Dream big. Do big stuff. It's just one of those nights where you just don't want it to end.[93]*

And with that, he had addressed the troops one last time. Travis smiled, looked around the room, and handed over the mic.

Since then, the Uber alumni have spread throughout the tech industry. There have been several dozen new startups—in categories like scooters, virtual kitchens, car rental, payments, data infrastructure, cannabis, and furniture, just to name a few. Many have joined as executives for Silicon Valley's hottest new generation of startups. And some, like myself, have joined venture capital firms to invest in the next Ubers, Dropboxes, and Slacks. It is part of the Silicon Valley circle of life that this happens—that tiny, high-energy startups eventually grow to be large and unwieldy, and the most entrepreneurial employees go on to spread their know-how, money, and energy into brand-new companies. Companies like YouTube, Instagram, LinkedIn, WhatsApp, and Salesforce were founded by alumni of PayPal, Google, Yahoo, and Oracle, and Uber's alumni are repeating the same pattern.

Uber alumni are spreading some of the biggest lessons we learned about network effects: launching new markets, scaling through hypergrowth, making big bets with products, competing fiercely with rivals, and more. The network effects that drove Uber are highly relevant to many products in the technology industry, and this means that as technology transforms the world at large, network effects will become central across product categories, geographies, and industries.

But the Uber alumni are not the only ones to watch.

Over the past decade, the industry has seen an incredible amount of innovation in all corners of the economy. Networked products have reinvented software at its core—with the web browser, smartphone, video, and communication leading the charge. But we've also seen network effects reorganize entire industries in a way that combines both software and an enormous amount of offline logistical work—whether that's e-commerce, job marketplaces, or trucking.

Crypto looks to be one of the most important new technologies emerging, and has networks at its core. Bitcoin has created an alternative to traditional currencies, but in my opinion, it's even more exciting to see the trend of crypto becoming infused into every aspect of software. This will redefine gaming, social networks, marketplaces, and many other product categories, so that every software developer will have to think about network effects as part of building products.

All of these trends are why I've sought to unite a framework of ideas built on examples from the distant past—telephones, credit cards, and coupons—and from the modern era of networked products like messaging apps, marketplaces, workplace collaboration, social networks, and more. A very wide swath of products will be redefined by network effects in the coming years.

It's not just the ex-Uber network who will lead the charge, but rather, the alumni of all the companies mentioned in this book—Slack, Dropbox, Twitch, Microsoft, Zoom, Airbnb, PayPal, and dozens of others—who have learned about the power of viral growth, launching new markets, accelerating engagement, and the ways that network effects can offer a huge advantage. They will spread these ideas into the next generation of networked products that will transform entire industries.

ACKNOWLEDGMENTS

Prior to this book, my entire experience of writing had revolved around an erratically published newsletter and random tweets whenever I felt like it. This project ended up being something else—months of research followed by years of writing, and finally, a furious spurt of editing. It was like me saying, "I like to go for jogs around the neighborhood," and then signing up to run an ultramarathon. Yet through this project, I have connected with an incredible number of people—interview subjects, thought partners, and many readers of many partially finished drafts. I want to take a moment to express my gratitude.

First, a deep thank-you to my mentor and lifelong friend Bill Gossman, whom I first met as a college intern in Seattle. It was through our chats and what I learned in the first few years of my career that set me on my career path. His direct advice and guidance kicked off my adventures in Silicon Valley, and ultimately, this book.

I had a tremendous amount of support from many friends and colleagues at Andreessen Horowitz. Hanne Winarsky helped me navigate through the beginning phases, including the initial book proposal. Li Jin spearheaded much of the early research, joining many dozens of interviews, and was an essential thought partner. Olivia Moore very generously provided detailed notes, questions, and challenges as I rounded the corner toward a final draft. Katie Baynes and Margit Wennmachers have been crucial in working through both the content of the book and how I'll tell the world about it. Greg Truesdell has been my collaborator on endless iterations of design. My fellow authors at the firm, Scott Kupor and Ben Horowitz, gave me a preview of the entire first-time author journey, and provided guidance along the way. My frequent conversations with Jeff Jordan, Marc Andreessen, and Chris Dixon helped me form key ideas that I touch on throughout. And a shout-out to Connie Chan, Jonathan Lai, D'arcy Coolican, and the many folks on the Consumer investing team that shouldered the load while I was off during nights and weekends writing away. I am lucky to be surrounded by an amazing and supportive team.

A long list of reviewers helped me refine my writing. In particular, I am grateful for the long hours spent by Ada and Sachin, my sister and brother-in-law, who read deeply and commented thoroughly—their insights and questions are baked into many of the key chapters. As I like to say sometimes, thanks, useful sister! I am thankful for my close friend and consigliere Bubba Murarka, who has taken so much time on both this, and all the other many projects we work on together. To the ex-Uber crew, I appreciate the thorough read (and more general commentary) from the trenches: Chris Nakutis Taylor, Jahan Khanna, Ilya Abyzov, Alex Czarnecki, Shalin Mantri, Zoran Martinovic, William Barnes, Logan Lindsell, Chan Park, Ben Chiang, Aaron Schildkrout, Josh Mohrer, Brian Tolkin, Adam Grenier, and Kenny D'Amica, among others.

There is a long list of the many incredible people I interviewed as part of my research. Thank you Steve Huffman, Sean Rad, Steve Chen, Jon Badeen, Kevin Lin, Emmett Shear, Andy Johns, Jonathan Abrams, Paul Davison, Rohan Seth, and Max Levchin—these folks have all had a hand in creating some of the most iconic products in the past decade. Same with Drew Houston, Stewart Butterfield, Ali Rayl, Eric Yuan, Reid Hoffman, Brad Silverberg, and Steven Sinofsky—thank you. I had incredibly helpful conversations with Anand Iyer, Ale Resnik, Mike Ghaffary, Patrick Moran, Josh Wais, Jonathan Golden, Lenny Rachitsky, Jim Scheinman, Darius Contractor, Chrys Bader, Bryan Kim, and ChenLi Wang. They were all so generous with their time, educating me and contributing insights that have influenced my thinking. Thanks again.

I appreciate the advice from fellow authors Michael Ovitz, Seth Godin, Eric Ries, Elad Gil, and Ramit Sethi, who inspired me to start this project in the first place. I often refer to my notes from our conversations—it's been crucial in my journey as a first-time author. Finally, a big shout-out to my extraordinary editor Hollis Heimbouch and her team at Harper Business. Hollis's guidance and feedback during this multi-year process was indispensable as I made my way through the winding maze that is a first book. And thanks to Chris Parris-Lamb, my literary agent at the Gernert Company, who answered endless newbie questions at the start, and jumped in at all the pivotal moments.

NOTES

Thanks for reading this far!

1. Uber Inc., "Form S-1," filed April 11, 2019, https://www.sec.gov/Archives/edgar/data/1543151/000119312519103850/d647752ds1.htm.

2. American Telephone & Telegraph Company, "Annual Report for the Year Ending December 31, 1900," filed March 26, 1901, Google Books.

3. Bob Metcalfe, "Metcalfe's Law Recurses Down the Long Tail of Social Networking," August 2006, https://vcmike.wordpress.com/2006/08/18/metcalfe-social-networks/.

4. W. C. Allee and Edith S. Bowen, "Studies in animal aggregations: Mass protection against colloidal silver among goldfishes," *Journal of Experimental Zoology*, February 1932.

5. M. Kathryn Davis, "Sardine oil on troubled waters: The boom and bust of California's sardine industry 1905–1955," University of California, Berkeley, 2002.

6. Naval Ravikant, Twitter post, June 2017, https://twitter.com/naval/status/877467713811042304?lang=en.

7. Reid Hoffman, "The Big Pivot," Masters of Scale, Podcast audio, July 2019, https://mastersofscale.com/stewart-butterfield-the-big-pivot/.

8. Stewart Butterfield, interview with the author over videoconference, April 2020.

9.   First Round Review, "From 0 to $1B—Slack's Founder Shares Their Epic Launch Strategy," February 2015, https://review.firstround.com/From-0-to-1B-Slacks-Founder-Shares-Their-Epic-Launch-Strategy.

10. Eric Yuan, interview with the author, San Jose, February 2020.

11. Jonathan Golden, "Lessons Learned Scaling Airbnb 100X," Medium, August 2017, https://medium.com/@jgolden/lessons-learned-scaling-airbnb-100x-b862364fb3a7.

12. Chris Nakutis Taylor, interview with the author over videoconference, January 2019.

13. William Barnes, interview with the author over videoconference, January 2019.

14. Alex Rampell, "The Fresno Free-for-All Behind the Original Credit Card," September 2019, https://a16z.com/2019/09/18/history-of-the-credit-card/.

15. Joseph Nocera, *A Piece of the Action: How the Middle Class Joined the Money Class* (New York: Simon & Schuster, 1994).

16. Chris Dixon, "The next big thing will start out looking like a toy," January 2010, https://cdixon.org/2010/01/03/the-next-big-thing-will-start-out-looking-like-a-toy.

17. Wikipedia, "Wikipedia: Size comparisons," accessed May 2021, https://en.wikipedia.org/wiki/Wikipedia:Size_comparisons.

18. CBS News, "Meet the man behind a third of what's on Wikipedia," January 2019, https://www.cbsnews.com/news/meet-the-man-behind-a-third-of-whats-on-wikipedia/.

19. Bradley Horowitz, "Creators, Synthesizers, and Consumers," February 2006, https://web.archive.org/web/20210225130843/https://blog.elatable.com/2006/02/creators-synthesizers-and-consumers.html.

20. Evan Spiegel, remarks during the DLD conference, January 2020, Germany.

21. Sean Rad, interview with the author over videoconference, March 2019.

22. Jahan Khanna, interview with the author, San Francisco, December 2018.

23. Eric Yuan, interview with the author, San Jose, February 2020.

24. Rohan Seth and Paul Davison via email, February 2021.

25. Bubba Murarka via email, March 2021.

26. Marc Andreessen, "The only thing that matters," June 2007, https://pmarchive.com/guide_to_startups_part4.html.

27. Sean Rad, interview with the author over videoconference, March 2019.

28. Jonathan Badeen, interview with the author over videoconference, April 2019.

29. Bianca Bosker, "Here's One of the College Kids Helping Tinder Take Over Campuses," *Huffington Post*, July 2013, https://www.huffpost.com/entry/tinder-app-college-kids_n_3530585.

30. Reid Hoffman, interview with the author over videoconference, December 2020.

31. Lee Hower, "How did LinkedIn get its initial traction?" Quora, August 2010, https://www.quora.com/How-did-LinkedIn-product-get-its-initial-traction/answer/Lee-Hower?comment_id=69849&comment_type=2.

32. Harry McCracken, "How Gmail Happened: The Inside Story of Its Launch 10 Years Ago," *Time*, April 2014, https://time.com/43263/gmail-10th-anniversary/.

33. Libby Plummer, "Hipstamatic—Behind the Lens," Pocket-Lint, November 2010, https://www.pocket-lint.com/cameras/news/lomography/106994-hipstamatic-iphone-app-android-interview.

34. M. G. Siegler, "Apple's Apps of Year: Hipstamatic, Plants vs. Zombies, Flipboard, and Osmos," Techcrunch, December 2010, https://techcrunch.com/2010/12/09/apple-top-apps-2010/.

35.   James Estrin, "Finding the right tool to tell a war story," *New York Times*, November 2010.

36.   Kevin Systrom, "What is the genesis of Instagram?" Quora, January 2011, https://www.quora.com/What-is-the-genesis-of-Instagram /answer/Kevin-Systrom.

37.   Josh Constine, "Instagram hits 1 billion monthly users, up from 800M in September," Techcrunch, June 2018, https://techcrunch .com/2018/06/20/instagram-1-billion-users/.

38.   Robert J. Moore. "Instagram Now Adding 130,000 Users Per Week: An Analysis," Techcrunch, March 2011, https://techcrunch .com/2011/03/10/instagram-adding-130000-users-per-week/.

39.   Shutterstock, "What the Most Popular Instagram Filters Tell Us About Users," March 2018, https://www.shutterstock.com/blog /instagram-filters-user-study.

40.   Chris Dixon, "Come for the tool, stay for the network," published as a blog post, January 2015, https://cdixon.org/2015/01/31/come-for -the-tool-stay-for-the-network.

41.   Claude Hopkins, *My Life in Advertising* (New York: McGraw-Hill Education, 1966).

42.   Steve Huffman, interview with the author, San Francisco, March 2020.

43.   Jonathan Golden, "Lessons Learned Scaling Airbnb 100X," Medium, August 2017, https://medium.com/@jgolden/lessons-learned -scaling-airbnb-100x-b862364fb3a7.

44.   Lenny Rachitsky, "How today's fastest growing B2B businesses found their first ten customers," Substack, July 2020, https://www.lennys newsletter.com/p/how-todays-fastest-growing-b2b-businesses.

45.   Paul Graham, "Do things that don't scale," published on paulgraham .com, July 2013, http://paulgraham.com/ds.html.

46.   Dropbox Inc., "Form S-1," filed February 2018, https://www.sec.gov /Archives/edgar/data/1467623/000119312518055809/d451946ds1 .htm.

47.   Drew Houston, interview with the author, San Francisco, February 2020.

48.   Cade Metz, "The Epic Story of Dropbox's Exodus from the Amazon Cloud Empire," *Wired*, March 2016, https://www.wired.com/2016/03/epic-story-dropboxs-exodus-amazon-cloud-empire/.

49.   Drew Houston, "Dropbox Demo," YouTube video, September 2008, https://www.youtube.com/watch?v=7QmCUDHpNzE.

50.   Sarah Perez, "Nearly 1 in 4 people abandon mobile apps after only one use," Techcrunch, May 2016.

51.   Dan Frommer, "You really only use three apps on your phone," Quartz, September 2015, https://qz.com/508997/you-really-only-use-three-apps-on-your-phone/.

52.   Aatif Awan, interview with the author, Menlo Park, California, April 2019.

53.   Max Levchin, interview with the author via email, April 2021.

54.   David Sacks, "The Sharp Startup: When PayPal Found Product-Market Fit," Medium, November 2019, https://medium.com/craft-ventures/the-sharp-startup-when-paypal-found-product-market-fit-5ba47ad35d0b.

55.   K. V. Nagarajan, "The Code of Hammurabi: An economic interpretation," *International Journal of Business and Social Science* 2, no. 8 (May 2011): 108.

56.   Fareed Mosavat, interview with the author over videoconference, May 2020.

57.   Mike Wehner, "The unlikely father of esports streaming," Daily Dot, September 2015, https://web.archive.org/web/20201117135049/https://kernelmag.dailydot.com/issue-sections/features-issue-sections/14010/justin-tv-twitch-xarth/.

58.   Emmett Shear, interview with the author, San Francisco, March 2019.

59.   Kevin Lin, interview with the author, San Francisco, February 2020.

60. Steven Levy, "The Untold Story of Facebook's Most Controversial Growth Tool," Medium, February 2020, https://marker.medium .com/the-untold-history-of-facebooks-most-controversial-growth -tool-2ea3bfeaaa66.

61. David Ulevitch, interview with the author over videoconference, March 2021.

62. Eric Feng, "A stats-based look behind the venture capital curtain," Medium, September 2018, https://efeng.medium.com/a-stats-based -look-behind-the-venture-capital-curtain-91630b3239ae.

63. Ilya Strebulaev and Will Gornall, "How Much Does Venture Capital Drive the U. S. Economy?" Stanford GSB, October 2015, https:// www.gsb.stanford.edu/insights/how-much-does-venture-capital -drive-us-economy.

64. Neeraj Agrawal, "The SaaS Adventure," Techcrunch, February 2015, https://techcrunch.com/2015/02/01/the-saas-travel-adventure/.

65. Jeff Jordan, "A Recipe for Growth: Adding Layers to the Cake," a16z.com, January 2012, https://a16z.com/2012/01/18/a-recipe-for -growth-adding-layers-to-the-cake-2/.

66. Josh Constine, "9 highlights from Snapchat CEO's 6,000-word leaked memo on survival," Techcrunch, October 2018, https://tech crunch.com/2018/10/04/chat-not-snap/.

67. Bangaly Kaba, interview with the author, Menlo Park, California, December 2019.

68. Frank D'Angelo, "Happy Birthday, Digital Advertising," *AdAge*, October 2009, https://adage.com/article/digitalnext/happy-birthday -digital-advertising/139964.

69. Hannah Orenstein, "21 Vine Stars Formed a Secret Coalition and Quit the Platform Together Last Year," *Seventeen*, October 2016, https://www.seventeen.com/life/tech-social-media/news/a435 19/21-vine-stars-formed-a-secret-coalition-and-quit-the-app/.

70. Walter Isaacson, *The Innovators: How a Group of Inventors, Hack-*

ers, Geniuses, and Geeks Created the Digital Revolution (New York: Simon & Schuster, 2014).

71.   Adam D'Angelo, interview with the author over videoconference, April 2020.

72.   Michael Wesch, "YouTube and You: Experiences of Self-awareness in the Context Collapse of the Recording Webcam," *Explorations in Media Ecology*, 2009.

73.   Eugène François Vidocq, *Memoirs of Vidocq: Principal Agent of the French Police* (E. L. Carey and A. Hart, 1834).

74.   Reddit Inc., "Comments of Reddit, in the matter of Section 230 of the Communications Act of 1934, before the Federal Communications Commission," filed September 1, 2020, https://ecfsapi.fcc.gov /file/10902008029058/Reddit%20FCC%20Comment%20RM%20 11862.pdf.

75.   Steve Chen, interview with the author over videoconference, March 2020.

76.   Eugene Wei, "Status as a Service (StaaS)," published on eugenewei. com, February 2019, https://www.eugenewei.com/blog/2019/2/19 /status-as-a-service.

77.   Aatif Awan, interview with the author, Menlo Park, California, April 2019.

78.   TikTok Inc., "How TikTok recommends videos #ForYou," published on Tiktok.com, June 2020, https://newsroom.tiktok.com/en-us/how -tiktok-recommends-videos-for-you.

79.   Reid Hoffman and Chris Yeh, *Blitzscaling: The Lightning-Fast Path to Building Massively Valuable Companies* (New York: Currency, 2018).

80.   Robin Wauters, "After one year, Airbnb rival Wimdu is big. How big? $132 million a year big," TheNextWeb, March 2012, https:// thenextweb.com/news/after-one-year-airbnb-rival-wimdu-is-big -how-big-132-million-a-year-big.

81. Michael Schaecher, interview with the author, San Francisco, January 2020.

82. Brian Chesky, "Blitzscaling 18: Brian Chesky on Launching Airbnb," YouTube video, November 2015, https://www.youtube.com/watch?v=W608u6sBFpo.

83. Jonathan Golden, interview with the author over videoconference, February 2019.

84. Warren Buffett and Carol Loomis, "Mr. Buffett on the Stock Market," *Fortune*, November 1999, https://archive.fortune.com/magazines/fortune/fortune_archive/1999/11/22/269071/index.htm.

85. Andrew Parker, "The spawn of Craigslist," Tumblr, January 2010, https://thegongshow.tumblr.com/post/345941486/the-spawn-of-craigslist-like-most-vcs-that-focus.

86. Amir Efrati, "The Mounting Minuses at Google+," *Wall Street Journal*, February 2012, https://www.wsj.com/articles/SB10001424052970204653604577249341403742390.

87. 9to5Mac, October 2011, https://9to5mac.com/2011/10/21/jobs-original-vision-for-the-iphone-no-third-party-native-apps/.

88. Bessemer Venture Partners, "The Anti-Portfolio: Honoring the companies we missed," accessed June 2021, https://www.bvp.com/anti-portfolio/.

89. Fred Wilson, "Airbnb," posted on avc.com, March 2011, https://avc.com/2011/03/airbnb/.

90. Jahan Khanna, interview with the author, San Francisco, December 2018.

91. Brad Silverberg, interview with the author over videoconference, December 2020.

92. Steven Sinofsky, interview with the author over videoconference, November 2020.

93. Travis Kalanick, Uber Alumni Investing Club event, San Francisco, November 2018.

ABOUT THE AUTHOR

ANDREW CHEN is a general partner at Andreessen Horowitz, investing in early-stage consumer startups. He is a board member of fast-growing startups like Substack, Clubhouse, Z League, All Day Kitchens, Sleeper, Maven, and Reforge, and previously led the rider growth teams at Uber during their high-growth, pre-IPO years. He has a popular professional blog, and has been featured in *Wired*, the *Wall Street Journal*, and the *New York Times*. He holds a BS in applied mathematics from the University of Washington, where he graduated at the age of nineteen. He splits his time between San Francisco and Los Angeles.